D1206507

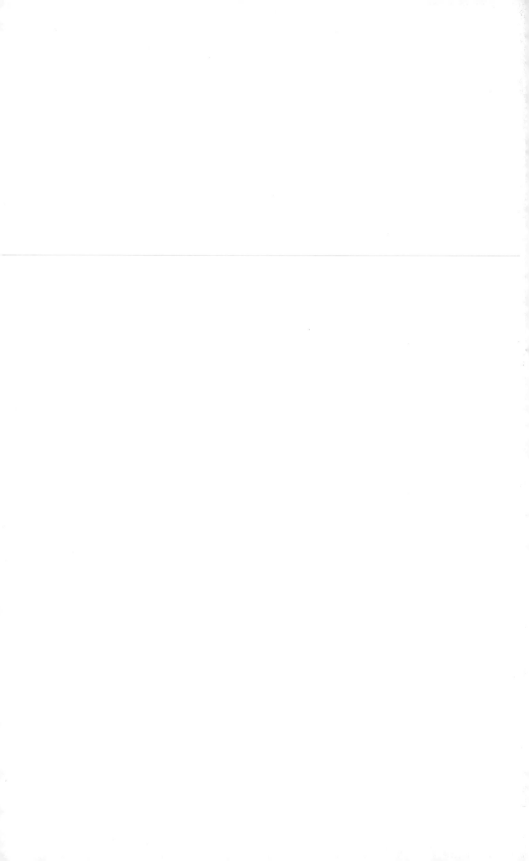

NOVEL THEORY AND TECHNOLOGY IN MODERNIST BRITAIN

Modernism reshaped novel theory, shifting criticism away from readers' experiences and toward the work as an object autonomous from any reader. *Novel Theory and Technology in Modernist Britain* excavates technology's crucial role in this evolution and offers a new history of modernism's vision of the novel. To many modernists, both novel and machine increasingly seemed to merge into the experiences of readers or users. But modernists also saw potential for a different understanding of technology – in premodern machines, or the technical functioning of technologies stripped of their current social roles. With chapters on Henry James, Ford Madox Ford, Wyndham Lewis, and Rebecca West, *Novel Theory* argues that, in these alternative visions of technology, modernists found models for how the novel might become an autonomous, intellectual object rather than a familiar experience, and articulated a future for the novel by imagining it as a new kind of machine.

HEATHER FIELDING is Associate Professor of English and Associate Dean of the Honors College at Purdue University Northwest in Westville and Hammond, Indiana.

NOVEL THEORY AND TECHNOLOGY IN MODERNIST BRITAIN

HEATHER FIELDING

Purdue University Northwest

CAMBRIDGE
UNIVERSITY PRESS

CAMBRIDGE
UNIVERSITY PRESS

University Printing House, Cambridge CB2 8BS, United Kingdom

One Liberty Plaza, 20th Floor, New York, NY 10006, USA

477 Williamstown Road, Port Melbourne, VIC 3207, Australia

314–321, 3rd Floor, Plot 3, Splendor Forum, Jasola District Centre,
New Delhi – 110025, India

79 Anson Road, #06-04/06, Singapore 079906

Cambridge University Press is part of the University of Cambridge.

It furthers the University's mission by disseminating knowledge in the pursuit of
education, learning, and research at the highest international levels of excellence.

www.cambridge.org
Information on this title: www.cambridge.org/9781108426046
DOI: 10.1017/9781108676083

© Heather Fielding 2018

This publication is in copyright. Subject to statutory exception
and to the provisions of relevant collective licensing agreements,
no reproduction of any part may take place without the written
permission of Cambridge University Press.

First published 2018

Printed in the United States of America by Sheridan Books, Inc.

A catalogue record for this publication is available from the British Library.

ISBN 978-1-108-42604-6 Hardback

Cambridge University Press has no responsibility for the persistence or
accuracy of URLs for external or third-party internet websites referred
to in this publication and does not guarantee that any content on
such websites is, or will remain, accurate or appropriate.

Contents

Acknowledgments

My early interest in literary studies was nurtured by a group of caring and talented English faculty at Tulane University: James Kilroy, Supriya Nair, Maaja Stewart, and, especially, Barry Ahearn. At Brown University, Mary Ann Doane and Kevin McLaughlin both provided helpful feedback on an early version of this material. I am fortunate to have studied with Tamar Katz: she is the kind of teacher whose comments from a decade ago continue to improve my writing.

I am grateful to many of my colleagues at Purdue University Northwest, formerly Purdue North Central, for their encouragement and friendship and for contributing to an intellectual culture supportive of humanities scholarship. Thanks are due in particular to Hui Chu, Assen Kokalov, Bethany Lee, Karen Bishop Morris, Richard Rupp, and Sarah White, as well as to Ron Corthell and Mike Lynn, whose mentorship has meant much to me over the years.

At Purdue Northwest, I have been fortunate to work with a group of amazing English majors and Honors College students. In a cultural climate that recognizes only those academic activities with measurable impact on specific employment outcomes or economic development, I have been buoyed by these students, who persist in intellectual curiosity, who find fulfilment and engagement in reading and learning about literary history, and who keep taking literature courses, running book groups after they graduate, and pursuing their intellectual interests throughout their lives. In particular, Eileen Long, Ashley Pezan, Kelsey Tabbert, and Alexis Ulrich continue to inspire my teaching and research.

This work was supported financially by a dissertation fellowship from Brown University, as well as by release time from Purdue University Northwest. I am also grateful to the PNW library – especially to Susie Anderson and her interlibrary loan skills – as well as to the Regenstein Library of the University of Chicago.

Thanks to Kevin Dettmar, Scott Klein, and Dan Punday, who read parts of this manuscript or my book proposal and offered useful feedback. Thanks also to Sarah Hardy, Lina Ibrahim, Bonnie Roos, and Paul Saint-Amour, who have offered much professional support. Two anonymous readers for Cambridge University Press helped me to improve the manuscript substantially and gave me the courage to make some significant changes. I owe much gratitude to my editor, Ray Ryan, for his support of this project.

My family has always encouraged my work, even though this book has been so long in the making. My parents, David and Suzanne Fielding, raised me to be capable of the kind of persistence scholarly writing requires. I thank them for their love, their patience, and their faith in me. My sister and brother-in-law, Erin and Cary Brooks, put up with a lot from me during the writing of this book. The dynamic duo of Lily and Caleb, my niece and nephew, give me hope for the future. I finish this project with thoughts of my grandmother, Valerie Frederick, and of the three people in my family who passed away while I was working on it: my grandfather, Ulysse Frederick; my aunt, Paula Lund; and my mother-in-law, Alcee Hecht.

I owe a great debt to my husband, Paul Hecht, who believes in me far more than I believe in myself, and whose enduring optimism sustains me. None of this work would have been possible without him, or without our girls, Franny, Winnie, and Agatha.

An earlier version of Chapter 1 appeared as "'The Projection of His Consciousness': James and Narrative Technology" in *Modern Language Quarterly* 70.2 (June 2009): 223–44. An earlier version of Chapter 3 appeared as "How the Taxi-Cab Driver Reads: Wyndham Lewis, Modernist Aesthetics, and the Novel as Machine" in the *Journal of Modern Literature* 38.1 (Fall 2014): 128–46. I am grateful to the publishers of these journals for permission to reprint this material here.

Introduction
Readers and Machines in Modernist Novel Theory

Literature's relationship with technology has seemed to have a teleology. As writers across the twentieth century incorporated technologies into their works not just thematically, as content, but as strategies, techniques, and media, the resulting texts became increasingly interactive. The more immersed the novel was in technology, the more writerly the reading experience became, and the more power and control accrued to the reader. The reader's experience came increasingly to define the text and its value. This narrative rose to prominence with Marshall McLuhan, who argued that the electric age would "cool" the media environment, producing more media that would require participation from audiences: computers, not print. The dominance of cool media would change society, McLuhan argued, so that "electrically contracted, the globe is no more than a village," where everyone participates in everything.[1]

The story would continue through the second half of the twentieth century, when hypertext was canonized as the first genre of fully electronic, computer-based literature. Hypertext, Robert Coover argued, "provides multiple paths between text segments."[2] Its webbed, multidirectional structure "presents a radically divergent technology, interactive and polyvocal, favoring a plurality of discourses over definitive utterance and freeing the reader from domination by the author."[3] In this democratic, nonhierarchical environment, "reader and writer are said to become co-learners or co-writers, as it were, fellow-travelers in the mapping and remapping of textual (and visual, kinetic and aural) components."[4]

Even after the first generation of hypertexts has become largely unreadable by contemporary computer systems, interactivity remains a defining characteristic of electronic literature. Certainly, the early theories of hypertext, offered by critics such as Coover and George Landow, have been thoroughly critiqued for ignoring the limitations on readers' choices that exist in the hypertext environment, as well as the choice and interactivity that even print can create.[5] Nonetheless, critics have continued to see the reader's active involvement in the work as an integral component of technology-based literature. Espen J. Aarseth, for instance, argues that the reader of an electronic text pursues an "ergodic" task: she must actively create a path through, because one is not provided in advance by the text itself.[6] The foreword to a 2015 anthology of criticism, *Interactive Digital Media: History, Theory and Practice*, provides another example. Nick Montfort justifies the title's key category as an inclusive term for describing electronic literature, even though "there are some related activities that would seem to be left out of IDN [interactive digital narrative] strictly interpreted," including "story generation systems that are noninteractive."[7] Electronic literature can be defined as interactive, Montfort demurs, because doing so excludes only a nonrepresentative minority of texts. And even though McLuhan's theory of cool media has fallen out of the mainstream, his historical projections are congruent with those of Lev Manovich, who notoriously set interactive and noninteractive media structures in opposition to each other in his 2001 book *The Language of New Media*. Interactive media – he calls them databases – present a set of choices that a user must order. Narrative media, by contrast, create an order in advance, making choices for the user. For him, database and narrative are "natural enemies," and database is winning: he argues that database, the coolest of genres in McLuhan's terms, would be the dominant genre of the twenty-first century.[8]

As electronic literature has continued to develop, however, a minor tradition of works specifically, pointedly designed against interactivity has emerged. Young-Hae Chang Heavy Industries (YHCHI) – the Seoul-based collaboration between Young-Hae Chang and Marc Voge – is the best known example. Their minimalist, Flash-based works pair jazz or electronic music with text that moves across the screen. YHCHI's texts make the reading process uncomfortable by removing any control the reader might have.[9] There is no capacity to pause, rewind, or fast-forward; the reader's choices are to stop the text by hitting the back button on the web browser or closing the window, or to let the text play on. The text moves at its own pace, one that is sometimes too slow for comfort, and sometimes a bit too fast for readers, especially for those struggling to apply techniques of close reading.[10] These texts actively frustrate any reader's attempts to skip to the end or to a favorite part, or to pause or review difficult sections. Some works, such as "Artist's Statement No. 45,730,944: The Perfect Artistic Web Site," are looped so that they continue replaying, complicating even the emotional payoff of getting to the end of a story. As Warren Liu puts it, YHCHI's works are focused on "address, rather than on exchange": these texts challenge a reader's desire to participate in them.[11]

YHCHI have defined their practice against the expectation that electronic literature should require a reader's choice and input, maintaining that theirs is a "simple technique that shuns interactivity."[12] By 2008, they presented this quality as the most well-known characteristic of their repertoire: "Those who are interested in our work know by now that we've never been big on interactivity."[13] YHCHI compare interactivity to "channel surfing," where a viewer has only fake choice between options fully determined in advance.[14] Channel-surfing is also the classic example of twentieth-century boredom and procrastination: an unproductive, emotionless activity that gives the watcher the ability to choose but results in her not actually watching any specific work. Channel-surfing is perhaps the best example of a kind of interaction between beholder and text that results in the text's disappearance – something YHCHI's works are designed to prevent.

This genre of machine-based literature that is self-consciously anti-interactive challenges McLuhan's teleological media narrative. These works suggest the possibility of an alternative history of literature and the machine, one that is not motivated by increasing interactivity. Such a history would be particularly modernist. Michael Fried differentiates between the central strains of modernism and postmodernism in terms of their relationship to what he calls "theatricality."[15] Postmodern texts are often theatrical in that they demand a "special complicity" from their beholder – something very close to interactivity.[16] The postmodern work is "an object in a *situation* – one that, virtually by definition, *includes the beholder*."[17] Postmodern works are directed toward a reader, whose response and involvement are constitutively part of the meaning of the work. Modernist texts, by contrast, tend to reject the viewing or reading experience as a component of the work of art. The work is defined by its autonomy from its beholder, who is irrelevant to the meaning and value of the work. Modernist works are anti-interactive, in this view. Certainly, modernism was a heterogeneous collection of modern*isms*, but it would still be accurate to say that a major strand of it was invested in anti-theatricality, and deeply concerned about what theatricality could do to art.

Gertrude Stein's aesthetic theory exemplifies anti-theatrical modernism. In her 1936 lecture "What Are Master-pieces and Why Are There So Few of Them," Stein argues that a true masterpiece can only exist as "the thing in itself."[18] The masterpiece can be defined in opposition to what

Stein calls "identity": how people exist in relation to time, other people, and memory. Nothing that is part of identity can ever be singular – "the thing in itself" – because identity is the state of being in relation to other people and things and one's own memories, so that "two [are] present instead of one."[19] For a work to be a masterpiece, it must escape from the world of identity; it must be self-contained.

Audiences, viewers, and readers are troubling to Stein's masterpiece, because they threaten to bring it into the world of identity, where, as Jennifer Ashton explains, it will be "the object of a *subject's experience*."[20] Works that are, by their nature, directed at an audience – oratory and letters are Stein's examples in this essay – cannot ever become masterpieces:

> One of the things that I discovered in lecturing was that gradually one ceased to hear what one said one heard what the audience hears one say, that is the reason that oratory is practically never a master-piece very rarely and vary rarely history, because history deals with people who are orators who hear not what they say but what their audience hears them say.[21]

When an audience receives a work, Stein claims, it is replaced, even to the speaker herself, by its reception. By contrast, Stein's masterpiece is ontologically independent and contained, in that it is not "for" anyone; by definition, it is something that can never exist as someone's experience of it.

YHCHI point toward Stein's aesthetics, and a specifically modernist trajectory for literature and technology emerges. Jessica Pressman reads the work of YHCHI as exemplary of what she calls "digital modernism": works of twenty-first-century electronic literature that return to modernist techniques and situate themselves in a modernist lineage. These contemporary digital works, Pressman argues, sometimes challenge the expectation that electronic literature is defined by "reader-controlled interactivity."[22] *Novel Theory and Technology in Modernist Britain* reveals the full significance of this connection. Building on Pressman's work, I excavate a significant tradition within modernism of theorists imagining technology as a source of strategies for making the novel anti-interactive and anti-theatrical. When YHCHI create electronic narrative works that use technology to resist interactivity, they not only gesture toward modernism, but enact what modernist novel theory envisioned.

This book focuses particularly on the novel because, especially in modernism, this genre had a particularly vexed relationship to reader interaction. For modernism, the idea that the work of art should be independent of its beholder was most readily associated with poetry, with imagism's valuation of the hard, static, visual object. This association continues: while YHCHI's works generally have narratives, they are definitely not novels and are most often aligned with concrete poetry. To thinkers such as Wyndham Lewis or Percy Lubbock, a poem could be reasonably thought of as a visual object that one looks at from afar, but the novel seemed to be a far more insistently temporal genre, one that must unfold over an extended series of pages as the reader turns them, borrowing the time of the reader's experience and merging with the reader. Yet modernist novel theory undertook precisely the challenge of designing an anti-theatrical novel: theorists such as Lewis, Lubbock, and Stein wanted to figure out how the novel might exist fully without needing to be lived by its reader.

Rethinking the novel's relationship to reading was an urgent task at this moment in history. In the years between Henry James's infamous critique of mass reading habits in "The Art of Fiction" (1884) and Q. D. Leavis's *Fiction and the Reading Public* (1932), novel theory in Britain was the site of deep concern about how readers treated novels. Increasingly, middlebrow reading tendencies encroached. Readers sought familiarity and closeness: they wanted to merge with novels, to become part of them, to live in and through them. Especially in what some writers diagnosed as the emotional poverty of the years following World War I, readers wanted to form emotional bonds with novels or to use them to provide experiences that were lacking in their lives. At stake was the relationship between the novel and the real world: does the novel's value derive from the role it plays in readers' lives? Or does the novel's value instead come from its form, often imagined as a quality that should distance the novel from its reader? These debates about form and character preoccupied British novel theory, especially in the 1920s, when it seemed to many critics that social forces were increasingly pushing the novel into life and away from form.

This study shows that for critics who were concerned by readers' growing desire to get closer and closer to the novel in order to make it fill gaps in their lives, the modern machine seemed to face a similar problem: instrumentalization. Both novel and machine were increasingly reduced to an instrument for meeting an end that had been determined in advance. The novel could be made to act as the friend a middlebrow reader needs; the machine had become a means to produce what we already know we desire. A novel that is a reader's old friend is always already familiar and thus loses the ability to communicate anything new or different. Like the novel, technology no longer seemed capable of bringing anything heterogeneous into the world, instead producing a society that hurries incessantly toward something that seems new but is really more of the same.

Yet these theorists also saw the potential for another, noninstrumental vision of technology – in the technical functioning of devices stripped of their current social function, for example, and in premodern machines. Conceptualized in a certain way, technologies might offer strategies for protecting the novel from the demands and desires of its readers, for designing a novel that could still unfold and "move" without requiring input from or the participation of a reader, for theorizing how the novel works without referring to how readers apprehend it, and for understanding how the novel produces knowledge. In making such arguments, these writers were also theorizing technology, this book argues. They intervened in debates about how to understand technology's defining qualities, and how to theorize machinery's effects on art, culture, and society. Such interventions can be found in the discourse of mainstream modernist novel theory, and not only at its avant-garde edges, where writers such as Bob Brown designed literal machines to develop reading practices appropriate to the Machine Age.[23] The modernist novel theory that emerges is also a theory of technology.

The Problem with Reading

Our well-rehearsed standard history of novel theory situates its origins in modernism, with Henry James and Percy Lubbock.[24] According to this history, reading was simply never a prominent category in thinking about the novel, at least until postmodernism began to allow us to recover from New Criticism's institutionalized critical practices. For contemporary historians of novel theory such as Dorothy J. Hale and Nicholas Dames, resisting or complicating this origin story has been an overriding priority. They trace an earlier history of thinking about the novel, and uncover layers of modernism's novel theory that do not fit into this narrative.[25] Expanding on their work, this book recuperates the complexity of the historically particular debates surrounding novel-reading in modernism. Whether theorists were excited or horrified by the modes of reading they saw in their culture, reading was a site of deep anxiety in both social and aesthetic terms, an issue requiring immediate critical attention and a new theory of the genre.

Modernism emerged out of a Victorian context in which reading was the dominant focus of thinking about the novel. For thinkers such as G. H. Lewes and Alexander Bain, one studied the novel by analyzing its physical and psychological effects on readers. The novel and its reader were deeply and inevitably intertwined, according to such a view. As Dames puts it, this criticism was concerned with what a novel does to a reader, not what it is on its own, and could even be described as a "physiology of the novel."[26]

Coming out of this tradition, critics in early twentieth-century Britain thought that readers' relationships to novels were in a state of flux. There was a common refrain in criticism during this period: that readers were being drawn ever closer toward an emotional and experiential bond with the novel. They wanted not only to grasp the novel, to hold on to it, but to turn it into an effect they could integrate into their lives. Critics across the spectrum diagnosed the rise of this phenomenon, whether they saw it as positive or negative, for aesthetics or for society. For those who were worried by this deepening proximity between reader and novel, there was also no simple way to avoid it or theorize it away: they almost obsessively returned to dwell on the intractability of the problem of reading.

For example, Q. D. Leavis thought that readers behaved differently toward novels following World War I. People were reading more than ever before, she argues in *Fiction and the Reading Public*, and more books were being written to meet the demands of the expanding literary public – a claim repeated frequently across novel criticism in the period.[27] While some might imagine that cinema and radio reduced the influence of the novel, Leavis thought that novels had become more important – perhaps even too important – to English society. Postwar England guaranteed a good readership for novels, Leavis argued, because people felt a deep gap in their lives that could best be filled by the novel: "fiction for very many people is a means of easing a desolating sense of isolation and compensates for the poverty of their emotional lives."[28] These readers demanded novels driven by characters they could think of as "real people," who could make them feel through a process of "emotional contagion."[29] And fiction could "provide compensation for life more effectively" than could its competitor media.[30] Readers needed to live through novels, to make up for what was lacking in their own lives. Highbrow modernist novels that refused to cater to such middlebrow desires would never find popular success, Leavis imagined. The common reader would certainly reject a work such as Virginia Woolf's *To the Lighthouse* because it emitted "no glow of companionship."[31]

It was the middlebrow novel, which emerged in the 1920s and became a dominant force in fiction in the 1930s, that fulfilled these readers' demands, in Leavis's view. While the division between the high modernist and middlebrow novel was certainly unstable and permeable, these two categories were often distinguished from each other on the basis of their relationship to reading. The middlebrow novel could be defined by the fact that it prioritized readability and accessibility: "I have trained myself to write quickly, punctually and readably to order over a wide range of subjects," wrote novelist Winifred Holtby.[32] The middle-brow novel aimed to open itself up to, not to protect itself from, its read-ers. It courted the affective relationship that readers so deeply desired, in Leavis's critique. As Storm Jameson put it, the writer "must think first how I can make you laugh or cry": whatever social, political, or intel-lectual aims a middlebrow novelist might have, the emotional engage-ment of the reader was essential.[33] The middlebrow novel, Leavis argued, existed to fill in the gaps in modern readers' experiences, "to pass time," to provide "the longest surcease from ennui at the least expenditure of time and money."[34] Such novels were "designed to be read in the face of lassitude and nervous fatigue," to inspire emotion rather than to require intellectual effort.[35] In turn, reading these novels fit into one's daily rou-tine. You read "in your bath, for instance, or late at night when you are too tired to go to bed, or in the odd quarter of an hour before lunch," as George Orwell put it.[36] Or you read "while you wait for the bus, while you strap-hang, in between the Boss's dictations, while you eat your ABC lunch," according to Graham Greene's description of other places where one might read the books appropriate for reading on a ship journey.[37] The middlebrow novel would be fully integrated into its readers' lives.

This study focuses on the period when the middlebrow was coming into its own and modernism was negotiating its relationship to these changing dynamics of novel-reading. This sense of growing proximity between readers and novels, the sense that the middlebrow mode of read-ing was beginning to dominate, was at the heart of one major critical debate in British modernism in the 1920s, over whether the novel should be understood as an aesthetic object governed by the externality of form or as an experience contiguous with the rest of life. Percy Lubbock's *The Craft of Fiction* (1921) exemplified the former position for many crit-ics, while E. M. Forster made the key statement on the novel as life in *Aspects of the Novel* (1927). By 1928, Edwin Muir described Lubbock's and Forster's work as setting up two critical poles between which critics must choose. Lubbock, he argues, goes almost too far toward analyzing the novel in formal terms, to the point that "difficulty in a novel becomes to him, one might almost say, an additional source of aesthetic enjoy-ment."[38] Forster, on the other hand, rejects structure and is "content so long as the novelist 'bounces' us into a belief in his characters and gives us 'life.'"[39] By 1932, Virginia Woolf would criticize the middlebrow writer for incoherently refusing to choose between these two sides: "The middlebrow is the man, or woman, of middlebred intelligence who ambles and saunters now on this side of the hedge, now on that, in pursuit of no single object, neither art itself nor life itself, but both mixed indistinguishably, and rather nastily, with money, fame, power, or prestige. The middlebrow curries favour with both sides equally."[40] The middlebrow writer would chase what sells and what reviewers, book clubs, and libraries would approve, Woolf implies. Such a writer would not see any tension between form and life, and thus could avoid making any honestly intellectual, aesthetic decision about where to position her work.

Lubbock sought to analyze form, and argued that to do so one must attempt to achieve distance from the novel rather than being absorbed by it. For him, point of view was the key technique of the novel. Lubbock thought that novels could be categorized by the kind of point of view they utilize – but the idea that all novels have a point of view implies that the novel, as a genre, always imposes some kind of mediating aperture between viewer-reader and subject matter. As the metaphor of point of view suggests, Lubbock imagined the novel as a visual object that one sees at a distance, rather than feeling up close, and thus the critic can subject it to critical scrutiny and create objective taxonomies. Forster critiqued the distancing procedures that Lubbock promoted, arguing that in "moving round books instead of through them," reader-critics had an incomplete and impoverished relationship to their subject matter.[41] For Forster, the novel cannot be separated from the reader's life and viewed, objectively, at a distance. Instead, it must be fully experienced and is embedded in and indissociable from life. In *Aspects of the Novel*, the most central category of the novel is character – and character for him just means "people" in literature. For Forster, novelistic characters differ from real people only in that they are described beyond the kind of evidence that is available to the historian, to reveal the inner life.[42] Beyond his famous categories of flat versus round, Forster refuses to typologize character, arguing instead that characters are as infinitely various as people.[43]

In Woolf's view, these two approaches were opposed primarily on the basis of where they positioned the reader with respect to the novel. In a 1922 essay, she criticized Lubbock's *The Craft of Fiction* for trying to interrupt the close relationship between reader and novel: "whenever Mr. Lubbock talks of form it is as if something were interposed between us and the book as we know it. We feel the presence of an alien substance which requires to be visualized imposing itself upon emotions which we feel naturally, and name simply, and range in final order by feeling their right relations to each other."[44] She sides largely with Forster, because he argues that criticism should "work[...] from the emotion outwards," through the closeness of feeling rather than the distance of sight.[45] Like Leavis, Woolf often argued that the modern reader wants to be the friend of the novel, but for her this could be a positive development: it brought readers into closer emotional connection with writers and encouraged a democratic feeling of equality between the parties.[46] Ironically, Leavis saw Woolf as just the sort of writer whose books would never be embraced by the common reader she so idealized, because those readers could not help but see the form of her high-modernist novels – and this would get in the way of them relating to the characters as real people.[47]

Critics on both sides of the debate thought that when readers related to characters as real people, they could no longer see the novel itself. They see only their own emotions, and the novel as an object disappears as a sort of mirage. In her 1922 review of *The Craft of Fiction*, Vernon Lee came out on the side of the novel of character in these terms. She preferred novels focused on characters, she argued, because they are more real and less like playing with dolls. Novelists who focus on character have access to what she called, adapting John Ruskin's term, "imagination penetrative."[48] Defined as a capacity for "otherness," this kind of imagination "allows us to witness even the drama of our own life as if it were the drama of others."[49] For Lee, Henry James, who is primarily interested in working out his novel's "logical mechanism," definitively lacks this capacity.[50] Lee's "imagination penetrative" was another version of the concept she is well-known for integrating into English aesthetics: empathy, translated from the German *Einfühlung*. Empathy is the "projection of our own dynamical and emotional experience into the seen form" and "attribution of our life to seen shapes": we feel something or have an experience, and then attribute that feeling or experience to the art object.[51] Reading works through a process like empathy, Lee argued: the novel itself is a screen onto which readers project their own feelings. The novel ceases to have an independent existence, and "lives in the mind which contemplates it."[52]

For Lee, the disappearance of the novel behind a reader's feelings is not a negative phenomenon but simply how aesthetic apprehension works. Lubbock largely agreed with Lee that the novel disappears when we read it – though for him this posed deeply troubling problems that needed to be solved. While Lubbock wanted to distance readers from novels, he shared with these other thinkers the sense that doing so was increasingly difficult. Indeed, he begins *The Craft of Fiction* under a sign of impossibility and failure. He reveals that he wants to think about a novel he knows well as "an old acquaintance," but the problem is that reading, getting close to a book and allowing it to pass through the reader into life, inevitably disrupts knowledge of the book.[53] It will turn out that a book cannot be an old friend – because it is impossible to know a book as well as one must know a person to call him or her a friend. "To grasp the shadowy and fantasmal form of a book, to hold it fast, to turn it over and survey it at leisure – that is the effort of a critic of books, and it is perpetually defeated," he laments.[54] He tries to imagine how one could adequately theorize the novel, to understand it, but the proximity involved in reading makes such a thing impossible: "Nothing, no power, will keep a book steady and motionless before us, so that we may have time to examine its shape and design. As quickly as we read, it melts and shifts in the memory."[55]

Lubbock here digs into a problem that obsessed novel theorists on both sides of the form–life debate: the idea that the novel by definition unfolds in time, as the reader turns its pages. For theorists on Forster's side, the novel's life derives largely from the temporality of reading. In a 1927 essay, Hugh Walpole, for example, suggests that time makes the novel into a living thing that ultimately cannot be studied scientifically:

> a book is not like a well-made box, so truly constructed that it will fulfill every charge made upon it; a book is a fluid, moving, uncertain thing that is glorious one moment and foolish the next, richly covered here and naked to all the winds there, so clearly intimate at this moment that your dearest friend is nothing to you and so stiffly distant at the next that you wonder whether you dare raise your hat to it.[56]

The novel, moving through time, is not the same from moment to moment, rendering it epistemologically "uncertain."

While Forster was very much not interested in formal definitions of the novel, he did argue that there were two constants across the genre: novels are about people, and there is always time. To deny time, he warns, is to become unintelligible. That is what Gertrude Stein did, Forster claims, with great cost to sense and meaning: in her work, "the order of the words in the sentences" was "abolished, which in turn entails the abolition of the order of the letters or sounds in the words."[57] Even for writers who do not go to Stein's extreme, to attempt to evade the gradual unfolding of a novel through time is to sacrifice the thing that makes characters live. In his critique of Henry James's *The Ambassadors* at the end of *Aspects of the Novel*, Forster argues that "[m]aimed creatures can alone breathe in Henry James's pages" – because James only believed in the novel as an aesthetic whole.[58] The characters are not real people; they are there merely to produce a "particular aesthetic effect" that is revealed only in the whole, rather than from part to part, as the reader progressively turns pages.[59] James, Forster argues, denies the "life" of the novel and the "humanity or the grossness of its material."[60] All of these theorists ultimately come to the same conclusion, whether it excites or appalls them: that the novel seems to require affective proximity from the reader due to the unavoidable, genre-defining fact that it must unfold in time.

The form-versus-life debate recapitulated an opposition that had structured thinking about modern poetry, especially in the era of imagism: classicism versus romanticism. T. E. Hulme opposed the hard, finite, aristocratic art of classicism to the democratic, imprecise, emotional art of romanticism.[61] Classical art one observes at a distance; Wyndham Lewis would argue that one can apply intellectual judgment to such works, which are best exemplified by the visual and plastic arts.[62] Romantic art one must feel; it draws people together, and is best exemplified by music.[63] Certainly, Lubbock's formalism, with its terms from the visual arts, draws on values associated with classicism while Forster's vision of the novel in life might be associated with romanticism. It is not, however, quite so straightforward to map these two debates onto one another, because the issue of reading gets in the way.

Hulme and Eliot almost exclusively applied classicism and romanticism to modern poetry, leaving the novel out of consideration. In fact, Hulme argued that while modern poetry – imagism, in particular – can achieve classicism, prose is inherently romantic. Reading prose is "something resembling reflex action in the body."[64] It happens "almost without thinking" and renders the kind of intellectual reflection that Lubbock's formalism requires quite impossible.[65] Modern poetry manages to avoid the unthinking temporal flow of prose: "while one [poetry] arrests your mind all the time with a picture, the other [prose] allows the mind to run along with the least possible effort to a conclusion."[66] In the most basic terms, poems are shorter than novels – they can arrest time rather than "run[ning] along." For Hulme, prose is also necessarily instrumental, unlike poetry. The prose work is an "old pot," but it does not matter much if words and images leak out, because the work is but "a train which delivers you at a destination."[67] The work itself is only a means to an end, and reading is the process by which one uses prose to get to that "destination."

Wyndham Lewis was the critic who most explicitly applied the terms of classicism and romanticism to the novel, especially in *Time and Western Man* (1927) – and in doing so he shared Lubbock's sense of failure. Like Lubbock, he found the temporal dimension of the novel to be inescapable, even though he idealized the static, classical work of art. For Lewis, the temporality of the novel linked it to music, which he saw as an inherently romantic form of art. These aural genres invariably require the spectator to come into close proximity with the work and even to merge with it, in opposition to the distancing visual arts:

> You move round the statue, but it is always there in its entirety before you: whereas the piece of music moves through you, as it were ... When you are half-way through you, if you did not remember what you had just heard, you would be in the position of a clock ticking its minutes, all the other ticks except the present one no longer existing: so it would be with the notes. You have to live the music.[68]

Narrative, like music, comes to life through the spectator and cannot fully exist without her. For Lewis, the novel's merging with the spectator makes it an anti-intellectual, "dumb" form, "a sprawling jelly of the vulgarest sentiment."[69] The novel thus seemed to be incompatible with Lewis's own aesthetic values. He would go on to spend much of his career attempting and then failing, in his own terms, to make the novel evade time, as Chapter 3 shows.

The ineluctable temporality associated with reading novels was a particular obstacle for critics who were working to professionalize literary study and to make literary criticism more scientific. I. A. Richards was at the center of such efforts in England, and was hired to teach the first course on the contemporary novel for the new English Literature Tripos at Cambridge in 1919. Richards planned a book on the novel that would come out of those lectures, but he never completed it and his drafts do not survive.[70] Richards denied that aesthetic experience was specific and special, strove to create precise definitions for critically vague categories such as "the beautiful," and used experimental, empirical methods.[71] In *Practical Criticism*, for instance, Richards tracked Cambridge students' responses to a variety of poems that had been stripped of their titles and authors' attributions. Richards's experimental method demanded simplification, as he warns at the start of *Principles of Literary Criticism* (1925), the companion volume of theory that accompanied *Practical Criticism*. To record empirical responses to aesthetic objects, one must start at "the smallest scale."[72] Nicholas Dames has suggested that for Richards, novels were ultimately too complex for his method to accommodate; their scale was simply too large.[73] In one of his few surviving comments on the novel, in a letter to Mansfield Forbes, Richards complains, "These damned 400-page novels take such a lot of time, and they are very rarely worth it. 31 hours for twopence!"[74] The temporal demands of the novel overwhelmed Richards's sense of the capabilities of his scientific method. Thus, he avoided publishing about the novel.

This study considers the efforts of four novelist-theorists who tackled the problem Richards could not face. Henry James, Ford Madox Ford, Wyndham Lewis, and Rebecca West all tried to figure out how the novel could enable a critical form of reading that would keep the reader at a distance, forcing her to see the novel as an aesthetic whole or an intellectual object rather than experiencing it. For each of these writers, protecting the novel from the middlebrow reader would involve aligning it more closely with criticism. As these writers described how the novel might be made to endure beyond its reading, how it might be rendered a formal object rather than a reader's experience, they imagined it as an intellectualized form, whose primary function would be epistemological, not affective. Such a novel would be particularly accessible to criticism. These writers were attempting to tackle the problems that Lubbock diagnosed: that the novel disappears while we read it and thus we cannot know it adequately. Such novels were designed to get the reader to engage as a critic – to back away from the text, to avoid emotional connection, to treat it as something other than a temporal experience. Rebecca West is the writer I examine who takes this line of thought the furthest. She so completely imagines the novel in epistemological terms that it ultimately becomes a form of knowledge-production. At that point, for her, the truly artistic novel becomes indistinguishable from criticism, the task of which ought to be purely epistemological. The more the novel attempts to open itself to criticism, the more it itself becomes intellectual. Methodologically, this study emphasizes these writers' literary and cultural criticism; it is more interested in how these writers conceptualized their own novels and those of other modernist writers, in what these writers attempted to do, than whether they achieved it. Yet the study also attempts to account for the proximity of fiction and criticism in these writers' work by reading their literary and critical texts next to each other, as coterminous, interpenetrated texts that often address the same questions and issues.

Novel Theory and Technology in Modernist Britain excavates the debates surrounding the reader's relationship to the novel in English novel theory, between Henry James's critique of reading in the late nineteenth century and Q. D. Leavis's pronouncement of the triumph of the middlebrow novel in the early 1930s. Modernist studies is ripe for such an archaeology, because novel theorists' resistance to reading has largely fallen out of critical consideration. Certainly, over the last twenty years, scholars have devoted much critical attention to modernism's relationship to its readership. Important studies have considered the complex publishing histories of modernist works, modernist writers' nuanced strategies for self-promotion and marketing, and modernism's symbiotic relationship with mass culture.[75] Modernist writers' critiques of, and complex relationship with, middlebrow reading habits are topics most often considered in studies of the middlebrow novel; these issues less frequently inform studies of high modernism itself.[76] In the current critical environment, we tend to see modernist writers' discomfort with mass readership and the middlebrow, ambivalence about their own popularity, and theoretical deconstructions of the act of reading as symptoms of an elitist pose. That is to say that we know, now, that modernist writers – including those who most vociferously argued that sequential reading destroys the integrity of the work – were strategically developing celebrity, building their brands, and devising new publishing strategies to engage with the marketplace.

As a field, modernist studies has perhaps moved far enough from Andreas Huyssen's notorious 1986 argument that there was a "great divide" between the autonomous, high modernist artwork and the debased, feminized mass cultural product to be able to return to claims for autonomy and against reading without being worried about uncritically buying into modernism's myths about itself.[77] This book builds upon several recent studies that devote new critical attention to modernism's arguments about the art object's separation from its beholder, its theories of textual integrity, and its complex claims for aesthetic autonomy. Jennifer Ashton, for instance, analyzes Gertrude Stein's arguments for the anti-theatricality of the art object. In doing so, Ashton aims to recuperate a specifically modernist Stein, against the postmodern version that dominates contemporary criticism, which sees her as a writer invested in indeterminacy and the opening of the literary text to the reader. Such visions of Stein, Ashton argues, are an effect of an increasing sense among critics that the divide between modernism and postmodernism is fictional, something that Ashton sees as a "historical misunderstanding," a flattening of literary history, and a sign of a "pervasive theoretical effort ... to displace what, in its broadest terms, we might call the 'meaning' of a text by the reader's experience of it."[78] Like Ashton, I aim to restore modernist novel theory's difficult, even tortured, rejection of reading as a particularly modernist position – and one that had at its core ideas about literature's relationship to technology that are also particularly modernist in their rejection of interactivity.

Other critics have revisited aesthetic autonomy by arguing that it constitutes not an ideological retreat from social reality, but instead a specific kind of engagement with the social. Lisa Siraganian reads modernist claims for autonomy as a rejection of a divide between aesthetics and politics. She argues that "[a]utonomy from the world was never, for the modernists, a failure of relation to it ... an art object's autonomy means not liberation from the whole world but freedom from others ascribing meanings to art objects."[79] Andrew Goldstone, similarly, reads "the aestheticist practices of modernism *as* its social program": aesthetic autonomy was not mere ideology but, instead, a "*mode of relation*" between literature and the social world.[80] What results is a useful, flexible way for critics to define modernism without having to choose between two explanations that, in Goldstone's view, have structured modernist studies: one that defines modernism from within art, as a rejection of earlier forms, and another that explains it contextually, as a way of dealing with social and historical change. Like Goldstone, this book aims to bridge the gap between these two definitions by reconsidering modernist claims for aesthetic autonomy to uncover "the social practices through which purely aesthetic or formal innovations *become* goals in themselves."[81]

Novel Theory and Technology in Modernist Britain contributes to these discussions by showing the specific forms aesthetic autonomy took in the modernist theory of the novel, where it was a complicated and fraught solution to a problem that is both social and aesthetic. Indeed, this book demonstrates that modernist claims for novelistic autonomy were particularly connected to the social world because these writers saw deep parallels between the current state of the novel and that of the machine. Technologies faced exactly the same set of problems: they merged with their reader or operator, were ineluctably bound to the forward progression of time, and could, as objects, disappear behind a user's desires and experiences. Yet, like the philosophers of technology who were working at the same time, these writers often found an alternative vision of technology – and a model for novelistic autonomy – lurking within the machines of the Machine Age. As these writers participated in contemporary debates about how to define and imagine the machine, they found in technology patterns for how to imagine a novel that could stay autonomous from its reader. Rather than theorizing the novel's retreat from the social world into an isolated and impermeable sphere, these writers drew the novel closer to the world – to the technology that increasingly structured modern existence – in their designs for autonomy. Theorizing autonomy in these terms tied the novel to the world – just not to the reader.

The Modernist Machine

Modernist writers who saw the novel getting increasingly close to its readers and problematically merging with life often thought that readers were treating novels the way they were accustomed to treating machines. For example, in *Fiction and the Reading Public*, Leavis writes that middlebrow reading works according to the "penny-in-the-slot-machine principle."[82] Anticipating Adorno and Horkheimer's account of the culture industry, Leavis argues that this kind of reading transforms the novel into a "piecemeal succession of immediate effects."[83] The reader, in turn, becomes unwilling or unable to see the novel as a whole textual object or to feel effects build up over time: "all our habits incline us toward preferring the immediate to the cumulative pleasure."[84] To read this way, Leavis implies, is to handle the novel as a machine.

Leavis's diagnosis of mechanical middlebrow reading – put a penny in a slot and an emotional effect pops out – coincides with the critique of instrumentality in the philosophy of technology. According to Martin Heidegger's well-known account in "The Question Concerning Technology" (1954), modernity entails a very particular understanding of technology's essence, one that he wants to show is historically relative, not itself the only way to understand technology. In modernity, Heidegger argues, technology is conceptualized as a pure means to an end that is always determined in advance.[85] Manufacturing epitomizes how the modern world understands all technology: it cannot create anything new, but only a set of predetermined, always already-known objects. The user of technology can only order from a menu, and the world is reduced to a "standing-reserve" of raw material.[86] As a consequence, our very understanding of causality is reduced, and we lose a sense of responsibility for the technological creations we usher into the world. In *Technics and Civilization* (1934), Lewis Mumford similarly argued that modern technology was governed by the paradigm of mechanization and its attendant standardization, epitomized by the mine and the military, which reduced the human being to a worker following orders, or what Wyndham Lewis would call a "machine-minder."[87] For both Mumford and Heidegger, the stakes of how we conceptualize technology extend far beyond technology itself, to the limits that define what we are able to think. As Mumford put it, "like all great changes, the introduction of the machine was essentially a change of mind."[88] But changing that mind-set would be profoundly difficult, as instrumentality and standardization actively prevent us from being able to think beyond their limits. As Heidegger argues, modern technology insistently moves toward regulating and blocking technology's unsettling aspects, which reveal that an alternative way of thinking about technology is possible. The writers I examine saw the novel as not just affected by, but deeply implicated in, this instrumental conception of technology.

For both novel and machine, one central consequence of instrumentalization is homogeneity. In Heidegger's account, *technē* loses its capacity for "revealing" and can no longer usher the new into the world.[89] Modernist novel theory similarly focused on homogeneity as an impact when the novel is instrumentalized by readers. When readers feel texts, they assimilate them to their own already felt emotional states – the "glow of companionship" described by Leavis.[90] When the work becomes part of the reader, it is brought into Stein's world of identity, which is governed by a logic of recognition: a reader encounters a work through the lens of her own memory, and the reader's sense of the world is reflected back to her through it. The work comes to her as something that is already familiar, and it cannot bring something entirely new into existence. What Stein diagnoses – the disappearance of the novel behind the reader's own experience – is remarkably similar to Vernon Lee's theory of empathy, where the reader projects her emotions onto a work. The only difference is that empathy is simply how aesthetic reception works, for Lee, while Stein strives for a different logic of reading, for the rare work, the "master-piece," that can escape the overwhelming logic of identity.

The novel and the machine seemed to be susceptible to being instrumentalized by their users in spectacularly similar ways, and it was increasingly difficult to conceptualize either as something other than an instrument. One particularly significant reason for this shared problem was time: the machine seemed to be as bound to forward temporal momentum as was the novel. Wyndham Lewis makes the claim for this similarity most explicitly. He argues that just as the novel must extend through time because it is only fully realized as a reader turns its pages, the machine is defined by its propensity to drive time forward, by the impetus to hurry onward toward something that seems new but really is not. Machine culture is ruled by a progress narrative, he claims, in which one innovation must be succeeded by another in a continual drive toward improvement and efficiency.[91] Lewis Mumford would share his diagnosis. In Mumford's history of technics, he emphasizes time as the foundation of modern technology: for him, the clock, not the engine, is the archetypal modern machine, the origin of the Machine Age.[92] Subjects are caught in the machine's time, striving to move forward without being left behind. The machine's mechanical forward momentum makes it difficult to think objectively about technology, to see its structure and its effects on society – just as, for Lewis or Lubbock, a reader cannot comprehend the novel as a cumulative whole because she experiences it piecemeal across an expanse of time.

The novel's structural relationship with the machine seemed to push it away from any possibility of an autonomous, independent existence as an object, away from form, toward its reader, toward life. But the thinkers I examine also saw the beginnings of other ways to understand technology. Like Heidegger, they envisioned what technology could be. For Heidegger, instrumentality was one among many roles that *technē* could play, not its final and ultimate role. Modern technology may be instrumentalized and rationalized, but some residue of an alternative, poetic conception of technology persists around the edges. Indeed, for the ancient Greeks, both art and technology were forms of *technē*. Both had the capacity for what Heidegger calls "bringing-forth," rather than just "challenging," which is what technology as manufacturing does: "What was art – perhaps only for that brief but magnificent age? Why did art bear the modest name *technē*? Because it was a revealing that brought forth and made present, and therefore belonged within *poiēsis*."[93] Art was *technē* because it helped new and heterogeneous creations emerge into the world, caring and taking responsibility for them. Technology could be imagined differently – and art is the site where a new vision of technology is possible.[94] For the theorists this book discusses, to reimagine the novel as a formal object that does not allow its readers to instrumentalize it involves re-conceptualizing what the machine means in modernity. The new novel required a new vision of technology and, at the same time, a new vision of technology would require a new kind of novel.

To think about how technology, differently understood, might ground a theory of art that separated the work from the beholder, we might well turn to Wilhelm Worringer's *Abstraction and Empathy* (1908), a text that influenced many of the writers this study examines. To be sure, Worringer does not discuss technology itself – a crucial point to which I will return. However, he does offer a related theory of art as inorganic, where that means that at its origin, art is motivated not by the desire to merge with nature through feeling, but rather by the need to remove objects from "the flux of the phenomena of the external world" in order to reveal their essential form.[95] His argument corresponds with the form side of the form-versus-life debates: art is essentially not about facilitating emotional experience for the beholder. He writes against a tradition of thought that, he argues, is difficult to resist: explaining art as imitation of nature. In this commonsense view, the beholder of an art object is moved by art that imitates nature because such works enable her to feel empathy with and to get closer to nature.[96] For modern theorists, it was tempting to see such organic empathy as the explanation for all art, as the universal structure of aesthetic experience. Worringer argues instead that art begins not with nature but with abstraction. Abstraction allows man to separate specific objects from the rest of life and from himself – from the "course of happening" – in order to situate each object in its "clear material individuality."[97] Looking at an object in this way, man can see the laws that make it "necessary and irrefragable," rather than arbitrary or random.[98] When man does not feel at home in the world, when he feels intimidated by the world around him, then "taking the individual thing of the external world out of its arbitrariness and seeming fortituousness" makes him happy because doing so allows him to locate "a point of tranquility" beyond the flux of the world.[99] By separating objects from the continuous flow of life, art gives him security, reminding him of the rules and laws that govern the world and allowing him to find a moment beyond the flux. We want organic art, Worringer argues, only in historical eras where we feel deeply happy with, and comfortable in, the world, where we already feel a sense of mastery over it.

In *Abstraction and Empathy*, Worringer never explicitly links the inorganic to machines or technology, though the link is implicit and would be followed up on by later critics, Lewis included.[100] This omission enables Worringer to provide a stable definition of the inorganic as the site of abstraction. Were he to take the next step of pursuing the connection between the inorganic and the machine, a can of worms would open: machines cannot always mean abstraction and form, since they are embedded in historical, social, and economic forces. In the Machine Age, after all, machines seemed to encourage or require their operators to merge with them into "machine-minders" – and to instigate a temporally driven culture in which it becomes increasingly difficult to abstract any object, to see it whole and discover its rules and regularity. Modernist novel theory took on this challenge. In order to imagine technology as a model for an abstract work of art, Lewis, for instance, attempted to recuperate an older, premodern vision of what the machine could be. He theorizes that "Every Age has been 'a Machine Age,'" insisting that modernity's version of technology is not the only possibility.[101] The machine might be instrumentalized today, but if we go back historically, the machine was not an instrument but an abstract, structured form that was powerfully independent of its beholder. If we think of the machine not as the automobile or the assembly line but as the totem pole, Lewis argues, it is possible to kill two birds with one stone: to think our way out of modern technology and to imagine how a work of art – even a novel – might escape the forces that pull it into life and into the reader's experience.

While Lewis wanted to return to an earlier, abstract vision of technology, in order to conceptualize how the novel might stay independent of its reader, the other writers this study considers imagined alternative strategies. Henry James saw potential in the way image-projection technologies associated with popular culture, such as the magic lantern and cinema, transferred autonomy away from their viewers. Ford Madox Ford imagined the telephone beyond its social function for promoting interpersonal communication and intimacy, as a device for connecting fragments of information. For James and Ford, film technology and the telephone, respectively, then become potential sources of remediation, models for restructuring the novel as an autonomous object that can move through time and come to life without requiring a reader's participation.[102] By contrast, Rebecca West focused on what it would mean for the novel to become part of the field of technics – what she understood as the source of all technological innovation, as the site where humanity stores its knowledge and uses it to adapt to the environment. As part of technics, the novel's essential task is to create knowledge, not to affect a reader emotionally. For each of these writers, reimagining technology was an essential task of theorizing the novel for the modernist era.

It was also a task that was particularly crucial for *British* modernists, something they often saw themselves as uniquely well-placed to tackle. This book's focus on British modernism deserves explanation. The bad middlebrow reader was particularly felt as a threat in British modernism of the 1920s. As Mary Grover notes, in the United States, the middlebrow was perceived in much more neutral terms; it was not until the 1960s that American high culture began to feel the middlebrow as a threat, rather than an educational opportunity.[103] At the same time, British writers in the early twentieth century found themselves at the

center of conflicting ideas about Britain's role in the world's technological future: did Britain have a particularly developed relationship to
technology, as the world's first industrialized nation? Or was the country's progress in aesthetics and technology hampered by traditionalism,
held back by its long history, as Gertrude Stein and Frederick Winslow
Taylor respectively radicalized aesthetics and manufacturing in the
United States?

Wyndham Lewis argued for the former position. In a nationalist moment in *BLAST I* (1914), Lewis claimed England as the birth-
place of the modern machine: "Machinery, trains, steam-ships, all that
distinguishes externally our time, came far more from here than anywhere else."[104] For Lewis, England's early technical innovation meant
that English writers had a duty not to get too excited over machinery
as such – the English have too much history with machines to worship
technology as a source of newness and cultural reinvigoration. Thus,
the English could not be futurists, he argued. Only a less industrialized
nation could become so worked up over something so passé: "The Latins
are at present, in ... their Futurist gush over machines, aeroplanes, etc.,
the most romantic and sentimental 'moderns' to be found."[105] Twenty
years later, Lewis would pinpoint the Soviet Union as the group that wor-
shipped modern technology: "in Moscow it is a matter of daily routine
to stick up gigantic posters of power-plants under the nose of the gaping
moujik ... and scream at him, over and over again – 'LOOK at the great
big powerful MACHINE, you idiot tiller of the stupid soil, you animated
sod! – BEHOLD – which can do a billion times as much horse-power of
work, you understand, in a *minute*, do you see, as *you* can do in a twelve-
month!'"[106] In his view, British modernists were well positioned to get
past worship to forge a new, more mature relationship with technology.

According to another view, though, the British represented the old
guard, who were incapable of fully appreciating new technical developments. Consider William Carlos Williams's 1929 response to Rebecca
West's essay criticizing James Joyce, "The Strange Necessity." Williams
alleges that being British, West cannot fully appreciate Joyce, representing as he does "the leap of a new force" with his "technical innovations in
literary form."[107] Joyce "is making a technical advance which she is afraid
to acknowledge."[108] The problem is that English criticism is married to
the past, to its tradition, what Williams calls its insular "mould" that is
"without further capacity for extension and nearly ready to be discarded
forever."[109] The job of the American modernist critic is to support Joyce
in breaking through England's old dominion: "this is the opportunity of

America! to see large, larger than England can."[110] Only the American can see the technical advance as such.

Williams's description of Joyce in this 1929 essay inadvertently recapitulates an argument Percy Lubbock made about James in 1921. Lubbock describes James as the great innovator of the novel, who "permanently enlarged" the resources of fiction.[111] For Lubbock, James helped to create an environment in which a novelist "is handling an instrument, it may be said, the capacity of which has been very elaborately tested."[112] Lubbock claims James and his technical innovation for British criticism, as Williams would claim Joyce for America. Against this backdrop of England's perceived traditionalism in an age of growing American power, and its historical status as technical innovator, it is perhaps not surprising that we see British critics claiming a technology of the novel for themselves.

In analyzing how modernist novel theory understood technology, I aim to contribute to a significant existing body of research that has made technology a central category of modernist studies. My work is particularly influenced by Friedrich Kittler's *Discourse Networks 1800/1900*, which argues that in the modernist period, media were conceptualized not as vehicles for subjective expression but as storage vessels for material inscriptions. In his theory, media texts in the discourse network of 1900 were designed primarily to store, not to communicate: "their indelible and indigestible existence on the page is all that the page conveys."[113] They stored meaningful data and they stored noise, and the difference between the two begins to unravel. The expressive author disappears, to be replaced by a writing body or a machine, as in automatic writing experiments, for example. Kittler's work helps to suggest why and how modernist novel theorists were drawn to technology as a way to reimagine how the novel might be rendered autonomous from its reader. At the same time, however, my work complicates Kittler's by focusing on how unstable the meaning of technology was during the modernist era. The concept of the discourse network implies a kind of determined univocality, such that, in Kittler's view, in the discourse network of 1900, technology necessarily means storage and the collapse of any difference between noise and meaning. Rather, I show that modernist writers were entering into a series of ongoing debates about the cultural and philosophical meaning of technology. If it were possible for technology to model an anti-instrumental vision of the novel, then doing so would require an intervention and a theory, because machines also seemed to be performing the exact opposite cultural work, at the same time.

This book also builds on the work of a newer generation of scholars who analyze formal connections between modernist literature and technologies. Sara Danius, for example, focuses on perception as the nexus where aesthetic form and technology merge. For her, "technology is in a specific sense *constitutive* of high-modernist aesthetics" because it created perceptual possibilities that modernists translated into formal practices.[114] More recently, Mark Goble has analyzed modernist formalism as an investment in medium-specificity. For him, modernism's formalist turn from semantic communication is complemented by a "commitment to the more sensuous and visceral experiences of other mediums," in order to expand literature's capacities.[115] Like Danius and Goble, I focus on how technology inflected modernism's understanding of literary form, but my project contributes a new focus on technology's role in theories of the novel as a genre. My research suggests that modernist theorists were invested in the novel's difference from other artistic forms, and that it was the novel's specificity that connected it so deeply to Machine-Age technology: both were incorporated into the progressive forward momentum of modern time and were susceptible to instrumentalization. From a viewpoint focused on modernist novel theory, the story Goble tells looks necessarily different: the strand of modernist novel theory I trace was not interested in translating the "sensuous and visceral experience" of technological media into novelistic form, but rather in using technology to imagine how the sensuous and visceral – how experience itself – might be stripped from the novel, leaving behind a static, whole object that invites no interaction from its reader.

Outline

The first two chapters of *Novel Theory and Technology in Modernist Britain* consider the work of modernist writers who reconceptualized two specific technologies and extrapolated how their techniques might enable the novel to resist the instrumentalizing tendencies of readers. The first chapter traces James's use of the metaphor of filmic projection in his late critical writing, where he proposed reorienting thinking about the novel away from reading. Certainly, projection is one of James's classic visual metaphors that serves to imagine distance between novel and reader, who is positioned as looking through an aperture onto a fictional scene. In his late criticism, especially the preface to *The Ambassadors*, James expands the metaphor of projection to imagine a fictional scene that has independence from the reader, whose view is not just mediated, but actively interrupted. As James develops the metaphor, he uses it to describe the transfer of autonomy from the reader, who no longer provides the energy to move from page to page and cannot skip ahead if she wants, to the text itself, which moves automatically, as a film projector moves frames of film. James's metaphorical system embeds the reader in a viewing or reading apparatus, imagining a form of aesthetic autonomy that is produced from a technical system of control rather than from purifying a subject's disembodied aesthetic vision. The chapter concludes by arguing that *The Ambassadors* associates a hallmark of James's late style – the tendency to delay tying pronouns and abstractions down to specific referents – with cinema. That technique, which interrupts the reader's view of the scene, emerges as a key site where the novel imagines itself as a device that controls the reader to ensure its own autonomy.

Ford Madox Ford shared James's concern about modern reading habits but for him, the key problem was information overload. Overwhelmed subjects had lost the ability to connect disparate fragments of information and competing points of view. They coped by assimilating fragments and facts into their daily routines, a defense mechanism that neutralizes information and prevents it from communicating anything new. Ford theorizes the impressionist novel as the last bastion of connective thought: it fragments, but then connects the pieces by emphasizing forward narrative movement. For Ford, it is crucial for this momentum to derive from inside the novel itself, not from the reader, who has lost the capacity to connect the fragments.

Ford shares with Lubbock and James an interest in theorizing how the novel can unfold over time, without moving through the reader to do so. But Ford shifts away from their visual metaphors, emphasizing instead the media channel implicit in his formulation that the novel must be "carried" forward. In his *Parade's End* series, he describes that channel as a telephone, which operates both as a narrative connector and a site of fragmentation. It is the series' explicit metaphor for its nonlinear time structure, in which single scenes are split into multiple disjointed perspectives and scattered across the text. Ford imagines the telephone as a figure for a narrative structure that cannot easily be pinned down by a reader accustomed to turning the shock of the news into a morning routine. In Ford's hands, the telephone figures a kind of textual movement that occurs within the novel.

The last two chapters move from examining modernist writers' theorizing of specific devices as models for the novel to examining their theories of technology itself. These chapters situate modernist novel theorists in the context of the philosophy of technology, beginning with Chapter 3's examination of Wyndham Lewis's fraught theory of the machine. For Lewis, the machine and the novel shared a very specific fate, because both were caught in an unstoppable forward temporal momentum – the time of the clock, of progress, of reading. This specifically modern temporality had profoundly negative consequences, in Lewis's view. The modern subject, captured by the rhythm of the machine, was reduced to the status of a "machine-minder." The novel, unable to escape the temporality of its reader's experience of reading, was constantly merging with its reader and could not stand on its own as an aesthetic object.

Lewis attempted to think his way out of this conundrum by theorizing how the novel and the machine could both be removed from modern temporality. The machine must be rethought in premodern terms as a specifically static, formal, geometric object – a work of primitive sculpture, not an automobile. To return to this older definition of the machine was also to link art and the machine together, by defining certain kinds of art as machines. Even the novel could, with difficulty, be imagined in these terms: thus Lewis's "taxi-cab driver test of fiction," which allows that the novel can be art if it can be adequately encountered as a cab driver flips to a random page and takes it in over the course of a single instant. While Lewis's test is strange and disastrous, it resonates with a common theme in modernist thinking about the novel, found in writers from Virginia Woolf to Joseph Frank: the idea that the novel cannot be adequately read, though it can be reread, so that the reader can see the whole without the disturbance of sequential unfolding. In these terms, circumventing the temporality of reading, the novel is a machine, and the machine is recuperated as a model for formal autonomy.

The final chapter broadens the discussion further, from the machine to what contemporary theorists call technics. It turns to Rebecca West's "The Strange Necessity," a long essay on James Joyce that takes as its specific object defining the novel as a mode of information-gathering. West's essay is an important and insufficiently read document in modernism's turn away from Victorian novel theory's investment in the reader. For West, the stakes of defining the novel in terms of information are significant: the novel becomes an experimental discourse that is part of what she calls the super-cortex, a transindividual field of knowledge-production that helps humans adapt to their environment without waiting on biological evolution to do so. West does not explicitly term this field technics, but philosopher of technology Bernard Stiegler would argue that technics must be defined in precisely this way.

Forty years after "The Strange Necessity," West returned to these ideas in a belligerent lecture on Marshall McLuhan. West argues that she articulated McLuhan's popular argument that media are "extensions of man" long before he did, in "The Strange Necessity," when she theorized the novel's position in the super-cortex. But crucially, then, West argues that McLuhan went too far when he promoted the cool, interactive medium in his vision of the electric, computerized future in the global village, where everyone would be intensively connected to everyone else. West, arguing for technics as the generation of usable knowledge and against technics as interactivity, precisely pinpoints modernism's technology against that of postmodernism.

The book ends with a conclusion that considers what happened to modernism's vision of a technologically enabled aesthetic autonomy. It argues that in the context of late modernism, which largely rejected the difficulty and perceived elitism of high modernism in order to appeal to a larger audience, the discourse linking technology and the novel's autonomy from its reader split apart. The conclusion traces the remains of that discourse across the work of three important figures in late modernism and early postmodernism: F. R. Leavis, Joseph Frank, and Marshall McLuhan. Leavis expanded upon the critique of Machine-Age culture that this book considers in Chapters 2 and 3: he imagines that mechanization has produced an anti-intellectual standardization coincident with a loss of cultural tradition and authority. But Leavis refuses to see aesthetic autonomy or formal experimentation as a potential antidote and insists that only a return to an "organic," agrarian world that he identifies with D. H. Lawrence can provide an alternative to debased modernity. Frank, writing at the height of New Criticism in the American academy, promoted the modernist novel's attempt to isolate itself from readers through spatial form, and occasionally described spatial form in technological terms, but he was deeply uninterested in the social or cultural effects of either reading or technology, and thus did not pursue the connection. McLuhan would inherit the largest share of the discourse this book has examined: he certainly pursued connections between technology and modernist form and analyzed how that form renovated the novel's relation to its readers. But, influenced by Leavis's valorization of agrarian society, McLuhan read modernism as the beginning of an electronic age that would retribalize the world through universal participation in everything, including the novel. He thus rejected the link between modernism, technology, and aesthetic autonomy posited by the novelist-theorists this study considers.

Ultimately, the writers this book examines offer a particularly modernist account of the novel's cultural significance in the Machine Age. To theorize a new kind of novel, one that did not need to move through a reader to exist and have meaning, and could not be used as a means to an already determined end, these writers thought it crucial to theorize a different vision of technology. For them, the novel was part of the field of technology, which shaped the novel's limits and possibilities. As it was overwhelmingly defined in modernity, technology was an instrument to a predetermined end, one that promoted homogeneity and sapped the capacity for critical thought. But these writers also thought that technologies had the potential to be static objects of intellection, modes of connecting the fragments of modern thought, sites where human knowledge is stored, and devices that resist the instrumentalizing impulses of mass culture. But in order to change the novel, it would be necessary to change technology at the same time. Aesthetic autonomy – in its particular guise within modernist novel theory – emerges as a complex strategy that deeply entangled the novel with the world even as its theorists strove to keep readers at a distance. The novel, as theorized by these writers, is particularly powerful and important as a site where modern subjects could rethink the essence of the technology that shaped their lives.

CHAPTER I

Point of View as Projector
Henry James, Percy Lubbock, and the Modernist Management of Reading

In "The Art of Fiction" (1884), Henry James contemptuously observes that "many people ... read novels as an exercise in skipping."[1] Readers who skip are not serious enough to comprehend an ambitious literary work, but more important, for James, is the fact that they literally "skip" the novel itself. They think a novel "depends on a 'happy ending'" and want the story to be so "full of incident ... that we shall wish to jump ahead, to see who was the mysterious stranger, and if the stolen will was ever found."[2] The novel becomes a mere means, an "exercise," which leads up to the sought-after conclusion: "The 'ending' of a novel is, for many persons, like that of a good dinner, a course of dessert and ices."[3] These readers find that the art of the novel – what James defines as "the search for form" – interferes with their childish pursuit of dessert: they "would all agree that the 'artistic' idea" is "host[ile] to a happy ending" and "might even in some cases render any ending at all impossible."[4] James alludes to the possibility that a special kind of "artistic" novel might be able to compensate for these distasteful habits by interfering with the end to which the rest of the text is subjugated.

"The Art of Fiction" is an early foundational document in the history of modernist novel theory. It constitutes a clear response to the mainstream of Victorian thinking about the novel, represented here by Walter Besant. "The Art of Fiction" is a rewriting of Besant's *The Art of Fiction* (1884), which argues that though a novel itself may be bad, it "is sure not to be badly read."[5] For Besant and other Victorian novel theorists, such as G. H. Lewes and Alexander Bain, the reader was the appropriate object of literary criticism, because the novel's significance and value lie in its effect on the reader. The reader cannot devalue the work; rather, there *is* no work, in a real sense, without readers, whose reading habits cannot be normatively judged. In *Principles of Success in Literature* (1865), Lewes defines popular success as "[r]igorously considered ... an absolute test" of the "merit" of a novel and dismisses concerns about the quality of the reading public as jealousy on the part of less successful writers.[6] Thus, he argues, "[t]he prosperity of a book lies in the minds of readers."[7] For these thinkers, the novel *is* its effects on readers. For James, the art of the novel, its value, lies instead in "the search for form" – and this he defines as a quality that is ultimately antagonistic toward the way readers read, frustrating their search for an affective payoff. This critique of reading set the stage for modernism's reorientation of novel theory toward form and away from reading as the object of criticism.

For James, the particular problem with reading, what form must work to solve, is a phenomenon that later critics would identify as instrumentalization. Fredric Jameson offers the detective story, that classic form of eagerly read middlebrow fiction, as a privileged example of instrumentalized art: "you read 'for the ending' – the bulk of the pages becoming sheer devalued means to an end – in this case, the 'solution.'"[8] When works are instrumentalized, they are integrated fully into the structure of the commodity, defined as "a thing, of whatever type, [that] has been reduced to a means for its own consumption."[9] Jameson draws on Theodor Adorno's argument that commodified music "forcibly retard[s]" its listener.[10] Rather than apprehending the particular qualities of the music, she can only experience the "cumulative success" of the work.[11] The music itself disappears behind the listening experience, which becomes more important than the work: "[t]hat it happens, that the music is listened to, this replaces the content itself."[12] For Adorno, the Hollywood movie most exemplifies this replacement of the text by its consumption. The most end-oriented of cultural products, its value is determined completely by its conclusion, which can be glimpsed in every moment of the text: "As soon as the film begins, it is quite clear how it will end, and who will be rewarded, punished, or forgotten."[13]

Percy Lubbock – who elevated the Jamesian novel to the centerpiece of a new theory of the novel and pushed James's critical apparatus even further toward the form side of the form-life debate of the 1920s – was particularly worried about the novel becoming "a means for its own consumption," as Jameson puts it.[14] For Lubbock, the problem is not just one particular bad style of reading, but reading itself, as a general practice: James's concern with average readers morphs into hopelessness about the possibility of anyone being able adequately to apprehend a novel. Because a novel unfolds gradually as we read, it is more or less impossible for us to understand it fully, to see it as an aesthetic whole, a true art object: "It is revealed little by little, page by page, and it is withdrawn as fast as it is revealed; as a whole, complete and perfect, it could only exist in a more tenacious memory than most of us have to rely on."[15] The problem of instrumentalization grows even more severe and intractable. To read is to skip the novel, even if one is trying to see the novel as a complete, integrated whole: he flatly states that "[w]e cannot remember the book."[16] There is no way to read without transforming the novel from an independent object into an experience of consumption.

For James and Lubbock, the novel can only be apprehended as a complete whole – it can only evade its own instrumentalization – if reading becomes more like looking, which would seem to position the reader at a distance from the text, rather than encouraging her to consume it. This is one motivation behind their key theoretical contribution: elevating point of view over reading as the central category of novel criticism. They focus on how the reader is positioned in relation to the novel's fictional world, not on reading as an experience: "the question of our relation to the story, how we are placed with regard to it, arises with the first word," Lubbock states.[17] He divides the novel into a series of categories – the dramatic, scenic, and pictorial – in terms of where the reader is situated: is the reader high up with a commanding view of a vast stretch of the fictional scene, or is she "straight in front of the action"?[18] Either way, the reader is a viewer looking at an external scene, not a child eagerly consuming a novel as though it were ice cream. This is a criticism focused on the way information becomes known, not on how that information affects a reader.[19] Rather than reading to get what she wants, the reader is distantly "placed," as Lubbock puts it, and observes a fictional world unfold before her without trying to use it for a purpose.

This chapter argues that in his late work, James pushes the distancing, mediating capacity of point of view even further than Lubbock would, by imagining it as a technology, an image-projection device. James finds in projection technologies such as the magic lantern strategies for how point of view might control what a reader can see, separating her from the novel and ensuring the novel's autonomy from her. As Mark Goble, Richard Menke, and Pamela Thurschwell have recently shown, James relished the aesthetic possibilities associated with the mediating prostheses of technology.[20] Goble in particular argues that the logic of technologically mediated, indirect, circuitous communication, exemplified in his analysis by the telegraph, pervades and structures James's late work. Building on these ideas, I trace James's theory of point of view as a visual technology that interrupts the reader's view of a fictional scene. In doing so, this chapter's contribution is to show that technological mediation was, for James, a strategy for generating aesthetic autonomy for the novel.[21] James is the place from which this book must begin because he initiates a way of thinking about the novel that would be developed further by writers in the 1920s: the idea that the novel can resist its incompetent readers or save itself from them by utilizing strategies drawn from contemporary discourses of technology.

The prefaces to the New York Edition of James's work (1907–9), where James aims to imagine, create, and train a readership adequate to his works, present point of view as a magic lantern that projects images.[22] As he develops this metaphor, especially in the preface to *The Ambassadors*, James emphasizes two key functions of point of view. First, the projected images move independently, on their own, rather than being motivated by an active reader. Second, projection is the prefaces' metaphor for how point of view manages what the reader can and cannot see of the fictional scene; point of view operates as a mediating aperture that distances the reader from the scene. The novels often actively block the reader's clear view, something James explores when, in a later essay, he turns the magic lantern into an airplane that drops shadows on the ground below, obscuring the reader's view. The reader may not be able to see the fictional scene clearly, but she can see the shadows or projected images themselves, and those shadows are point of view: they reveal nothing but how the viewpoint mediates the scene. As James puts it in one formulation, the point-of-view figure's consciousness is what is projected onto the fictional scene. In lieu of having a clear sight line of the novel's content, the viewer instead gains access to a view of the novel's form: we see the workings of point of view itself. With this technique, the novel is able to interrupt readers who want to get close to the text, who are so absorbed that they want to consume it. In turn, the novel attempts to replace regular reading with criticism, which, for James, sees past what most readers want to consume in order to comprehend the novel as a formal whole. Criticism, James argues, does not consume the novel, but rather ensures its duration beyond the moment of its consumption.

While the magic lantern is James's explicit referent, I argue that film is the apotheosis of his thinking about projection. For James, projection is a metaphor for how the novel can distance and detach the reader – and he sets the stage for later writers who would use the term theoretically to think about the reader's relationship to a text. In James's metaphorical system, projection has this distancing effect because the text can move itself along in the same way a projector moves frames of the film, without relying on the reader for its motive power. The idea that film transfers autonomy from the viewer, who no longer has control over the viewing experience, to the text itself, was a topic frequently discussed in modernist writing about film. But while most critics differentiated the difficult writing of modernism from the mass media of cinema on the basis of this control over viewing, James instead welcomes cinema as a model for novelistic structure. Even though the mechanical movement of the images in a film might seem to model a passive form of reading, for James that passivity requires the reader to stay detached and distant from the text, as a critic would. As the novel becomes a kind of image projector, it solves the problems Lubbock would identify as obstacles to criticism – that the reader has trouble seeing the novel as a whole and inevitably turns it into a means to achieve an experience. James envisions image projection as a way to shift control of the reading process from reader to text and, in the process, he makes his reader a component of a larger apparatus for reading. He thus imagines a form of aesthetic autonomy for the novel that does not involve empowering a pure aesthetic vision on the part of the reading subject, but instead requires controlling and managing that subject's view.

The chapter concludes by turning to the text of *The Ambassadors* (1903), which anticipates the image-projection metaphors of its preface. The novel links cinema to the aesthetics of delay that characterizes James's late style, where the narrative reveals basic information – the identity of a figure who has appeared, the content of a telegram – only after announcing the presence of that information. At its climax, the novel connects this strategy of delay to cinema when Strether realizes the sexual nature of Chad and Mme. de Vionnet's relationship. This scene is presented as a *tableau vivant* in which Strether, Chad, and Mme. de Vionnet move about within the frames of a painting. In the context of the preface's theory of image projection, the cinematic quality of this moving picture has to do with the way our view, even of this moment of revelation, is consistently delayed and blocked, as we see "figures" before they resolve into particular characters. Strether's view, at this point, casts moving shadows rather than operating as a clear aperture. Exactly at the kind of juicy moment to which a bad reader might want to skip, the novel inserts a mediating distance, one that interrupts the reader's view of the fictional scene even while the novel moves on. In turn, a major feature of James's late style – the broad use of pronouns and abstractions that are sometimes filled in later with content, sometimes not – emerges as a way James embeds readers into an apparatus that controls their view of the scene.

Defending the Novel against Consumption

In "The Art of Fiction," James imagines an innocent, earlier era of novel-reading, before he arrived on the scene, when no one wanted anything but to consume the novel: "there was a comfortable, good-humoured feeling abroad that a novel is a novel, as a pudding is a pudding, and ... our only business with it could be to swallow it."[23] In a later essay, "The New Novel" (1914), he would critique current writers who still thought in these regrettably old-fashioned terms. H. G. Wells, Arnold Bennett, and Hugh Walpole – these writers still wanted actively to aid readers who desired to consume the novel. In particular, James argues, they present their work as the mere "squeezing out to the utmost of the plump and more or less juicy orange," fictional material that is processed to make it easily digestible.[24] In the essay's other dominant metaphor, James suggests that these writers see their work as a "slice of life" that "pretends to be nothing else," although that is disingenuous, since there is "no question of a slice upon which the further question of where and how to cut it does not wait, the office of method, the idea of choice and comparison, hav[ing] occupied the ground from the first."[25] Such a novel invites its readers to treat reading as an opportunity for a meal: "The slice of life [is] devoured, the butter and the jam duly appreciated."[26] In both essays, readers long to eat bad novels, to take such works into their bodies and metabolize them.[27] Read this way, novels cannot be distant objects to be thought about; rather, they merge with their readers. Such works invite consumption because they do nothing to interfere with the reader's view of the fictional scene. These novels strive to present a crystal clear picture of their subject matter with no obvious form that would intervene between reader and subject.

Lubbock further develops James's argument in *The Craft of Fiction*, where consumption comes to define not just bad reading of bad novels, but the very process of reading itself. Lubbock argues that when we read, we recreate the novel inside our own minds: "These things take shape in the mind of the reader; they are re-created and set up where the mind's eye can rest on them."[28] As a result, the novel ceases to be an independent work of art but, through reading, comes to exist inside the reader. With such a close connection to the novel's fictional world, it is difficult for readers to avoid becoming immersed, "losing ourselves in the world of the novel."[29] We treat characters as though they were real people, getting to know them and imagining a full life out of our glimpses: "I, as I read, am aware of nothing but that a new acquaintance is gradually becoming better and better known to me."[30] We act as though we live in the world of the novel, as though the novel's fictional scene is real: we "complete, in our minds, the people and the scenes which the novelist describes – to give them real dimensions, to see round them, to make them 'real.'"[31] And as a result, our ability to understand and analyze the work suffers – we cannot see the novel as a whole, complete aesthetic object. Lubbock strains against this mode of reading that seems frustratingly inevitable. He tries to forge a critical method that would allow the novel to maintain independence from the reader, to avoid merging into the reader's life.

For James, criticism is one key line of defense against the full consumption of the novel by readers. In "The Future of the Novel" (1899), he argues that most novels effectively disappear soon after being published: "What at least is already very plain is that practically the great majority of volumes printed within a year cease to exist as the hour passes, and give up by that circumstance all claim to a career, to being accounted or provided for."[32] These novels might still be read, but they are consumed in the process. It is criticism, not regular reading, that accounts and provides for novels, making them endure and allowing them to be a part of the future of the novel – criticism can give a novel "a present and a past."[33] James describes criticism's nurturing capacity: it helps to enlarge the capacity and range of the novel, encouraging it to experiment rather than "only to go straight before it," a path that would make the novel's future "in very truth more and more ... negligible."[34] Criticism helps the novel endure beyond the moment of its consumption by transforming reading into a different kind of process. The absorptive, consuming function of reading can be made intellectual and self-aware: "The effect, if not the prime office, of criticism is to make our absorption and our enjoyment of the things that feed the mind as aware of itself as possible, since that awareness quickens the mental demand."[35] With a healthy criticism, "we cease to be only instinctive and at the mercy of chance": both the reading and the writing of novels can be made intentional and mindful.[36]

In *The Craft of Fiction*, Lubbock imagines that the critic is able to evade the consumptive pull of reading because she must stay at a distance from a novel's fictional world. If the reader can maintain sufficient distance from the novel's scene – she "must stand above it" – she has a chance of being able to see the novel's form.[37] From this distance, the reader may be able to "watch the book itself, rather than the scenes and figures it suggests," and thus avoid being "swayed and beset" by the content of the novel, which she must try to see as "objects, yes, completed and detached."[38] So many readers focus their attention on "something more, something other, than the novel itself − ... its life-like effects."[39] A better criticism must maintain distance in order to see the book as itself, a "whole and single" object, rather than "a continuous, endless scene, in which the eye is caught in a thousand directions at once, with nothing to hold it to a fixed centre."[40]

For James, the novel can encourage critical, rather than consumptive, instrumentalizing reading, by manipulating point of view, which is the technique through which a novel can best reveal its form − the book itself rather than its subject matter, as Lubbock puts it. In "The New Novel," James suggests that Joseph Conrad's complex narrative schemes work to this effect. In his reading of *Chance*, James analyzes Conrad's doubled narrative system, which focalizes the story through both Marlow and an omniscient narrator who "sets Marlow's omniscience in motion."[41] Although James criticizes Conrad's system for being too cumbersome, he also praises it for making form itself visible and thus impeding readers inclined to skip the novel to get to the point.[42] In this case, Conrad generates such a complex point of view that it ceases to be a device for accessing a fictional scene but becomes the main scene itself: he makes narrators "almost more numerous and quite emphatically more material than the creatures and the production itself in whom and which we by the general law of fiction expect such agents to lose themselves."[43] The extra layer of narration calls attention to the formal shape of the novel, as a dirty pane of glass might force a viewer to remember that she is looking through a window: "Nothing could well interest us more than to see the exemplary value of attention, attention given by the author and asked of the reader, attested in a case in which it has had almost unspeakable difficulties to struggle with − since so we are moved to qualify the particular difficulty Mr. Conrad has 'elected' to face: the claim for method in itself."[44] Conrad utilizes point of view to turn the reader into a critic, by forcing attention to the formal shape of the novel and preventing her from losing herself in the fictional world.

James most fully explores point of view as a mediating function that creates distance and imposes form between a reader and a fictional scene in the prefaces to the New York edition. To do so, he develops a series of metaphors that describe point of view as a technology. Certainly, James frames his argument about point of view in terms of "centers of consciousness," a term that would seem to imply that point of view is a psychological principle, that the narrating subject's psychology organizes the novel. But the prefaces consistently use metaphors of visual technology to imagine the center of consciousness as an optical lens rather than a unit of psychology. In the preface to *The Portrait of a Lady*, for example, James famously describes that novel's center of consciousness, Isabel Archer, as "a pair of eyes," "a field-glass," and a "window": a device that "forms, again and again, for observation, a unique instrument, insuring to the person making use of it an impression distinct from every other."[45] In *What Maisie Knew*, the transparent, neutral "field-glass" of *Portrait* mutates into a hallucinogenic magic lantern:

> It was to be the fate of this patient little girl to see much more than, at first, she understood, but also, even at first, to understand much more than any little girl, however patient, had perhaps ever understood before … She was taken into the confidence of passions on which she fixed just the stare she might have had for images bounding across the wall in the slide of a magic-lantern. Her little world was phantasmagoric – strange shadows dancing on a sheet.[46]

Maisie's world will seem phantasmagoric – to her and to the reader – because, as the point-of-view character, she is an optical medium, as James points out in the preface: "I should have to stretch the matter to what my wondering witness materially and inevitably *saw*; a great deal of which quantity she either wouldn't understand at all or would quite misunderstand."[47] As Christina Britzolakis notes, James here "define[s] narrative point of view as a technological prosthesis" rather than a psychological property.[48] As a prosthesis, point of view is not an internal, psychological capacity of a narrator to whom we can grow close, whom we can treat as a real person, but instead a technical tool used to control a reader's level of engagement, to manipulate what she sees, and to keep her at a distance.

The magic lantern is crucial for James's development of his concept of point of view in the preface to *The Ambassadors*. He uses the metaphor to suggest how separate the reader is from the fictional scene, how much her view is mediated and controlled and how that setup makes it impossible for her to consume the scene. Initially, the preface to *The Ambassadors* explores the idea that the image projected – the fictional scene – might move on its own, gaining a degree of autonomy rather than passively waiting to be seen or consumed by a reader. In this version of the metaphor, the real person who inspired Strether projects an image of a fictional scene featuring Strether the character: it is the man's "charming office to project upon that wide field of the artist's vision – which hangs there ever in place like the white sheet suspended for the figures of a child's magic-lantern – a more fantastic and more move-able shadow."[49] James, as reader-author, is entirely passive; he does not watch, and instead his vision is "the white sheet" that simply "hangs" in place. What James emphasizes, against his own passivity, is the projected shadow's ability to move itself – it is not only "strange," like the shadows Maisie sees, but also "moveable." As the metaphor develops, this capacity for autonomous movement only intensifies. To explain his own eagerness and excitement as he explores the story thus suggested, James transforms the magic-lantern show into a problematic chase scene. His role becomes active and intense, as he "look[s] for the unseen and the occult, in a scheme half-grasped, by the light or, so to speak, by the clinging scent, of the gage already in hand."[50] The projected shadows attempt to get away, as James pursues, rather than passively watching. According to a racist metonymy that transforms the dark shadow into a black slave, this "game of difficulty breathlessly played" turns into a "dreadful old pursuit of the hidden slave with bloodhounds and the rag of association."[51] The pro-jected shadows evade the vision of their aggressive pursuer, move on their own, and struggle to secure and maintain their autonomy.

The preface proceeds to tone down the violence and oppression of this image by shifting focus from the fleeing fictional scene and the reader-author who chases it to how point of view limits, and even blocks, how much the reader can see of that scene. The preface turns to Strether the character, who mediates the reader's view of the novel's fictional world, controlling how much she is able to see of the scene that is now protected from her interventions.

> The novel's plot was to be so much this worthy's [Strether's] intimate adventure that even the projection of his consciousness upon it from beginning to end without intermission or deviation would probably still leave a part of its value for him, and *a fortiori* for ourselves, unexpressed. I might, however, express every grain of it that there would be room for – on condition of contriving a splendid particular economy.[52]

James imagines Strether's consciousness as an image that will be projected onto the novel's subject matter, rather than a clear portal or viewpoint through which a reader looks. That projected consciousness interferes with any spectator's observation of the novel's subject matter itself: it "would probably still leave a part of its value for [Strether], and *a fortiori* for ourselves, unexpressed." Through Strether's point of view, the novel omits information rather than transmitting it, presenting only what "there would be room for." Whereas through Maisie we watch "strange shadows" and "images," and through Isabel we look out on "the human scene," through Strether we see only a generalized, abstract, content-less "it." As Lubbock puts it, "Henry James knows all there is to know of Strether, but he most carefully refrains from using his knowledge."[53] Strether's consciousness tightly manages what the reader knows, and in the process, shelters the novel from readers who might treat it like a commodity to be consumed. It is not the content of the novel itself that is controlled, but the reader's view of it. Underneath the abstraction of "it," the novel runs off on its own.

This, James writes, is the more "sedentary part" of the compositional adventure, and "involves as much ciphering, of sorts, as would merit the highest salary paid to a chief accountant."[54] As the fictional scene runs off on its own, the pursuer, the reader-author figure, stops chasing and returns to a more passive role, becoming an accountant at his desk. His task is to use the point-of-view figure to transform the fictional scene into something more abstract, "it." At its next stage, the preface suggests that the "ciphering" function of point of view aims to substitute "the story of one's story itself" for "the story of one's hero": to make the novel's method, its form, visible in the place of the content of the fictional scene.[55] Later in the preface, James almost explicitly aligns the novel's accountant, its cipherer, with Maria Gostrey, the *ficelle* figure whose job is to solicit information from the center of consciousness so that the writer can avoid long passages of exposition. Maria Gostrey, James writes, has been "pre-engaged at a high salary," pointing back to his mention of the chief accountant's pay grade.[56]

> Through the *ficelle*, the task of the novel is to project imaginatively, for my hero, a relation that has nothing to do with the matter (the matter of my subject) but has everything to do with the manner (the manner of my presentation of the same) and yet to treat it ... as if it were important and essential.[57]

"[T]he manner of my presentation," form, is projected onto the novel's "matter" and displaces the specific content that makes up the novel's plot. Rather than enabling the reader to get closer to Strether, to learn more about his background and his thoughts, instead the *ficelle* facilitates the elision of that novelistic content behind a meta-level analysis of the novel's form. The *ficelle* gives James an alibi for making the novel be about its own form – something, he admits, "the dire paucity of readers ever recognising": the thing he's most looking for, the thing he's adventuring after, is not something a reader is ever going to notice.[58] That is to say, the more the novel considers its own form, the less readers will want to jump ahead; even further, the less they will like to read the novel at all. In this sense, James's claim that Maria is "the reader's friend," although she looks like Strether's friend, is ironic – she is on the writer's payroll, after all.[59]

In this complex narrative, the preface uses the figure of the magic lantern to suggest the autonomy of the fictional scene from the reader-author, who turns momentarily into an active, authoritarian figure before returning to a position of passive watching. The projected image, the fictional world, proceeds to run off on its own, to move by itself, of its own accord. At the same time, the preface imagines projecting Strether's consciousness onto the scene, supporting the scene's autonomy by controlling the reader's view of it. The novel manipulates its point of view in order to require the reader to disengage from the fictional scene, drawing her attention to an abstracted outline rather than a full picture. As a result, that reader can see the form, the shape, the whole of the novel, rather than getting sucked into its story, wanting to be friends with its characters, jumping to the end to see what happens. Imagined in these terms, projection gives the reader access to a critical view of the novel as an aesthetic object, a view that Lubbock worried was difficult to attain.

In "The New Novel," James would return to the figure of image projection to further develop the idea that point of view can block a reader's view of a fictional scene, substituting in its place a view of the novel's form. He gets there, in his discussion of Conrad's use of Marlow as a narrator, by using the image of an airplane flying high above the ground to describe the mediating distance imposed between a reader and a fictional scene by the doubled narrative system. Marlow functions as

> a prolonged hovering flight of the subjective over the outstretched ground of the case exposed. We make out this ground but through the shadow cast by the flight, clarify it though the real author visibly reminds himself again and again that he must – all the more that, as if by some tremendous forecast of future applied science, the upper aeroplane causes another, as we have said, to depend from it and that one still another; these dropping shadow after shadow.[60]

Conrad's innovation is to interrupt the reader's view of the diegetic world: the airplane operates as a visual technology that "casts" an interfering "shadow" between reader and scene, much as the magic lantern produced "strange shadows dancing on a sheet" in front of Maisie.[61]

With the airplane metaphor, the essay also returns to the aggression suggested by the preface's description of the fictional scene as a slave running away from violent oppression. Here, the novel's point-of-view system does not just interfere with the reader's view, but becomes openly antagonistic toward the fictional scene: these airborne narrators are destructive precursors to aerial bombardiers. While "The New Novel" predates the first aerial bombings of World War I by one year, it was clear by then that the airplane would be a technology of war. In 1913, for example, the *London Times* asked, "Shall we try for the ownership of this weapon, or wait till we have felt the prick of it against our own men first?"[62] At the other pole from a romantic "flight of fancy," the airborne narrators now drop "shadow after shadow" as though they were bombs. These airplanes produce the "perfect eventual obscuration" of the ground beneath – the novel's subject matter – in a frenzy of destruction that figures how the novel uses point of view to control the reader's access to the fictional scene.[63] Such a novel gives the reader only a deeply obscured view, and forces the reader to notice the aggressive way in which her view is managed. A novel whose point of view can be figured by a warplane cannot be a passive object of consumption, a pudding that easily slides down the metaphorical throat of an eager reader who does what she wants to the novel. A reader cannot take up residence in such a novel's almost inaccessible – indeed almost bombed-out – fictional world. And yet it is significant that the destruction of the fictional world is perpetrated, in James's scenario, not by any reader, but by the novel's own point-of-view system: still the novel forecloses any possibility of the reader's interference.

The fictional world of *Chance* is all but destroyed by Conrad's complex system of point of view, but the reader does get access to something else in return: the form of the novel. *Chance* "sets in motion more than anything else a drama in which his own system and his combined eccentricities of recital represent the protagonist in face of powers leagued against it, and of which the dénouement gives us the system fighting in triumph, though with its back desperately to the wall, and laying the powers piled up at its feet": Conrad's formal system itself is the main character of this novel, and the novel's plot is supplanted by the story of the form itself.[64] As a reader, this is what James sees when he looks at the novel: "This frankly has been *our* spectacle, our suspense and our thrill."[65] A reader like James can see such a novel intellectually, with detachment. She cannot consume the novel – that possibility has been foreclosed, James's metaphor suggests. Through its careful management of point of view, *Chance* becomes a novel that is simultaneously a work of criticism.

It forestalls the possibility of being consumed, earning itself a future. At the same time, it also forces self-awareness, by not allowing the reader to see past or through its formal, technical system.

Projection and the Moving Image

In the years following the prefaces, projection would become a key term in a series of critical debates within modernism about the relationship between beholder and art object. The figure was claimed both by theorists who promoted the active, intense interpenetration of text and reader and by those who, like James, argued instead for the opposite – for the work's autonomy and detachment from the reader. These divergent theories of reading can be exemplified by how they understand the metaphor of magic-lantern projection. At stake was whether projection placed an interfering, technical medium between work and beholder, or instead enabled their greater proximity. In the first English discussions of empathy as aesthetic response in the 1910s, for example, Vernon Lee theorized the apprehension of aesthetic objects as "this projection of our own dynamical and emotional experience into the seen form."[66] When we ascribe beauty, for instance, to a work, we are engaging in "sympathising projection": we project our own subjective experiences onto it, imagining them as qualities that inhere in the object itself.[67] The nature of aesthetic experience is that we are "projected out of ourselves," onto the work.[68] If we take her metaphor of projection seriously, she seems to be suggesting that the beholder looks at the art object, but sees only a projected image of herself. For Lee, it is impossible for the beholder to ever see the work for what it is on its own, because the work is nothing on its own.

H. D., writing several decades later, would build on the idea that through figurative projection, the text loses an independent, objective existence, and merges with the reader. For her, that merging would not involve the reader projecting herself onto the work, but rather the writer projecting her private experience into the world so that the reader can engage fully and deeply with it. For H. D., the magic lantern's projected images "open the boundaries of the self": "The dream-picture focussed and projected by the mind, may perhaps achieve something of the character of a magic-lantern slide and may 'come true' in the projection."[69] In "The Dream" (1941), H. D. opposes two conceptions of memory in these terms: a "flat picture" in which subjective material stays private and contained and a "projected" picture in which that same material becomes an open, readable, three-dimensional document.[70] Projection is the opening of a door to the extrasubjective world:

> The dream, the memory, the unexpected related memories must be allowed to sway backward and forward, as if the sheet or screen upon which they are projected, blows and is rippled in the wind of whatever emotion or idea is entering a door, left open. The wind blows through the door, from outside, through long, long corridors of personal memory, of biological and of race-memory. Shut the door and you have a neat flat picture. Leave all the doors open and you are almost out-of-doors.[71]

H. D. conceives of projection as an intimate, visceral, even erotic interpenetration of reader and author.[72] H. D. and Lee thus appropriate the figure of magic-lantern projection to articulate a relationship between beholder and work or reader and novel that would horrify James. The preface to *The Ambassadors* rejects the idea that the novel could "project" its fictional world so as to fully envelop the reader, as well as the idea that the reader can "project" her own feelings to fully cover the novel.

James was not the only thinker on the other side of this aesthetic debate to claim the term, theorizing the artwork's detachment from its beholder as a form of projection. When other writers used the figure as James did, they also emphasized the magic lantern's prosthetic qualities – its artificial technicity, its status as a visual medium that intervenes between beholder and work. Consider José Ortega y Gassett's 1925 reworking of the figure as a metaphor for the dehumanization of art. Like James, he underlines the visuality of the magic lantern and the detachment it implies. When the spectator is linked to the work visually, she is necessarily removed from it: "Seeing requires distance. Each art operates a magic lantern that removes and transfigures its objects. On its screen they stand aloof, inmates of an inaccessible world, in an absolute distance. When this derealization is lacking, an awkward perplexity arises: we do not know whether to 'live' the things or to observe them."[73] For Ortega, the magic lantern figures the distancing of the work of art from lived reality. The reader is then able to maintain an attitude of observation, rather than being forced to "live" the work – which is exactly what a spectator had to do under Lee's version of projection. Earlier, Ortega differentiated modernism from realism through a similar "optical problem" that emphasized the distancing properties of a properly modernist form of vision: "to see the garden and to see the windowpane are two incompatible operations which exclude one another."[74] To see – and then inevitably feel – the garden is to fall into the trap of realism and to engage a work through sympathy; as a consequence, "a work of art vanishes from sight."[75] To focus instead on the window is to apprehend a work in a modernist fashion, for James or Ortega. Windows inspire no emotions and, in terms that resonate with James's working of the metaphor, interfere not only with our ability to feel anything from a novel, but even with our ability simply to see its content.

Projection thus emerges as a key term in modernist aesthetics, and especially in the theory of the novel. Two diametrically opposed versions of projection circulated in modernist aesthetic theory, and these critics articulated their vision of how aesthetic apprehension works through different accounts of what happens when an image is projected. James set the stage for these discussions in claiming projection as a distancing form of point of view that controls access to fictional information and structures the reading experience to keep the novel from yielding its value immediately. In his version, the image casts an impenetrable shadow over the content, making it difficult to reach the end or payoff that is, for many readers, the novel's reason for being and the sole source of its value.

James's discussion of projection also reaches out toward another debate within modernist aesthetics, concerning the differences between how literature and film set up the experience of their beholder: although the magic lantern is his explicit referent, he develops the projection metaphor in a way that emphasizes its potential connection to the still emergent technology of cinema. The preface to *The Ambassadors* defines the magic lantern by its ability to produce shadows that are not "strange" but "moveable" – so much so that they might even be imagined as the shadows beneath an airplane traveling overhead.[76] The most important characteristic of these images is that they travel before a passive, detached viewer who is not actively involved in the fictional scene, and who is thus able to see the work as a complete aesthetic object. In emphasizing the magic lantern's independence from the viewer and its autonomous movement, James points away from the nineteenth century's phantasmagoria exhibitions and toward film.

James's work – especially the prefaces – has more often been considered in relation to photography; he invited this context when he illustrated the New York edition with photographs. In James's terms, the photograph and the magic lantern do share an important function: each abstracts what it represents. Stuart Burrows has shown how James often understands the photograph to have the power to "stereotype," requiring the "sacrifice of specificity" in its representation of the world.[77] For example, the photograph in the frontispiece of the New York edition of

The Golden Bowl need not detract from the novel because it represents "no particular thing in the text, but only of the type or idea of this or that thing."[78] It represents neither a real place nor the store within the novel where Amerigo finds the golden bowl: "the small shop was but a shop of the mind, of the author's projected world, in which objects are primarily related to each other, and therefore not 'taken from' a particular establishment anywhere, only an image distilled and intensified, as it were, from a drop of the essence of such establishments in general."[79] While both visual media "distill" what they represent, there is a crucial difference in how they do so. The photograph, necessarily a single image, takes the multiplicity of views available in the world and condenses them into one picture. The magic lantern, by contrast, necessarily entails movement between multiple projected images, its "moveable shadow."[80] Film, not photography, is its fullest manifestation.

That movement is crucial: for James, the magic lantern points toward a mode of reading in which the reader watches a text that moves on its own, at a distance, allowing no intervention. Later modernist writers would imagine film in precisely these terms, though, unlike James, they wanted reading to be entirely different from this kind of experience. These writers rejected analogies between film and literature because a film-goer has less authority to manipulate the medium than does a novel-reader. As Virginia Woolf puts it, a reader "can pause; he can ponder; he can compare," but the spectator of a film has no such control: though a viewer "can see them once he can never see them twice, and ... one picture must follow another without stopping."[81] Christopher Isherwood's novel about the British film industry, *Prater Violet*, similarly emphasizes film's unstoppable mechanical momentum: "The film is an infernal machine. Once it is ignited and set in motion, it revolves with an enormous dynamism. It cannot pause. It cannot apologize. It cannot retract anything. It cannot wait for you to understand it. It cannot explain itself."[82] In contrast to this mechanically driven model of apprehension, Isherwood's novel describes viewing a painting and reading a book as activities controlled by the spectator, not the text: "you can just glance at it, or you can stare at the left-hand corner or half an hour ... The author can't stop you from skimming it, or starting at the last chapter and reading backwards. The point is, you choose your approach."[83] Woolf and Isherwood argue that while books will "wait for you to understand" – to "ponder" and "compare," to replay a scene – film will not. The reader is the most important part of reading – her experience and her comprehension are what matter. By contrast, the film operates with autonomy from its viewer. The film "cannot apologize ... [i]t cannot explain itself" – the viewer's opinions and experiences simply do not matter. Literature's malleability enables readers to move forward or backward at any speed they wish, in order to ensure their comprehension; the film mechanism is utterly indifferent to viewers and what they might understand.

Maria DiBattista and David Trotter have examined these arguments about film's automatic movement in the interest of reappraising the long-standing critical tendency to use film as a descriptor of modernist literary form, especially through the trope of montage. DiBattista and Trotter both suggest that film, understood as a deeply automatic, mass-cultural technology, operated as a foil to modernist literature. In Trotter's reading, modernists were often critical of film's automatic structure: "Modernism was not the product of a machine age. It was (among many other things) a wilful enquiry into the age's wilful absorption in the kinds of automatic behavior exemplified by machinery in general" and film in particular.[84] For James, however, film's automatic movement is an attractive metaphor because of how it shifts the location of autonomy in the viewing situation. Woolf and Isherwood expect the reader of a novel to have autonomy over her own reading experience; we might expect the viewer of a photograph to have the same degree of control. The viewer of the film might be understood to have much less autonomy. The ability to move, to set something in motion, to control the viewing experience, transfers from the viewer to the projector. The projector and the images it moves have autonomy – from the grasp of the distant viewer, who cannot control their movement. Instead, the novel must evade that reader; it runs away. The autonomy of the image from its distant reader translates into the automatic movement of the frames of film: the projector moves the frames of film in an incessant progression, regardless of whether the reader would be better served by watching a scene again, pausing, or skipping to the end.[85]

This idea that the motive force for the novel's movement might derive not from the reader but from the text itself is particularly explicit in Lubbock's writing. He begins *The Craft of Fiction* worried that the novel constantly moves as we read it. The novel's movement makes it challenging for a critic to see its form: "Nothing, no power, will keep a book steady and motionless before us, so that we may have time to examine its shape and design."[86] Jamesian point of view emerges as the solution to this problem, because the novel begins to internalize the movement of the novel in reading.

What Lubbock values is "dramatization": James dramatizes what earlier writers from Flaubert to Thackeray would have presented in a scenic or pictorial way. Dramatization is about movement, for Lubbock: rather than being a still picture, the Jamesian novel moves on its own – like film. Lubbock does not go so far as to explicitly use cinema as a metaphor, despite the profusion of visual images in the text, but his language suggests his interest in positioning the reader to see the characters – especially the characters' minds – move on their own:

> the difference is that instead of receiving his report we now see him in the act of judging and reflecting; his consciousness, no longer a matter of hearsay, a matter for which we must take his word, is now before us in its original agitation. Here is a spectacle for the reader, with no obtrusive interpreter, no transmitter of light, no conductor of meaning. This man's interior life is cast into the world of independent, rounded objects; it is given room to show itself, it appears, it *acts*.[87]

We don't have someone else telling us what a Strether thinks – instead we *see* him thinking. His thinking is dramatized visually as movement, as action, such that we don't need reading to make the novel move, to bring it to life:

> Just as the writer of a play embodies his subject in visible action and audible speech, so the novelist, dealing with a situation like Strether's, represents it by means of the movement that flickers over the surface of his mind.[88]

This flickering movement repeats the image from the beginning of *The Craft of Fiction*, when Lubbock describes how difficult it is to keep a book "steady and motionless" before us so that we can see its form. Here, he displaces this troubling "movement" – the temporal movement of the reader's mind is "solved" by relocating it inside of the novel, containing it. The motive power comes from *inside* the text. The text itself does the agitating, the acting, the flickering, leaving the reader and author securely outside as parties observing a spectacle.[89] Lubbock is not imagining the characters as real here. Rather, they are technically generated by the optical apparatus of point of view: "enable an onlooker to see round the object, to left and right, as far as possible, just as with two eyes, stereoscopically, we shape and solidify the flat impression of a sphere."[90] The viewer's visual capacity is embedded into the apparatus, "enabled" by the text to see a particular kind of image: it moves and the viewer watches. In turn, the viewer can see form, which is redefined in filmic rather than photographic terms, emphasizing how the novel transmits itself: "Not as a single form, however, but as a moving stream of impressions, paid out of the volume in a slender thread as we turn the pages – that is how the book reaches us."[91] Film becomes the perfect metaphor for describing the novel's tight control over what the reader can see.

These filmic metaphors that describe how the novel reduces the autonomy of the reader, who no longer has the capacity to look however she chooses, can be understood in terms of the discourse of the management of perception that emerged in the nineteenth century. Jonathan Crary has traced, during that period, a shift from a camera-obscura model of visual perception – in which vision is an objective and fixed process directed at an object – to a model in which vision was "subjectified," reimagined as a fully physiological capacity that has less to do with the seen object than with the sensory capacity of the subject.[92] Vision was instrumentalized, and became a sense that could be trained and manipulated; the viewer became part of a viewing apparatus.[93] Crary exemplifies this shift in models of vision through the difference between the panorama and the multimedia diorama. In the former, the viewer has the freedom to look however she wants. By contrast, the latter device requires the viewer to sit on a moving platform; the viewer's visual capacity is managed and organized in a specific way. For Crary, the diorama "removed that autonomy from the observer," positioning her as a component of an adjustable, controllable device.[94] James's image-projection metaphor situates the novel in this discourse; for him, the novel, like the diorama, must locate its viewer within the textual apparatus, as one component of a larger technical system. He seeks to take control of the viewing experience away from the viewer and to locate it in the novel itself. While both photography and film are part of the new model of subjectified, trainable vision in Crary's history, James's system of metaphors sets up the projection of movable images as the height of the control of the viewer's vision.

As Crary points out, modernist theories of aesthetic autonomy are usually considered in opposition to this discourse, which reduces perception to a physiological capacity that is subject to measurement, training, and management. For many modernists, aesthetic autonomy would accompany a mode of vision that is precisely disembodied, as a "retreat from the anguish of a modernized world that was making the body into an apparatus of predictable reflex activity."[95] Chapter 3 will trace one exemplary attempt in the work of Wyndham Lewis, who argued that aesthetic object must be perceived in an instant, because otherwise the object becomes part of the subject's embodied, temporal experience. James's and Lubbock's attempts to imagine how the novel might evade consumption by real readers – how it might escape the forgetfulness associated with temporal extension, how it might correct readers' inability to see the whole – are certainly attempts to separate aesthetic perception from the flawed human body. But this is why it is so significant that James envisions technologies of image projection – the magic lantern, cinema, even the airplane – as models for how to correct readers' faulty habits. Rather than positing a purified realm of pure intellection, James instead locates the reader within a prosthetic, technological apparatus. What the reader is allowed to see, and how she is able to respond, are all carefully controlled. In Crary's terms, then, James participates in the "instrumentalizing of human vision as a component of machinic arrangements": for the novel to achieve autonomy, the viewer must lose it and be reduced to an instrument.[96] For James, the techniques of managing embodied vision precisely become a resource for preserving the autonomy of the literary text from a too-active, too-greedy reader.

The Ambassadors, Ambiguity, and Cinematic Movement

For James, the novel functions cinematically when it interferes with the reader's ability to apprehend the fictional scene. The novel moves on, independent of what a reader may or may not understand; autonomy shifts from the reader, whose view is now closely managed, to the text itself. Perhaps the strongest evidence that, for James, cinema models this control over the viewer is to be found in *The Ambassadors* itself. The novel links an important scene that is described in cinematic terms to one of the characteristic devices of James's late style: the delay generated when we are told that narrative information exists before we learn what that specific information is. The preface's theory of projection offers a way to understand why this association makes sense: by pointing to the abstract exterior of information without revealing its content, the novel exercises tight control over the reader's vision, reducing that reader's autonomy over the reading situation and distancing her from the scene as the text takes control and moves on, underneath the abstractions, regardless of what the reader knows. In drawing this evidence from the novel, my aim is not to use the literary text merely to exemplify the claims laid forth in James's literary criticism, but rather to treat the novel and the preface as continuous. To do so is consistent with the theory laid out in the preface, which describes how point of view projects form onto content – to interrupt a reader's view of the fictional scene in order to push to the front the view a critic ought to take.[97] In these terms, the novel not only promotes a critical view, but begins to resemble criticism itself.

The novel's climax is, famously, a cinematic *tableau vivant*, a moving picture in which Strether imagines himself walking around inside a favorite painting. Strether leaves Paris for the countryside, where he runs into Chad and Mme. de Vionnet, the woman who is the cause of Chad's rebellious desire to stay in Paris and not return to Woollett to run the family business. Strether planned his trip out of town explicitly as the recreation of a Lambinet painting he remembers from long ago: "he had gone forth under the impulse" to spend a day devoted "to that French ruralism, with its cool special green, into which he had hitherto looked only through the little oblong window of the picture-frame."[98] He finds a charming inn along a river as he "continued in the picture" and "all the while not once overstepped the oblong gilt frame."[99] Strether then sees two figures come into view, rowing toward him on the river – Chad and Mme. de Vionnet. The two have obviously spent the night together because, although they pretend to have just come down from Paris that day, they are both in shirtsleeves. Thus, in one shocking moment, Strether realizes that he has misread the affair between Chad and Mme. de Vionnet – their "virtuous attachment" has been reduced to banal adultery.[100] The lovers' entrance is also explicitly described as the painting moving: "It was suddenly as if these figures, or something like them, had been wanted in the picture, had been wanted, more or less, all day, and had now drifted into sight, with the slow current, on purpose to fill up the measure."[101] Strether becomes their "spectator" as they row toward him, and the language of painting is replaced by that of the vaguer "picture."[102]

Jonathan Freedman has recently laid out the case for reading this moment as cinematic, despite the dearth of explicit references to cinema in James's work. Freedman argues that throughout the novel, Paris has been characterized as a place of optical illusions – certainly, late in the novel Strether reflects that perhaps he was so often mistaken because "[o]f course I moved among miracles. It was all phantasmagoric."[103] This scene on the river, then, would be the culmination of the novel's optical illusions: a *tableau vivant* that moves and is ultimately, Freedman argues, "a kind of silent movie."[104] Indeed, as Freedman points out, George Méliès, who was working at the same time as James, imagined his illusion-centered films precisely as moving *tableaux vivants*.[105] For Freedman, thus, the scene on the river is cinematic because it is part of the culture of "beautiful and brilliant illusions that challenge the very order of the empirical world as we see and experience it" – because the scene on the river is one of the series of illusions that Chad and his ambassadors have used to trick and manipulate Strether.[106]

But read through the projection metaphor of the preface, however, the cinematic qualities of this scene seem to depend not so much on the production of an illusion as on the way the novel manages the reader's view of the scene. Initially, before the lovers appear, the novel describes the fictional picture as an aesthetic whole that is perfect because of its economy, what it leaves out. The full drama of the novel is condensed into an image through which Strether walks:

> They were few and simple, scant and humble, but they were *the thing* ... 'The' thing was the thing that implied the greatest number of other things of the sort he had had to tackle; and it was queer, of course, but so it was – the implication here was complete ... The text was simply, when condensed, that in *these* places such things were, and that if it was in them one elected to move about, one had to make one's account with what one lighted on.[107]

This is a picture of a complete whole built out of what, in the preface, James calls "ciphers," which hide specific referents behind abstractions. This whole is not static but in motion – and Strether is walking around in it – because every "thing" could be filled in by a number of different referents that the reader cannot see. The difference between a specific thing and "the thing that implied the greatest number of other things" is the novel moving, refusing to be pinned down or to give itself over immediately to a reader who wants to know what Strether is talking about. This is a whole that has already been subjected to the process of accounting James describes in the preface, the process that hides information about the fictional scene from the reader, while forcing her to see the novel's form – here, that complete whole – instead. What he finds in this final picture is an economized, condensed, ciphered, accounted for version of the whole novel, the whole novel translated into a "thing" that moves. And as much as Paris is a site of illusion and cinematic, optical trickery, as Freedman argues, it is also "the empire of 'things'" that are disorienting because they refuse to stay still.[108] As Mme. de Vionnet complains, Paris is "this tiresome place, where everything is always changing."[109]

The centrality of movement to the climax is further suggested by the source material recycled in the moving-picture metaphor. Early in the novel, before he meets Chad and Mme. de Vionnet in Paris, Strether reflects that his whole life has been a picture: "It was at present as if the backward picture had hung there, the long crooked course, gray in the shadow of his solitude."[110] If Strether's life is a picture, at this point early in the novel, it is a singularly static one: his point is that he feels trapped, as though his doom is inevitable, made certain by his earlier choices. He is stuck at the end of a course, in an exhausted picture that cannot move any longer. Over the course of the novel, the very nature of this picture will change, until we reach the dynamic motion of the climax's *tableau vivant*. This passage directly anticipates the language of the preface as well, where James's artistic vision "hangs there ever in place like the white sheet suspended for the figures of a child's magic lantern – a more fantastic and more moveable shadow."[111] Here, though, there are no moving shadows projected on the gray sheet by his "empty present," which is peopled only by the easily identifiable figures of Mrs. Newsome, Waymarsh, and Maria Gostrey: "though there had been people enough all round it, there had been but three or four persons *in* it."[112] There is no one else, and at this point the novel's economy is spare enough that Strether's picture cannot have "things" or "figures" whose referent can be deferred. This image emphasizes Strether's feelings of being pinned down, entrapped, impoverished: the novel cannot move forward, choosing from an available roster of "things."

The climax transforms the "backward picture" into an entirely different visual system that requires movement and refuses so easily to reveal its entire economy. When Strether sees them on the river, Chad and Mme. de Vionnet come into view as "things" that necessarily move and change:

> What he saw was exactly the right thing – a boat advancing round the bend and containing a man who held the paddles and a lady, at the stern, with a pink parasol. It was suddenly as if these figures, or something like them, had been wanted in the picture, had been wanted, more or less, all day, and had now drifted into sight, with the slow current, on purpose to fill up the measure.[113]

Before Strether realizes who these two figures really are, he sees them as abstractions – "figures," "the right thing," "a man," "a lady."[114] Psychologically, this delay is Strether's shock, his unwillingness to believe what he is seeing, but the prefaces suggest a more literal interpretation.[115] This is a moment where Strether's optical point of view is projected on top of the fictional scene, and the result omits information but produces a condensed visual picture, an aesthetic whole. The novel asks the reader to see how these abstract images "fill up the measure" of the picture, before seeing two characters she knows: to see them as part of an aesthetic whole that moves, but is nonetheless complete. The novel momentarily blocks the reader's view: she sees "two figures" for a moment, before they resolve into the specific figures of Chad and Mme. de Vionnet. At this moment, certainly the juiciest in the whole novel, where Strether comes face-to-face with sexual impropriety, the novel pauses our view, showing us the aesthetic object rather than letting us get to the point.[116]

Delayed realizations, in which a character is confronted with an abstracted view of something they more fully grasp at a later point, are a dominant feature of James's late style and especially of *The Ambassadors*. The novel associates this technique with Strether's particular point of view – Strether, James warns us in the preface, is "our belated man of the world."[117] He does not learn about Mme. de Vionnet's existence until quite late, a revelation "so long and so oddly delayed."[118] Strether thrives on "his postponements," and is always one step behind his own novel, which runs on as he holds the reader back.[119] Strether understands the world at a delay, but more strikingly, this is how he relates to himself. From his earliest conversations with Miss Gostrey at the beginning of the novel, Strether comprehends his own behavior only retrospectively: "It was not till after he had spoken that he became aware of how much there had been in him of response."[120] Chatting with Miss Gostrey later, he makes a comment and it is only when she laughs that he understands his own meaning: "He saw now how he meant it as a joke."[121] When he meets Miss Barrace, he initially sees her as part of a trick played on him by Chad's friends: "why Miss Barrace should have been in particular the note of a 'trap' Strether could not on the spot have explained; he blinked in the light of a conviction that he should know later on, and know well."[122] To fully understand his own reasoning, why he thinks what he does, he will have to wait until later, for the novel to move on.

Strether's belatedness is how the novel justifies its tactic of delaying the reader's access to narrative information – where we are given access to an "it" or a similar abstraction, which will be filled in with specific content only later, or even never. One notable example of this technique can be found just at the moment Strether first meets Chad's friend Little Bilham, momentarily mistaking him for Chad. Strether's conversation with Little Bilham takes place off-screen, so to speak, without the novel providing a scenic account of it. The text provides no information about this conversation until Book Three; for several pages, there is a gap between what the narrator and the reader know and what Strether knows. As Maud Ellmann remarks, it is as though "[t]he prose itself is missing its appointments with reality."[123] This gap cannot be accounted for by the idea that Strether provides an aperture through which we see the scene: we are precisely prevented from seeing what Strether sees or knowing what he knows; what we do know, however, is *that* Strether knows. We see the outline of his knowledge, but not the content. The last sentence of Book Two describes Strether's plan to disclose his encounter with Little Bilham to his friend Waymarsh: "However, he would tell him all about it"; the very beginning of Book Three makes an almost identical claim: "Strether told Waymarsh all about it."[124] We see an abstract version of what Strether sees – his vision minus its content, transformed, like the content of the book in James's analysis in the preface, into an "it." The novel's delay tactic might be interpreted psychologically, as a sign of Strether's growing inner conflict, but in the terms James lays out in the preface, what we have here is Strether's consciousness being projected onto the scene of the novel rather than functioning as a clear portal through which we see the fictional scene. Such an explanation also helps to make sense of the fact that sometimes Strether knows what content lurks behind the abstraction, as in the case with Little Bilham, and sometimes he does not, as when the lovers row into his view at the climax – but the technique is the same. Either way Strether's consciousness subtracts information about that scene, encoding those contents behind the abstraction "it," allowing us to see the "it" but not its referent. This structure of delay permeates the novel, such that, for example, several times Strether encounters another character but sees only a man, or a woman, or a "figure," initially, until he later determines who exactly is there. This occurs, for instance, when Chad makes a surprise appearance at the opera – Strether sees a "solid stranger" who only later resolves into Chad – and when Strether runs into Mme. de Vionnet at Notre Dame, seeing only "a lady" the first several times he notes her as he walks around the cathedral.[125] The novel subtracts specificity from something concrete, the "stereotyping" function James associates with photography – but even further, the novel then moves on, regardless of what the reader knows.

Delayed understanding is specifically linked to the movement of images in a series of passages following Strether's initial sighting of Chad at the opera. At first, James invokes the metaphor of a flash of light to describe Strether's seemingly immediate understanding that Chad has profoundly changed: Strether "saw him, in short, in a flash."[126] As we might expect, though, the flash of insight and illumination will turn out to be illusory, as further, even contradictory flashes follow this one while Strether takes in the Parisian atmosphere, walking with Chad down a street filled with "expressive sound, projected light."[127] The second flash is "a quick ray" of understanding: "The intimation had, the next thing, in a flash, taken on a name – a name on which our friend seized as he asked himself if he were not, perhaps, really dealing with an irreducible young pagan ... The idea was a clue and, instead of darkening the prospect, projected a certain clearness."[128] Within three pages, he has reversed this moment of insight, deciding that Chad is not a "young pagan" after all. Strether changes his mind and experiences confusion, but not because these flashing images hide the truth: Chad "had in every way the air of trying to live, reflectively, into the square, bright picture."[129] Rather, it is the movement of the images, the fact that Strether sees a series of flashes, that prevents his understanding from stabilizing into any definitive, single enlightenment. Whatever Strether knows at any one point is just one flashing image, one abstracted "thing" that will continue to change and move and be filled in with different specific referents.

James imagines this kind of delayed access to content in terms of cinema in one of his very few explicit mentions of the device, his 1909 short story "Crapy Cornelia." The story uses the cinematic close-up to figure the protagonist's delayed recognition that a woman he meets at his girlfriend's home is actually his former fiancée, whom he has not seen in some time. All he sees, initially, is the woman's hat:

> The incongruous object was a woman's head, crowned with a little sparsely feathered black hat, an ornament quite unlike those the women mostly noticed by White-Mason were now 'wearing', and that grew and grew, that came nearer and nearer, while it met his eyes, after the manner of images in the kinematograph. It had presently loomed so large that he saw nothing else.[130]

At this first moment, Cornelia Rasch's hat plays the role of the "figures" of *The Ambassadors*: it takes the place of the actual person seen by White-Mason.

As the scene develops, the cinematic close-up morphs into another of James's image-projection metaphors, the airplane that projects (or "drops") shadows.

> It was in the course of another minute the most extraordinary thing in the world: everything had altered, dropped, darkened, disappeared; his imagination had spread its wings only to feel them flop all grotesquely at its sides as he recognised in his hostess's quiet companion, the oppressive alien who hadn't indeed interfered with his fanciful flight, though she had prevented his immediate declaration and brought about the thud, not to say the felt violent shock, of his fall to earth, the perfectly plain identity

of Cornelia Rasch. It was she who had remained there at attention; it was
she their companion hadn't introduced; it was she he had forborne to face
with his fear of incivility. He stared at her – everything else went.[131]

He sees "the most extraordinary thing in the world," which projects darkening shadows onto the real person, preventing him from realizing who
she is. Then the flight of his imagination is truncated and he drops to
earth, seeing the real woman in front of him. Just as in *The Ambassadors*
and in his critical writing, James here imagines cinema as the projection
of the point-of-view figure's consciousness onto the fictional scene, a
technique that produces the view of an abstraction, a "thing," rather than
that of the dramatic scene itself.[132] In turn, the workings of point of view
draw our attention, as the point of view drops obscuring shadows rather
than showing us a clear view of a fictional scene.

The images these repeated moments of delay, where an abstraction is not immediately filled in with content, function as "the evocation of a spectacle to
which we are emphatically denied visual access but to which we are nonetheless attracted and enticed."[133] These words are Crary's, as he describes
the "perpetual play of attraction and absence" in the paintings of George
Seurat, who, like James, explored the aesthetic potential of techniques of
perceptual management.[134] Crary here describes Seurat's *Parade de cirque*,
which portrays a circus sideshow meant to attract a crowd's attention to
the main stage act – but the painting is organized to close off our view
of that scene. Crary argues that Seurat draws his viewer's attention only
to refuse access to the scene in order to expose the emptiness of modern
spectacle – that we are paying attention to nothing. The management
of attention itself becomes the point. James similarly attracts our attention to something we cannot fully see, and hollows out the very thing he
invites us to see. For him, if the reader's view is interrupted, if she sees
an "it" or a "thing" instead of specific content, then the novel achieves a
degree of autonomy from that reader. This strategy deflects our view from
the fictional scene to the way we are placed before it, from the fullness of
content to the emptiness of form, from the affect-producing, titillating,
engaging content a reader is anxious to view to the dead, intellectualized
outline of form.

The novel concludes with a prime example of this technique of suspen-
sion, one that it associates almost explicitly with the projection of form
on top of content. The final scene, between Maria Gostrey and Strether,
is not portrayed explicitly as cinematic or phantasmagoric. However,
drawing on the metaphoric theory James begins in the novel and lays out
in the preface, this scene might be the most cinematic of them all: "the

article" – the abstract term Strether uses to describe the object manu-factured by the factory at Woollett, the source of the Newsome family fortune – is never filled in with content. Initially, Strether describes the factory in this way: "But above all it's a thing. The article produced."[135] Again, he gives us an abstracted, content-less version of what he knows. "The article," as it is repeatedly referred to, is particularly empty, even self-referential, since "the" is, of course, an article. At the very end of the text, though, Strether is perfectly willing and able to state the name of the factory's product. But this time, Maria Gostrey won't let him tell her: "she not only had no wish to know, but she wouldn't know for the world."[136] Here Maria Gostrey begins to function in her capacity as *ficelle*, just as James promised in the preface: in preferring not to fill "the article" in with content, she maintains the cipher through which the manner of presentation overtakes the matter of the novel. In the pref-ace, James reads this moment in the novel as the perfect finale because it functions "to give or add nothing whatever" – Strether's knowledge is not revealed, and nothing disrupts the aesthetic whole of the novel.[137] Strether and Maria Gostrey began this conversation early in the novel, at the start of the second book, and "the article" has stayed empty, without content, since then. Two pages from the end, Maria Gostrey notes, in free indirect discourse, that the actual thing manufactured "didn't signify now."[138] The novel – and Maria – have moved on, regardless of whether the reader knows. At this point in the novel, Strether suggests that nam-ing the article would provide "a great commentary on everything," but while the text points to the availability of this commentary it refuses to fill that structure in with content.[139] What finally operates as a "great commentary on everything" is not the article itself but the fact that the novel moves on – to its conclusion – without revealing what the article is. The empty, abstracted term almost explicitly becomes the novel's critical account of itself, its final comment on its own form.

In a mocking dialogue in *Boon* (1915), H. G. Wells would criticize the superficiality of James's work, "the elaborate, copious emptiness of the whole Henry James exploit."[140] That emptiness is the shape of aesthetic autonomy – for James, a condition achieved by imagining point of view not as a clear portal through which a reader sees a scene but rather as a device for managing a reader's view. In his theory of point of view as a form of image projection, James imagines that the point of view is pro-jected on top of a fictional scene, interrupting the reader's view, such that she sees only the empty outline of a projected shadow, rather than the full scene below. The reader becomes part of a technological apparatus for viewing; autonomy shifts from the viewer, who no longer has the authority to control the pace or depth of her viewing, to the text itself, which is freed to move like the frames of a film, regardless of how much a viewer might like to skip to the end or to pause or rewind. What the reader is able to see, from within this apparatus, is the form of the novel, its aesthetic shape and its method. This mode of viewing that James associates with cinema solves the problem Lubbock would go on to identify with reading – that because the novel moves, no reader can see the whole. This reader can see the whole, if nothing else. What it takes to ensure the novel's autonomy from its reader and to enable that reader to see the formal outline rather than the fullness of affect-producing content is the mediating distance James finds modeled in technology.

CHAPTER 2

What Carries the Novel
Ford Madox Ford, Impressionist Connectivity, and the Telephone

Like Henry James, Ford Madox Ford was deeply concerned about the state of modern reading. For him, bad reading was indicative of a much larger social problem diagnosed by a range of modernist thinkers: information overload. T. S. Eliot described the problem at the beginning of *The Sacred Wood* (1920): "The vast accumulations of knowledge – or at least of information – deposited by the nineteenth century have been responsible for an equally vast ignorance."[1] For Ford, similarly, the surfeit of information made it all but impossible for the modern subject to understand the world around her.

Ford argued in *The Critical Attitude* (1911) that the Victorians were led by "Great Figures," public intellectuals such as Darwin, Ruskin, or Carlyle, who were the moral authorities of the age and led people through forests of competing facts.[2] In the twentieth century, he claimed, the Great Figure shattered into innumerable figures: facts, statistics, information. These were, for example, the facts Dowell encourages his heart-patient wife to think about in order to keep herself calm in *The Good Soldier* (1915): "She would talk about William the Silent, about Gustave the Loquacious, about Paris frocks, about how the poor dressed in 1337, about Fantin Latour, about the Paris-Lyons-Mediterranée train-de-luxe, about whether it would be worth while to get off at Tarascon and go across the windswept suspension-bridge over the Rhone to take another look at Beaucaire."[3] These lists of facts also, of course, provide a cover that enables Florence to hide her affair with Edward Ashburnham, and, in turn, allow Dowell to dissimulate his own role in the deaths that follow.

The resulting situation of information overload combined with ignorance and uncertainty describes the state of the modern subject: "so many small things crave for our attention that it has become almost impossible to see any pattern in the carpet. We may contemplate life steadily enough to-day: it is impossible to see it whole."[4] Ford imagines the individual's relationship to information much as Lubbock envisioned the average reader's relationship to the novel: she is incapable of holding any whole in her mind. This modern subject is too distracted by facts, too consumed in communication, ever to be able adequately to comprehend the world around her. For Ford, this problem extends beyond reading to characterize man's relationship to life itself.

Ford was invested in tackling the problem of information overload and wanted to improve the public's capacity for thinking, both through his work in publishing and through the impressionist novel itself. *The English Review*, which Ford edited between December 1908 and February 1910, was one of his key strategies in this regard: it was designed as a broad-ranging periodical that would reform the public sphere by guiding its readers through diverging viewpoints, in a disinterested, critical, rational way. Mark Morrisson has traced Ford's plans to create, in *The English Review*, a space for rational discussion of opposing viewpoints, where consensus might be formed, even in a society increasingly fragmented and factionalized.[5] The impressionist novel was another site where new kinds of thinking could be imagined. As Mark Wollaeger has shown, "Ford's impression is meant to counter the unmanageable welter of modern facts by transforming them into assimilable information."[6] Rather than just recording an ever more immediate and fragmented reality, the impression was a "utopian information technology" that would "reinvest dead facts with coherent value," Wollaeger argues.[7]

Ford's tetralogy about World War I, *Parade's End* (1924–8), thematizes the crisis in connective thinking and communication that Ford diagnosed in his cultural criticism. While the novels' hero, Christopher Tietjens, strives to improve communication and thought against the pressures of the war, and idealizes both peace and true love as deep, direct conversations, the novels never allow this dream to come to fruition, even as the war ends and Christopher is reunited with his lover. Against Christopher's ideal, the novels imagine, as an alternative, the telephone conversation. Not only does the telephone require a mediating distance, but it also inflicts explosive interruptions that align it with the violence of the front. Nonetheless, the telephone is also a technology of connectivity. Thematically, the novels use the phone to map the expansive network of the war's effects, which connect the front to the base depot, the living to the dead, and soldiers to civilians back in England. Ford builds on a Victorian tradition of using the telegraph as a figure for a connective web that links all the parts of society together. Reimagined for the era of World War I, Ford's telephone becomes the series' privileged metaphor for the kind of connective thinking, enabled by impressionism, that is appropriate to the age of profound fragmentation.

In the first volume, *Some Do Not* ..., the telephone is a central figure for one of impressionism's techniques for representing a fragmented reality but also synthesizing the pieces. In *Joseph Conrad: A Personal Remembrance* (1924), Ford argues that the novel must break apart narrative unities such as conversations – this is an essential component of *progression d'effet*, which is the novel's sense of momentum. Scattering these pieces creates what Ford calls a "live scene" that gives the narrative a sense of time and movement separate from that of the story.[8] These fragments, dispersed but retaining links to their other pieces, generate an electric field of connectivity: this is how the impression restores connective thinking. *Some Do Not* ... performs a specific version of this technique: the novel breaks scenes or events into two versions, associated with the isolated points of view of different characters. But it then disjoins those versions of a scene from each other, separating the parts across expanses of narrative time in a technique that accounts for the deeply confusing chronology of the first volume. Sometimes these two versions are actually the two sides of telephone conversations, and Ford explicitly uses the telephone as a metaphor to describe a similar structure within Christopher Tietjens's shell-shocked mind, when, at the end of the first novel, he repeats a line of dialogue from the beginning and imagines that the repetitions are connected by a telephone. The narrative logic Ford associates with the telephone in these instances – where a scene is broken into two sides and scattered across narrative time – expands far beyond any specific diegetic telephones and describes the structure of much of the first volume.

When *Some Do Not* ... fragments scenes in this way, it generates a particular kind of connectivity, one that accomplishes the forward momentum Ford lays out as a primary goal. The pieces of split scenes are often separated by expanses of analepsis, and the repetition of the other side creates what Gérard Genette describes as "dispatching" moments that bring the narrative back to its present, allowing it to escape the retrospective pull and move forward.[9] In the terms of Ford's theory of impressionism, the particularly crucial characteristic of this narration is that the forward momentum of the novel derives from its own formal structure. The novel does not wait for its reader to "carry" it forward, as middlebrow novels do, in Ford's analysis. The reader will only see what she wants to if left in charge, assimilating the novel to her own experience – thus the novel must "carry" itself. Momentum, he suggests, cannot be generated by linear storytelling or by activating a reader's expectations: the narration must have its own, independent sense of momentum that comes out of how it assembles broken pieces of narrative material. Ford's formula that the novel must be "carried" relies on what linguists call a conduit metaphor, and for him, this conduit must be located inside the novel, not outside, in its reader. The narrative mode *Parade's End* associates with the telephone "carries" the novel ahead without inducing the kind of homogeneity Ford thinks occurs when a reader does the carrying. These fragments create a dense narrativity, as each piece points across the novel to its other pieces. What results is a text characterized by an internal dynamism such that individual narrative events remain different from themselves, as they point to their other pieces at other moments across the novel.

Building on Morrisson's and Wollaeger's accounts of Ford's strategies for improving modern thinking, this chapter argues that for Ford, the impressionist novel could generate connective momentum only if it attained a kind of autonomy from its reader. The novel would have to carry itself, to connect its fragments as though it had a telephone line running through its interior. Like James, Ford imagines how the novel might take over a function that otherwise would belong to the reader. Like James, Ford aims to transfer autonomy from the reader to the novel itself, and like James he turns to technological media to describe the automatic functioning of the novel, how it can move itself forward without relying on a reader to do so, in the process modeling connective thought for the modern reader. His idea that the novel can carry itself shares much with James's vision of novelist projection, though he shifts this idea out of James's and Lubbock's visual register, since he is more interested in connection and communication.

In recuperating Ford's theory that the novel must "carry" or move itself, this chapter challenges a significant strain of thinking about impressionism, best exemplified by Wolfgang Iser. He introduces the chapter on realism in *The Implied Reader* with a quotation from Ford: "You must have your eyes forever on your Reader. That alone constitutes ... Technique!"[10] In Iser's view, Ford is articulating perhaps the only rule that has defined the novel as a genre during its entire history: the novel is always shaped by its interactions with its reader. Novels come fully into being only when they are read, he argues, and a novel is therefore more a "living event" than a discrete object.[11] According to his narrative of literary history, it is modernism – whose exemplary fictional texts are full of ambiguities and indeterminacies that a reader must fill in – where fiction fulfills its genre's revolutionary promise as a participatory medium of communication. Iser argues that in eighteenth- and nineteenth-century novels, the reader is pedagogically guided by an author whose train of thought she follows. But by the twentieth century, Iser claims, the writer stops holding the reader's hand and "compel[s] the reader to view things for himself and discover his own reality."[12] The modernist novel makes a feature of all novels visible: they are dependent on readers to be realized.

Iser cites only this one line from Ford, opening a chapter with a quotation he sees as self-evidently supporting his postmodern theory of the reader-driven novel. But he is able to invoke Ford so casually because his view coincides with a long tradition of scholarship, in which epistemological uncertainty and skepticism are impressionism's grounding principles.[13] Even Ian Watt – whose theory of the novel is, in other contexts, directly opposed to that of Iser – argues that "the reader must be put in the posture of actively seeking to fill the gaps in a text which has provoked him to experience an absence of connecting meanings."[14] The impressionist novel would seem to demand a particularly active reading in which the reader puts together the novel's pieces to achieve a larger meaning that the text itself refuses to provide.[15]

This chapter excavates a particularly modernist, anti-theatrical layer of Ford's literary theory that pushes directly against such a vision of deep and necessary reader-text interaction. Ford sees the impressionist novel as connecting parts into a whole in a way that creates the dynamic "liveness" Iser associates with the reading of a novel, but through narrative technique alone. For a critic such as Iser, the novel is completed in the reading process when a reader "realizes" what is written, something that involves filling in the gaps that novels invariably leave. In Ford's theory, the novel's "liveness" comes from the same operation, but the novel does it to itself, and thus maintains a certain autonomy from its reader.

The Crisis of Connected Thought and the "Intimate Conversation"

Ford presents his version of the modernist narrative of information overload in *The Critical Attitude*, which Robert Green calls "very plainly a manifesto, a call for action."[16] In his vision of modernity, subjects are constantly bombarded by facts and ideas that interfere with real knowledge: "the trouble to-day with the poet, as with all the rest of the world, is that we know too much."[17] When the mind is constantly distracted by all this information, there is an end of "connected thought" because "the public brain cannot by any possibility, under the perpetual claims, under the perpetual assaults upon its attention, remain for very long steadfast to any particular subject."[18] In what Ford calls "this gnat's dance" of the modern mind, sustained reflection on anything significant becomes impossible: "We have hardly ever time to think long thoughts, but an infinite number of small things are presented for our cursory reflections."[19]

Ford reserves particular ire for the newspaper, which has taught its readers to be comfortable facing incommensurable, disconnected views and information: "although in the one column of a newspaper, as it were, we may read the altruist dogma that the province of good government is to work for the greatest good of the greatest number, in another column or half-way down the same column under another heading we shall see advocated the employment of the lethal chamber for the feeble-minded."[20] There is no intellectual authority guiding readers through these unrelated, conflicting, or incompatible ideas and facts, and readers do not labor to make connections between the pieces. Confronted with this constant flow of information, "there is an end of generalisations," a habit of mind that would assist the subject in fitting these fragments together into a whole.[21] The result, Ford argues, is the lack of a "critical attitude" in England – the ability to think in a disinterested, objective way and to look at the whole, rather than getting lost in details. The problem transcends the newspaper, in Ford's mind, and has infected all of public discourse, including virtually all genres of writing popular at that moment in England. The memoir and historical writing, for example, string together facts and anecdotes, and are genres of "'ana' – of tit-bits."[22] These genres are popular today, he argues, because they ultimately just collect and display facts and figures instead of promoting thought about them. That is the job of art, for Ford: "to awaken thought in the unthinking."[23]

To cope with all of the "figures" they are daily confronted with, readers assimilate data to what is already familiar, homogenizing anything that might be different. The newspaper, for example, can be made safe and manageable only if its meaning is that you read it with your toast and tea: "nowadays, even in remote country districts, the Englishman is overwhelmed every morning with a white spray of facts – facts more or less new, more or less important, more or less veracious."[24] News, no matter how disturbing or contradictory or puzzling, becomes a fully domesticated part of the Englishman's myopic daily routine.

The urgent rhythm of the news became part of English daily life during the Boer War, when "the Englishman found a necessity for existence in the snatching of news, turning swiftly from one short sensational para-graph to another, and filling his mind with the sharp facets of facts hardly at all related the one with the other."[25] Although these constantly chang-ing news stories purport to communicate information about a conflict taking place far away, they become so essentially ingrained in the English reader's daily routine that the real "event" at stake is not the war but the imperative to "snatch" more news. The newspaper instrumentalizes deaths on a foreign battlefield, transforming them into so many means to the end of selling newspapers and continuing the news cycle. Here we might recall Walter Benjamin's "The Storyteller" (1936), which links the waning of storytelling to the rise of news. Benjamin argues that no mat-ter where reported events might have taken place, news only comes from nearby. It is "understandable in itself," "shot through with explanation" – in direct opposition to the story, which a storyteller strives to keep "free from explanation as one reproduces it."[26] Unlike the story, the news can never communicate anything the reader does not already know, because it belongs to a fully instrumentalized category: there is always news, and it is an established and absolutely familiar part of daily life.

As news becomes routinized and the Figure fragments into figures, readers' appetite for more news grows. Subjects find themselves in a state of constant and incessant communication, although nothing new can be communicated: "the world appears to be so full of a number of things material, technical, or of gossip that there is no necessity, in whatever rank of life, for conversation to flag for one minute."[27] As a result, the social function of art – which used to be "the promotion of expression between man and man" – must change: to be socially meaningful, art has to do something other than simply promote yet more communica-tion.[28] But at the same time, modern culture cannot be improved by a Victorian-style Figure – what Galsworthy and Wells try to be, in Ford's view. Instead, modernity needs a new kind of guide that must render "life as it is."[29] The impressionist novel – "absolutely the only vehicle for the thought of our day" – has the greatest potential for recuperating con-nected thought and rejuvenating meaningful communication.[30]

This crisis of communication is a central subject of *Parade's End*. Christopher Tietjens might once have had the capacity to become one of the Great Figures who could guide social opinion. He is, of course, the self-styled last Tory, a man of principle who belongs to the landed gentry of a prelapsarian eighteenth century. He is also a figure for holis-tic knowledge and integrated communication. Christopher "knew all knowledge," as one character puts it: before the war, he tabulates errors in the Encyclopaedia Britannica, and he is the journalist Mrs. Wannop's human Wikipedia, providing her with facts for her articles.[31] Even after experiencing shell shock during his first tour of duty, he alone can solve a conflict that threatens British and French cooperation because he knows all about factors affecting coal prices – and can talk to a duchess about it, in French. In *No More Parades*, Christopher proves himself as the master of the army's bureaucratic communication channels, managing to move his drafts of soldiers out at record pace. In *A Man Could Stand Up–*, we see Christopher commanding a unit in the trenches, dedicating himself to getting his men to communicate with the units on either side of them: communication "was a mania with Tietjens. If he had had his way he would keep the battalion day and night at communication drill."[32]

The version of modernity faced by this eighteenth-century hero is one of fragmented information and pathological styles of communication. He devotes himself to training his men to communicate, because the subject had been removed from training curricula with the advent of trench warfare, becoming the "heel of Achilles" of his unit.[33] In his social life, people talk too much, spreading endless amounts of gossip – that he had slept with Valentine Wannop, that she had a child with him (years before she actually does), that he is a socialist. Against this flood of misinformation, Christopher opposes himself to gossip: "*I stand for monogamy and chastity. And for no talking about it.*"[34] Before the war, he works in the government statistics office, where he tries to explain the real, holistic meaning behind his figures to politicians who refuse to listen. Christopher's bosses resist his attempts to tell the truth about the statistics he collects, because they prefer to instrumentalize the data: they cook the numbers to prove whatever they have already decided they know. Perhaps the biggest blow to knowledge and communication is the war itself. After he experiences shell shock during his first tour of duty, Christopher loses the memory of three weeks. Huge gaps appear in his knowledge-base, and he resorts to reading the Encyclopaedia Britannica to build it back up.

In the midst of the horrors of the war, Tietjens idealizes a certain kind of communication. He defines peace, in fact, as the possibility of conversation: "For the Lincolnshire sergeant-major the word Peace meant that a man could stand up on a hill. For him [Tietjens] it meant someone to talk to."[35] That someone to talk to would be Valentine Wannop, because love, too, Tietjens defines as communication, "the intimate conversation that means the final communion of your souls."[36] If the war would end, "he could be sitting talking to her for whole afternoons. That was what a young woman was for. You seduced a young woman in order to be able to finish your talks with her."[37] Christopher insists several times that his vision of "the final intimate conversation" requires him and Valentine to be in the same place, to live together in a fantasy of a direct, immediate, complete union: "You can't finish talks at street corners; in museums; even in drawing-rooms," he thinks to himself; "You can't talk unless you live together."[38] The novel seems to move itself toward this end – armistice, peace, someone to talk to, Christopher's union with Valentine – despite all of the obstacles Tietjens must face down, including shell shock, his wife's machinations to get him in trouble, government incompetence, a military that is the tool of interfering civilians, politicians, and military brass who have no problem sacrificing men's lives (or even the entire country of France) for personal gain or to make a point.

But Christopher's tantalizing vision of real communication never comes to fruition. The third novel, *A Man Could Stand Up–*, concludes with the newly reunited Christopher and Valentine trying and failing to talk amidst myriad distractions, as Mrs. Wannop calls on the phone and Christopher's soldiers show up for an impromptu Armistice Day party. Valentine and Christopher are finally in the same space, but even then, they do not get the chance for meaningful dialogue. The final volume, *The Last Post*, hardly shows Valentine and Christopher together at all, much less in some "final intimate conversation." Christopher and Valentine move in together and at the end of the last novel she is pregnant, but we witness no conversations between the two of them during the entire volume. Christopher barely appears in the novel at all – he is off at his ancestral home, Groby, where American tenants have partially destroyed the house by chopping down an old tree. He speaks only one line of dialogue in the whole novel, on the last page, before he dashes off again. The war ends, but the conditions of the armistice are so appalling to Christopher's brother Mark, who is the head of the transportation ministry, that he has a stroke and stops talking altogether. The long-sought intimate conversation never happens, or at least cannot be portrayed by the novels. Christopher's ideal of the "intimate conversation" – world peace and true love combined – is ultimately a dream, one that is out of line with modern reality. This dream resonates with the moment early in *The Good Soldier* when John Dowell imagines that he is sitting by a fireside, having an intimate chat with an interlocutor, to whom he tells his story.[39] Of course, Dowell's telling of his story is largely an exercise in manipulation: a fake, debased version of Christopher's vision of real intimacy.

Impressionism and Telephonic Connectivity

In *Parade's End*, the telephone provides a decidedly nonutopian alternative to Christopher's dream of immediate conversation. Throughout the series, telephones do not just impose technological mediation, but are agents of psychic and even physical violence. Yet at the same time, the telephone plays a crucial role in the series' attempt to portray the social scope of the war, to understand the war holistically. The telephone links the deeply separated parts of society back together, a role it also performs at the level of the fractured individual psyche. Most importantly for my purposes, though, is that *Parade's End* uses the figure of the telephone to justify its own impressionist form, which, Ford insists, must fracture narrative unities to generate a new kind of dispersed connective energy.

The telephone might be thought of as a twentieth-century, postwar heir to the Victorian legacy of the telegraph. Victorian writers often invoked the telegraph to describe exactly the kind of unifying, connective thinking Ford saw as the necessary antidote to modernity's overwhelming flood of facts. The telegraph was a common metaphor for structures resembling *Middlemarch*'s unseen web that connects disparate people and parts of society together, making them all legible to an omniscient narrator. Another example can be found in Dickens's memoranda book, where he jotted down ideas for a telegraphic novel:

> Open the story by bringing two strongly contrasted places and strongly contrasted sets of people, into the connexion necessary for the story, by means of an electric message. Describe the message – *be* the message – flashing along through space – over the earth, and under the sea.[40]

Dickens imagines the telegraph as a social unifier, a device that, like realist narration, could create or at least expose invisible bonds that connect all aspects of society together. As Richard Menke and Elizabeth Ermarth have argued, it was common for both telegraphy and the realist novel to be thought of in this way, as agents of social unification.[41] In Ford's discourse about the impossibility of connected thought in the twentieth century, he laments the absence of just such a unifying force in society – a Figure that would put the pieces of culture together for the overwhelmed citizen.

The telephone belongs to the era of figures without a Figure, of fragmentation. Telephones will also have a unifying capacity, as I will suggest in a moment, but whatever coherence they produce is grounded, initially, in the violent fragmentation that Ford associates with the war.[42] Especially in its last two volumes, *Parade's End* imagines the telephone as a technology that belongs to the cacophony of the front. The telephone speaks in onomatopoeia – "Drrinn; drinnnn; drRinn," "quack" – that is matched only by the language of the guns and shells heard by Christopher at the front: "Tidy-sized shells began to drop among them saying: 'Wee … ee … ry … Whack!'"[43] Cannons are similarly articulate: "A large cannon, nearer than the one that had lately spoken, but as it were with a larger but softer voice, remarked 'Phohhhhhhhhh.'"[44]

The connection between gun and phone is not only sonic, though – phones communicate with dramatic, even lethal violence in *Parade's End*. Valentine experiences the telephone as a cannon that "*blew you out of its mouth*" when the manipulative Lady Ethel calls to inform her that Christopher is back from the front.[45] Valentine responds with violence as well, breaking the phone: "She marched straight at the telephone that was by now uttering long, tinny, night-jar's calls and, with one snap, pulled the receiver right off the twisted, green-blue cord."[46] In *The Last Post*, Mark Tietjens is so shocked and horrified by the news he receives over the phone about the conditions of the armistice that he has a stroke that leaves him paralyzed and mute. His wife, who answers the call, retorts: "I am Lady Mark Tietjens. You have murdered my husband. Clear yourself from off my line, murderer!"[47] He will not speak again until he utters his final words before dying at the end of the novel. Mark here suffers a fate similar to that of a character in one of Ford's much earlier novels, *A Call* (1910). In that novel, Dudley Leicester has a nervous breakdown after a shocking phone call, accusing him of adultery: "And suddenly, in the thick darkness, whirring as if it were a scream," the phone rings.[48] "No doubt it was the shock of hearing the voice on the telephone that actually induced the state of mind," his doctor remarks, suspecting a "lesion in the brain" caused in almost direct physical terms by a weaponized phone line.[49] We might be reminded here of Walter Benjamin's reflections on the "devastation [the telephone] once wreaked in family circles."[50] He remembers phone calls driving his father into a frenzied rage, which he feared would physically endanger the operator at the other end: "My heart would pound; I was certain that the employee on the other end was in danger of a stroke."[51] Like Ford, Benjamin imagines the phone as capable of transmitting, across a distance, not just words but violence that can shatter a body.

But that same fragmenting force also generates a larger connection that helps Ford to accomplish one of the goals of the series: to portray what Paul Saint-Amour describes as the "social totality" of the war, to map the whole network of the war.[52] "More than any other

English-language fiction about the war," Saint-Amour writes, *Parade's End* "connects not just battlefront to home front and trench to ministry, but the front and reserve lines to the bivouac metropolis of barracks, base depots, and headquarters, all joined by an octopoid war bureaucracy and by complex networks of communication, transport, command, and control."[53] The telephone is the essential technology for mapping the world of the war in *Parade's End*. In the second volume, *No More Parades*, Christopher's job is to manage one of these key linkages mentioned by Saint-Amour: he is stationed at a base depot, preparing troops arriving from Britain and from the colonies to ship out to the French front. He gets this job due to his "trustworthiness amongst innumerable figures and messages," and his main task is to cope with "the telephone going like hell" as he negotiates the bureaucracy to manage the movement of the troops.[54] Even when Sylvia shows up and he has to decamp for her hotel room to deal with his failing marriage, he is called away to the phone at least three times over the night to keep the troops moving. Not only does the phone link the various layers of the war theater to each other, but it also links the front to England. When Ford describes the violence Mark and Valentine experience from the ringing of the phone in terms that resonate with his description of the shells falling and cannons firing, he establishes continuity between the psychic experience of soldiers and women and men back in England. The telephone maps another connection as well, between the war dead and the living. The cord of a telephone morphs into an umbilical cord that joins the dead at the front to the survivors of the war: "But your dead ... *yours* ... your own. As if joined to your own identity by a black cord ..."[55] The telephone connects London to the front, the base depot to the rest of the war bureaucracy, the living to the dead.[56]

For the subjects who have experienced the fragmenting violence of war, the phone would even link the parts of their psyches back together again. In the first volume, *Some Do Not ...*, Ford imagines the telephone as binding the pieces of Christopher's shell-shocked mind. During his first tour of duty, he loses the memory of three weeks of his life; neither he nor the novel can remember what happened. At the end of the novel, Christopher repeats to himself a significant, identity-defining line he uttered at the very beginning: "I stand for monogamy and chastity. And for no talking about it."[57] He then thinks to himself: "His voice – his own voice – came to him as if from the end of a long-distance telephone. A damn long-distance one! Ten years ..."[58] This telephone connects the pieces of Christopher Tietjens across a gulf of time, the historical depth of which has been exacerbated by the violence of the war. Christopher's subjectivity fragments into two pieces that are no longer organically connected. For *Some Do Not ...*, the telephone is the figure that describes how these fragmented pieces of Christopher attach back together.

But as much as the device rejoins the parts of the character, on another level it also connects the disjointed pieces of the novel – these bits of repeated dialogue, one at the start and one at the end – to each other. It is this telephonic connection that will be most significant for considering the novel's impressionist form. In this instance, Christopher the character makes the connection between bits of dialogue explicit: he recalls having uttered the same lines earlier, and imagines that he is having a conversation with himself across the length of the novel. But in other instances, a similar and equally telephonic structure moves from the diegetic world of the character out to the level of form, when actual conversations, or even scenes, are split apart and separated across the narrative. Ford narrates an actual and important diegetic telephone conversation this way. In this example, Christopher has been helping to provide information to Valentine Wannop's mother, the journalist.[59] Because of the impact his shell shock has had on his memory, it takes him a while to remember a piece of information for which Mrs. Wannop has asked over the phone. They hang up; he then remembers the information and immediately goes to call her back. In this first version, our perspective is limited to that of Sylvia, who overhears Christopher's side of the conversation. The same scene repeats, about a hundred pages later, from Valentine Wannop's point of view, as she overhears her mother's side.[60] Certainly, the fact that we are at one level removed from the actual conversation, in the mind of characters overhearing rather than those speaking, emphasizes how far away we are from Christopher's ideal communion, how much mediation is involved. Even further, one conversation, one moment of story time, is broken into two separate pieces, which are then dislocated from each other at different moments of narrative time. The novel treats the conversation as though it was the lines uttered by a psychically fractured Christopher – two parts of a whole that no longer fit together immediately, but are instead separated over a distance.

When the novel splits up the halves of this single conversation, it executes a version of one of the key principles of Ford's impressionism, *progression d'effet*. In his book on Conrad, Ford defines the concept as being that "every word set on paper – *every* word set on paper – must carry the story forward and that, as the story progressed, the story must be carried forward faster and faster and with more and more intensity."[61]

This sense of momentum must be generated through an "indirect, inter-rupted method" that represents the fragmentary reality of real life – "the complexity, the tantalisation, the shimmering, the haze, that life is."[62] Splitting apart the pieces of a conversation such that speeches do not respond to each other is a crucial, defining technique of the impression-ist novel, for Ford: "no speech of one character should ever answer the speech that goes before it," to avoid "a certain dullness."[63] It is the break-ing up of what otherwise might be thought of as narrative unities – such as conversations, scenes, moments of story time – that will in fact gener-ate this momentum, which does not come from the story being narrated but must be a formal function of the narration itself, of the way elements of the story are broken up in narration. Thus the principle exploits the difference between the chronology of the story's events and how they are narrated in the novel. As Tim Armstrong puts it, "[t]his does not mean that the 'pace' of events speeds up; it is the narrative which has a life."[64]

Fracturing otherwise unified pieces of narrative creates a "live scene," in which every broken piece is almost electrified by its contrast with all the pieces around it. Ford's example has to do with how a writer might render a conversation between himself and his neighbor, Mr. Slack, who has a boring story to relate about exhibiting his flowers at a garden show. The writer cannot simply lay out Mr. Slack's story. Instead:

> if you carefully broke up petunias, statuary, and flower-show motives and put them down in little shreds, one contrasting with the other, you would arrive at something much more coloured, animated, lifelike and interest-ing ... Into that live scene you could then drop the piece of news that you wanted to convey and so you would carry the chapter a good many stages forward.[65]

This mosaic of fragments creates an atmosphere conducive to moving a novel along. The scene produces momentum by arranging fragments into a formally complex work – a whole composed of parts that exist in dialectical tension with each other, such that no part can stand in for the whole and the whole is more than the sum of its parts. In turn, this new aesthetic whole, the "live scene," necessarily establishes connection between these "little shreds"; connecting these fragments creates the energy, the "liveness," that will enable the scene to catapult the narrative forward.

This is exactly what happens when Ford splits apart the pieces of the telephone conversation, and it is a technique that appears across the novel. The novel breaks open moments of story time – single scenes – into views from different perspectives, and then scatters them across narrative time. The logic of this structure is telephonic: in *Parade's End*, he imagines the telephone as a device of explosive interruption that, equally, connects the shreds of the unities that have been smashed. The telephone puts Valentine in the mouth of a metaphorical cannon, but then connects the pieces of Christopher's mind together again. Pieces of dialogue are separated across narrative time from their responses: this is the structure of the long-distance telephone line that Christopher sees as his identity, and it is also the structure of the novel's narration of Christopher's conversation with Mrs. Wannop. This telephonic logic spreads out far beyond the explicit diegetic mentions of the telephone. This structure pervades *Some Do Not ...* at different levels, with scenes split by a few pages or hundreds. One example occurs in a well-known passage at the very beginning of the novel, when Ford evokes the soon-to-be-punctured normalcy of 1912. Tietjens and his friend Macmaster are in a railway carriage on their way to Rye. The scene is narrated in the third person through the perspective of Tietjens, as the novel clearly indicates in indirect discourse: "the train ran as smoothly – Tietjens remembered thinking – as British gilt-edged securities."[66] The novel's disordered chronology is apparent even within this phrase in its first paragraph – when is this remembering happening, since we are in the novel's present? A few pages later, after an analepsis of four months to when Tietjens's wife first left him, the novel returns us to the same scene in the railway carriage, but in Macmaster's point of view: "In the train, from beneath his pile of polished dressing and despatch cases ... Macmaster looked across at his friend."[67] With this technique, the novel uses narrative time to induce deep divisions within story time.

In other words, the novel prioritizes the arrangement of events in narrative time over story time, sujet over fabula, and in the process gives the narrative its own, independent sense of temporality. Because these shifts are usually not clearly marked, this technique is responsible for much of the volume's out-of-order narration, which caused Thomas Moser to give up on outlining its story sequentially, claiming the text's chronology "reveals almost total confusion."[68] These time shifts are more disorienting than those in *The Good Soldier* because they are not confined to a single character's narration and cannot be accounted for by a subject's failing memory or by his manipulations. These time shifts happen at a level beyond that of the individual subject, and constitute an attempt both to portray the fragmentation of the world and to connect the pieces back together again. This technique is part of what several critics have analyzed as the series' project of breaking down omniscience and denying full knowledge to any point of view, each of which becomes increasingly private and isolated.[69] Yet what results is not only the deconstruction of any communal vision of reality. Ford's narration fragments once unified scenes, but then it also self-consciously ties together the split pieces, establishing a specifically impressionist kind of connectivity.

In the examples I have considered, the novel's present moment – the railway journey, the telephone call – is fragmented into pieces that, separated from each other or laid out in contrast, produce the "live scene" that Ford describes in *Joseph Conrad*: the "little shreds, one contrasting with the other" are the various pieces of a scene which are broken apart from each other, mixed in with the narration of other scenes.[70] The "liveness" of the narration comes from the fact that those broken pieces are clearly incomplete, separated from, yet connected to, the other bits of narration that make up a full account of a scene. Theodor Adorno might call these moments parataxis: wholes that are "composed of the dissociations between the discrete parts."[71] What results is that one part of a scene may be separated from another piece, may appear as a fragment, but it nonetheless points to that other piece and leads us to wait for its disjoined partner to occur at a later moment; it implies the whole that it does not fully constitute.

Unmoored from their simultaneity in story time, the sides of the conversation or pieces of a scene become disconnected, floating fragments. James Joyce had used the telephone as a thematic justification for similar fragmentation in the "Wandering Rocks" chapter of *Ulysses*, which narrates just one half of a telephone conversation. Joyce prevents the two sides of the conversation from occurring in the same narrative moment and in so doing, Sara Danius argues, he splits perception from knowledge: we hear the words, but do not know what's being communicated.[72] A telephone conversation is narrated from the perspective of someone standing next to the desk of Miss Dunne, Blazes Boylan's secretary:

> —Hello. Yes, sir. No, sir. Yes, sir. I'll ring them up after five. Only those two, sir, for Belfast and Liverpool. All right, sir. Then I can go after six if you're not back. A quarter after. Yes, sir. Twentyseven and six. I'll tell him. Yes: one, seven, six.[73]

We never hear the other side of the conversation, and the conversation itself matters more as perceptual data than as functional narrative information. These words create an atmosphere rather than *doing* anything; they create no connections. *Some Do Not ...* does not so radically split sense from perception, and each side does provide content. Nonetheless, it flirts with this vision of the telephone by keeping the two sides at a distance from each other, preventing the reader from putting the two halves together for an expanse of narrative time and forestalling the kind of unmediated conversation of which Tietjens dreams, where both parties are present together and meaningfully communicate.

Yet unlike *Ulysses*, this novel provides access to the other half of the scene or conversation, forging connective pathways between the pieces it has fragmented. Ford might have belatedly drawn on the way early narrative film directors used the telephone. As Tom Gunning has shown, the telephone provided a crucial thematic motivation for film directors experimenting with continuity, in the period when narrative conventions in film were just being established.[74] In particular, Gunning suggests that with D. W. Griffith's 1911 film *The Lonedale Operator*, the basic shot–countershot structure of parallel editing emerged as the dominant strategy for portraying telephone conversations. The film establishes a pattern of alternation between the two ends of the conversation: it follows the back-and-forth movement between the parties and constructs a continuous narrative out of pieces taking place in different spaces but simultaneous time, as an alternative to an earlier strategy that split the screen to show both parties at the same time.[75] The telephone provided diegetic justification for the film to link events taking place in discontinuous spaces. In *Some Do Not ...*, Ford generates a sort of temporal version of the shot-countershot structure: the shot and countershot are separated not by space but by expanses of narrative time, yet the narrative must connect the pieces for its story to make sense. Gunning theorizes the alternation of sides of a conversation in cinema as producing a kind of "narrative omnipresence" that sees a hidden web of relationships, establishing connective pathways between disparate fragments of material.[76] *Some Do Not ...* similarly uses this telephonic structure to reveal unexpected connective paths that narrative time has hidden.

In *Some Do Not ...*, the telephone is thus an alibi for the narrative's fragmentation of this scene into two parts, but also for how the novel connects those two pieces back together again. The novel combines the fragmenting force Danius diagnoses in *Ulysses* together with the connective force Gunning finds in early cinema. In her analysis of the telephone in Heidegger's work, Avital Ronell has described the device as a textual "shredder" that splits a whole conversation into two distinct fragments located at a physical remove from each other.[77] While it breaks a temporal unity – a single conversation – into pieces, it also keeps those fragments in connection with each other: "the telephone line holds together what it separates," and "[b]eing on the telephone will come to mean, therefore, that contact is never constant nor is the break clean."[78] A telephone conversation might be understood as connecting two parties together, two parties that nonetheless maintain their separateness. According to this logic, telephony fragments what would otherwise be whole, yet the separation it promotes can never be complete. The shredded pieces are forever connected. It is perhaps not surprising that the telephone becomes a privileged figure in Ford's performance of impressionism in *Parade's End*, given how similar Ronell's theory of the device is to the theory of the impression, as articulated by Jesse Matz: "It does not choose surfaces and fragments over depths and wholes but makes surfaces show depths, makes fragments suggest wholes, and devotes itself to the undoing of such distinctions."[79]

The Novel Moves

In Ford's theory of impressionism, momentum is a critical concern. It is momentum that gives the novel this capacity to reform thinking: narrative moves forward, from one page to the next, in the process creating a train of thought that connects ideas. For Ford, momentum is how one gets out of the stagnating quicksand of disconnected thoughts: momentum *is* connectivity between the thoughts, words, images, and stories contained in a novel. Anything that retards the novel or might "make him pause and so slow down the story" must be cut, Ford insists.[80] Thus, his brand of impressionism holds two principles in tension: the need to portray the fragmentation of modern life, and the need to move quickly ahead. These two objectives may sometimes come into conflict, Ford acknowledges, but there is no ambiguity about which one should take precedence: "the sense of reality must stand down before the necessity to get on."[81]

The narrative strategy that Ford associates with the telephone generates momentum in a specific way: by repeating a single scene from multiple points of view, the novel marks the present. After this present moment – the train journey, or the phone call – is narrated from a specific character's point of view, various quantities of analepsis tend to follow, in which the character thinks about what happened earlier that day, or months ago, et cetera. Repeating the scene of the railway journey or the telephone conversation from another point of view establishes its temporal primacy, its status as what Genette calls the "base position" or "first narrative."[82] Those repetitions say to the reader: you've been pulled backward enough; it's time to get going now. Bringing us back to the present, they provide a basis from which the story can be advanced. Consider the example of Christopher's phone call to Mrs. Wannop, when he provides her with information for her articles. In between the two repetitions of the scene, one from Sylvia's perspective and one from Valentine's, the novel goes back in time, most notably to fill in what has happened with Macmaster since Christopher went away to war. He has secretly married Edith Ethel, who persuades Valentine to attend Macmaster's parties with her as a cover, while also repeatedly making slanderous claims about Christopher to others. After the repetition of the phone call, we stay in the present and move forward into new time: Valentine goes to meet Christopher at the War Office. In another example – the train journey with which the novel begins – the repetition of the scene, this time from Macmaster's perspective, gets the novel out of several pages of analepsis to several months earlier, when Sylvia had left Christopher. The novel then proceeds to narrate what actually happens after Christopher and Macmaster have arrived at Rye.

A more complex example will help to clarify. Chapter 3 shows Christopher working in his hotel room at night in Rye, when he is interrupted by Macmaster arriving home for the evening; this moment, which will be renarrated twenty pages later, functions as the plot's present tense. Initially, this scene is narrated from Christopher's point of view, but it switches after a few pages of dialogue into the other character's mind. From there, in Macmaster's point of view, the novel proceeds to narrate several other events – his dinner with the General, his meeting with Edith Ethel (all earlier on the same day). The next chapter moves back to Christopher's point of view and narrates the climactic scene when he first meets Valentine Wannop, his future love and suffragette, as she and her friend accost Mr. Waterhouse, a judge, on the golf course. In story time, that scene happens after Macmaster's meeting with Edith Ethel, but before his dinner with the General, which in turn precedes his interrupting Christopher's thoughts when he arrives back at the hotel that night. The narration of the meeting with the suffragettes on the golf course is followed, still in Christopher's point of view, by his dinner with Mr. Waterhouse, all before concluding back at the moment when Macmaster interrupts Christopher's work at night – a scene that is now narrated from Christopher's point of view. Having returned us to the narrative's base position, following a great deal of analeptic recall, the novel will proceed, at the opening of the next chapter, to move forward through time to the next morning, thus escaping the retrospective pull.

The narrative present or base point operates as what Genette calls, turning to a notable telephonic metaphor, "a sort of indispensable transfer point or – if one may say so – ... a *dispatching* narrative": to move ahead, we must return to this point.[83]

In the third volume, *A Man Could Stand Up –*, the telephone almost explicitly becomes a thematic force for forward narrative movement. Valentine and Christopher are radically split apart in this volume, which alternates between two temporally and spatially different moments: Valentine on Armistice Day and Christopher at the front several months prior. The two wind up in the same building at the end of the novel because of telephone calls that work as what Barthes would call "cardinal functions."[84] Barthes's primary example of a cardinal function is, not incidentally, a telephone ringing, which creates a "hinge" that advances a narrative by necessitating that something must happen.[85] When the phone rings, in his example, the character will either answer or not answer. In Barthes's theory, functions are opposed to indices, which do not initiate a sequence of action but instead create atmosphere, define a character, et cetera. Valentine, in particular, answers a series of calls that instigate the narrative's progress toward its end, her union with Christopher. Because she answers these calls from two conniving manipulators (Sylvia, in *Some Do Not ...*, and Edith Ethel, in *A Man Could Stand Up–*), she is duped into meeting with Christopher and providing more fodder to the gossips spreading tales about an affair that hasn't actually happened. In both cases, Valentine feels the way these calls move her toward an ending that seems to exist outside of her own will. The call that opens *A Man Could Stand Up–*, comes from Edith Ethel, who, for her own selfish reasons, urges Valentine to go to see Christopher, whom she has not seen since the end of the first volume. This call reminds Valentine of the one she received from Sylvia in the first volume, because both of these calls seem to her to function as Destiny: "the depths of the telephone began, for Valentine, to assume an aspect that, years ago it had used to have – of being a part of the supernatural paraphernalia of inscrutable Destiny."[86] Later, after she goes to see Christopher at Gray's Inn, the telephone will become "a machine of Destiny" again when her mother, talking to Valentine and then to Christopher, refuses to order Valentine home in order to prevent her from sleeping with a married man.[87] The telephone is *Parade's End*'s figure for the forces that move the novel toward its end.

The crucial characteristic of this kind of narrative movement is that it is built into the structure of the novel itself, rather than relying on something outside of the novel – the reader – for that motive force. When Ford theorized the movement or momentum of the novel in his discussion of *progression d'effet*, he insists that the novel's form "carr[ies] the chapter" ahead.[88] Ford's "carrying" is what linguists call a conduit metaphor: it imagines a medium through which the story must move. In his classic analysis, Michael Reddy shows that such metaphors derive from the common understanding that "language functions like a conduit, transferring thoughts bodily from one person to another."[89] Here is one of Reddy's examples, utilizing Ford's privileged verb: "His words carry little in the way of recognizable meaning."[90] The conduit metaphor describes communication as mediation: ideas, stories, or words preexist the moment of their expression, and are inserted into some kind of vehicle through which they will be expressed (one puts ideas into words, for instance).

One of the features that differentiates the impressionist novel from other genres is, indeed, that its conduit is located fully inside the novel, in its form, rather than operating primarily as the link between the novel's meaning and an external reader. For example, Ford contrasts the necessity for words to act as vehicles carrying the novel with the kind of mediation inherent to the romance: "in the Romance it matters little of what the tale-teller discourses, so long as he can retain the interest of the reader; in the Novel every word – *every word* – must be one that carries the story forward to its appointed end."[91] In the romance, the writer's job is to create a strong external conduit to the reader. What moves through the conduit is nearly irrelevant, and certainly cannot communicate anything significant or new. The novel, instead, carries itself through an internal conduit. The content of the story is still carried, just not toward a reader but toward the end of the novel: "every word set on paper – *every word set on paper* – must carry the story forward."[92] The conduit, what moves through the conduit, and its destination are all fully inside the novel. The novel's terminus – where the content goes as it moves through the conduit – is not the external party of the reader, but rather a point further on in the novel itself. The conduit's function is not to promote more communication of insignificant and homogeneous content, but instead to generate forward momentum that connects fragments.

That momentum was quite difficult to maintain, Ford thought. Even the most conscious of modern novelists – Conrad himself – was not immune to the cultural pressure to get lost in details. Once that happens, the novelist winds up relying on the reader to connect the details for him: the conduit moves outside of the novel and connects the novel to the reader rather than linking textual pieces into a critical, meaningful whole. Conrad often went into great detail about a scene, but without establishing connective momentum, Ford thought. As a result, the reader was left to connect the pieces on her own. The problem was that he was a bit too "scrupulous" in obeying another impressionist principle, justification: "that which happens in [the story] must seem to be the only thing that could have happened."[93] Go too far in that direction, and even a Conrad novel can turn into a work of middlebrow detective fiction, Ford argues in an essay in *The Critical Attitude*. In reading a hypothetical Conrad whodunit,

> [w]e should be conducted to the door of a house where the crime was to be committed ... The door would open upon a black hall and there the episode would end. The point would be that Mr. Conrad would by this time so entirely have identified us with the spirit of the expedition that we should take up the tale for ourselves. We should go up the creaking stairs ... ; we should push open the door and in the shadow of the bed-curtains we should perceive a sleeping form. But Mr. Conrad, having dropped his story with the knocker upon the front door, would begin his next chapter with an observation from Inspector Frost, of the Secret Service.[94]

The reader, not the words of the novel, carry the story forward: "we should take up the tale for ourselves." In turn, relying on the reader means that the novel is likely to have less momentum, as justification is also "apt to have the grave defect of holding a story back very considerably."[95]

What is ultimately at stake is that Conrad can turn his story over to the reader because nothing significant, unexpected, or interesting is happening. The reader takes over not by rewriting the novel in her head or filling in something unexpected, but by moving over territory that is so inevitable that it doesn't need to be written. When one turns the novel over to the reader, the novel stops communicating anything new; the "live scene" stops living. The result is identical to what happens when Englishmen read the news: the reader carries the novel, assimilating it to her routine just as she does with the morning paper. The reader gets too close to the novel, abdicating that attitude of detachment and distance that is necessary to maintain a "critical attitude." The reader reflects herself, and her own experiences, onto the text.

By contrast, the successful novel that provides its own momentum extirpates itself from that routine. Such a novel can provide a new and different experience outside of daily life, "making [the reader] entirely insensitive to his surroundings" as he reads.[96] The reader must not be doing the work, and he should not even notice that anything is happening: he should be "entirely oblivious of the fact that the author exists – even of the fact that he is reading a book."[97] The liveness of the text, its dynamism and movement, must be created entirely by the novel itself. If the text moves itself, it can display another form of thought to readers who will be tempted to read it according to their ordinary habits. This is why a conduit metaphor is so central to Ford's vision of impressionism: he takes the idea that the text moves from point to point and relocates the movement inside the text itself. Such a text can be more than a homogeneous record of habit and routine. Imagining the text as an internally moving document becomes, thus, a way to create that "critical attitude" in readers. If we read this telephone in terms of the conduit metaphor elaborated in his critical writing, then the carrying device is working inside of the novel, carrying the novel to the end of its plot, advancing the story. The text still moves – just within its own boundaries, not toward an outside reader. The story is still "brought to life" – just by itself, not by an external reader, who would not be able to connect the fragments anyway.

This is Ford's particular version of the aesthetic autonomy of the novel. Conduit metaphors like the one in his formula for how the novel "carries" itself have long been associated with claims for aesthetic autonomy, and structure the idea that the work of art "contains" meaning that can be transmitted and exists outside of either reader or author.[98] Critiques of the conduit model of communication are a mainstay of poststructuralist theory – Derrida's classic argument that speech did not preexist writing is one example. Iser in particular critiques a conduit-based understanding of literary communication, in which the novel is a complete whole prior to its transmission to a reader. He argues instead for a theatrical position in which meaning is created by reader and text together: the novel "is not to be identified either with the reality of the text or with the individual disposition of the reader."[99] Rather, "the literary text needs the reader's imagination, which gives shape to the interaction of correlatives foreshadowed in structure by the sequence of the sentences."[100]

Rejecting conduit metaphors, Iser claims the text needs the reader to "give shape" to its ideas. To argue for the text's independence from a reader, Ford invokes a conduit metaphor – but goes even further, to reimagine the conduit so that it does not connect the text to its reader, but parts of the text to each other. The conduit, thus, becomes a site where the novel models connectivity between disparate facts for its reader, who, in Ford's view, would not be able to connect the pieces herself. The story still moves through a conduit, still undergoes a mediating process of transportation, but all of that happens within the novel. As a result, the novel does not rely on the reader for it to be "carried." Rather, it shows the reader how to think from a "critical attitude" so that she can construct an interconnected whole out of disparate pieces.

Parade's End makes itself "live" and maintains its heterogeneity in the moments where it repeats scenes, such as when we watch Sylvia overhear Christopher on the phone with Mrs. Wannop and then, one hundred pages later, see Valentine's version of the same scene. These telephonic moments keep the scene in question from stabilizing, because we expect it to repeat in a different form later on. Each piece of a scene resembles a part of a conversation that makes us expect a reply. As Derrida argues in his reading of the Penelope chapter of Joyce's *Ulysses*, a single piece of a conversation – for example, the famous "yes" that concludes the novel – "never comes alone": "A certain narrativity is to be found at the simple core of the simplest *yes*."[101] The single side of the conversation is "haunted" by an "essential repetition ... which parasites it like its mimetic, mechanical double, like its incessant parody."[102] In Ford's novel, this haunting narrativity is everywhere. Each of these telephonic moments is necessarily open to the new though connected to what went before.

The doubled scenes in *Some Do Not ...* create this sense of narrativity and risk because, thus fractured and dispersed, they will necessarily be in flux. These scenes in the novel's present tense never congeal into static objects, something inevitable or fully "justified" that a reader can take over, because they keep changing across the novel. The most extreme example of this strategy occurs near the end of the novel, when Christopher and his brother encounter Valentine at the War Office as she stares in horror at the list of war dead:

> They turned the corner of the arch. Like something fitting in, exact and expected, Valentine Wannop stood looking at the lists of casualties ... With the same air of finding Christopher Tietjens fit in exactly to an expected landscape she turned on him. Her face was blue-white and distorted. She ran upon him and exclaimed: "Look at this horror! And you in that foul uniform can support it!"[103]

Two chapters and fifty pages later, the novel returns to this same scene, but it replaces the first version's omniscience with a narration that is radically limited to Valentine's point of view:

> She was looking at patterned deaths under a little green roof, such as they put over bird shelters. Her heart stopped! Before, she had been breathless! She was going mad. She was dying ... All these deaths! ... Perhaps he

wouldn't come ... He was immediately framed by the sordid stones. She ran upon him and said something; with a mad hatred. All these deaths and he and his like responsible! ... But he! He! He! He![104]

The novel shreds the scene into two versions that are quite different, in both form and content. The first passage, the event's first iteration, emphasizes how, for each of the characters, the scene "fit in exactly to an expected landscape." The second version disrupts the sense of a puzzle with all the pieces in the right place, since it focuses on the incommensurability of the Christopher Valentine knows and the horrors of the war in which he participated. But despite this opposition, the two versions still belong together; the chronology of the novel can only be unraveled if these two scenes are matched together.

Examples proliferate across the novel, such as in Christopher's phone call to Mrs. Wannop. Sylvia overhears him telling Mrs. Wannop about the Congress of Vienna, and then consulting with her on a possible article about illegitimate children of British soldiers in France: soldiers don't sleep with their mistresses if they are decent, but if they do, it is because they might not have another chance, he claims. Sylvia has an epiphany – "Listening to that conversation had extraordinarily cleared Sylvia's mind" – and realizes two things.[105] First, she is finally convinced that he actually does have shell shock: "His going at once to the telephone, as soon as he was in the possession of the name 'Metternich,' had at last convinced her that he had not been, for the last four months, acting hypochondriacal or merely lying to obtain sympathy or extended sick leave."[106] Second, she finally realizes that he has not slept with Valentine Wannop: "she knew – she had known at once from the suddenly changed inflection of Tietjens' voice ... that Tietjens himself had thought twice."[107] Valentine overhears the same conversation between Christopher and her mother and experiences only uncertainty about Christopher's nature and the fate of their relationship. There must have been "[a] message to me" in Christopher's theory of war babies, Valentine thinks – but she cannot tell whether he is the sort who would refrain out of decency or take his last chance.[108] As in the example of the War Office encounter, this scene dissolves into two incommensurable, opposed halves that no longer occupy the same moment in narrative time – and yet they are forever connected to each other.

In this bifurcated form, the narrative event remains permanently different from itself. Indeed, the event keeps happening, in different places across the narrative, in different ways. As Genette remarks in his analysis of a similar pattern in Proust, one piece "seems as if snatched from the text of the first section. A striking example of migration, or, if one wishes, of narrative scattering."[109] A single scene "takes place" at several different places in the novel; the scene is always moving, and cannot be pinned down. The novelistic event that is in motion operates as a defense against readers who would, out of habit, see only what they expect. The event – the conversation, the railway journey, or the visit to the War Office – cannot be transformed into a "thing," because it keeps changing. No definitive, single, identifiable version of those repeated events is available. Thus, such a narrative mode corrects for what Ford considers to be the failing of the newspaper, the romance, and most novels, which are all problematically subsumed by a reader who reflects her own experience onto them, ultimately rendering them fully homogeneous. In these novels, by contrast, each event is internally heterogenous, different from itself. Where the news, for example, occludes all distance, transforming the battles of the Boer War into the daily routine of a family in the English countryside, the structure of Ford's novel generates distance even within the confines of a single event or conversation.

It is fitting then, perhaps, that this telephonic structure does not persist in the same form across the entire tetralogy. None of the three volumes that follow *Some Do Not …* pursue its experiments with time-shifting to the same degree, though each of them experiments in other ways. In a well-known reading, Vincent Sherry argues that the series tries on and then discards a large number of modernist formal innovations, ultimately rejecting formal experiment itself as a path promising compensation or renewal, by the end of the 1920s.[110] The radical, unmarked time-shifting Ford associates with the telephone is one formal strategy that the series pursues and then abandons – but it is nonetheless a significant, if short-lived experiment because it is so closely tied to the theory of impressionism that Ford offers in his book on Conrad.

Some version of the first novel's time experiments persists into the third volume, *A Man Could Stand Up–*, which still associates the telephone both with momentum and with uncertainty generated within single narrative events. However, those characteristics move from the narrative's structure into the character's – Valentine's – consciousness. This volume exposes Valentine's isolation by often limiting our view of these scenes to hers – those scenes do not later repeat from another point of view, as they would have in the earlier novel. Two key diegetic telephone calls in the third volume produce the sense of mutability and multiplicity within every moment of time in the narrative, but that mutability moves inside her mind and becomes part of her experience. It is Valentine who repeatedly receives phone calls in this volume, and every time, Ford portrays her as torn between competing events taking place at the same time, showing the limits of her ability to experience everything happening in a single moment. The call that opens the novel, from Edith Ethel, takes place "amidst intolerable noises from, on the one hand the street and, on the other, from the large and voluminously echoing playground": Valentine thus has a difficult time figuring out who is calling, and about what.[111] She has "tantalisingly half-remembered" the voice on the line, but cannot put the pieces together for another five pages.[112] The problem is that while Edith Ethel drones on through the phone, the noises around Valentine resolve into a massive event, one of the "universal experiences": Armistice Day, announced by some sound – "maroons or aircraft guns or sirens ... the sound for which the ears of a world had waited for years, for a generation" – that she fails to hear.[113] This span of time splits into two different occurrences that compete for Valentine's attention, as two sounds she is not able to hear at the same time.

Later on, the same structure repeats; Christopher is on the phone this time, with Valentine's mother, while Valentine answers the door to find Captain McKechnie, who comes in to wait for Christopher. One part of her mind is connected, almost telepathically, to the conversation going on upstairs: "A sort of wireless emanation seemed to connect her with the upper conversation. She was aware of it going on, through the wall above, diagonally; then through the ceiling in perpendicular waves. It seemed to work inside her head, her end of it, like waves, churning her mind."[114] Although she cannot actually hear their words, the phone conversation moves through Valentine's mind; she internalizes this media channel much as Christopher did when he felt as though there were a long-distance line inside his mind. If that channel connected the fragmented pieces of Christopher across the gulf of his shell shock, this channel connects Valentine to a conversation happening elsewhere, to another event happening in another place. And just as she cannot hear her mother's conversation, so she cannot actually make any sense out of Captain McKechnie's babble either, although it is being spouted right in front of her: "He spoke so inexhaustibly and fast, and his topics changed so quickly that she could do no more than let the words go into her ears."[115] In both of these instances, Valentine winds up in two places at once, such that her experience of a single span of narrative time is bifurcated. As a result, she fully experiences neither event: she will hear about Christopher's conversation later, and she "listened to the words and stored them up" as Captain McKechnie talks.[116] For the reader these experiences are less temporally complex than they would have been in *Some Do Not ...*, but for Valentine they are not fully completed as they happen; these events keep happening.

Ford's experiments with a dynamic, internally moving narrative form continue to haunt the series, even after they seem to be abandoned following *Some Do Not ...* Even if he did not pursue these experiments to the end, this first novel offered a site for his theory of the impressionist novel that "carries" itself to be fully performed. By imagining the novel as a dynamic, moving text that cannot be pinned down, Ford aimed to improve thinking, to instill a critical attitude, and to enable the communication of real, new knowledge. The novel with a textual conduit in its interior would remain ever different from itself and open to the new, and would resist the pull toward homogeneity associated with a culture overloaded by information and pervaded by too much communication. Such a novel would accurately represent the fragmentation of knowledge and perspective in modernity, but would nonetheless reveal the latent connections between the pieces, thus modeling for its readers a way to stitch the fragments into a meaningful, synthesized whole. Reading this telephonic narrative structure in relation to Ford's theory of impressionism, this chapter offers an alternative to Iser's vision that the impressionist novel invites its reader to exercise a heavy hand, to intervene to provide the whole to which the fragments of the novel refuse to give us access. The whole is there, and the fragments are connected – we just need to follow along as the novel carries itself.

CHAPTER 3

"Every Age has been 'a Machine Age'"
Wyndham Lewis and the Novel's
Technological Temporality

Thus far, this study has argued that modernist writers thought specific technologies modeled ways of engineering the novel to protect itself from the bad habits of modern middlebrow readers, who manhandle novels to produce desired emotions. In the process, both James and Ford theorized the specific technologies they connected to novelistic form, negotiating a field of potential conceptualizations of each device. These writers participated in reimagining these technologies in the fullest sense, including the ways of knowing they imply and their relationship to aesthetic techniques.

The final two chapters expand this discussion from specific devices to the category of technology itself. These chapters excavate the depth of modernist thinking on this topic – about what defines technology, and about the epistemological and social implications of the category. For Wyndham Lewis, technology is a particular relation to temporality that structures human experience. Art – the novel in particular – is a form of technology, in these terms, and a privileged site where technology's essence might be changed. For Rebecca West, technology is a mode of human adaptation of the world. Like Lewis, she situates art – and again, the novel in particular – within the field of technology, as a way of gathering information about the world and adapting to it without waiting for biological evolution. Lewis and West go a step beyond James and Ford, theorizing the novel not as a homologue to a particular device but as an integral component of technology itself.

Lewis's central place in this study is, perhaps, not surprising, because critics have long described him as "the most technophilic of high modernists."[1] Such readings often link Lewis to the protofascist side of modernism that thought technology could elevate the elite individual into a superhuman soldier. These accounts also often observe that Lewis's prose is mechanical or machinelike, and certainly the language of the machine peppers critical descriptions of his works. Fredric Jameson's

Fables of Aggression: Wyndham Lewis, the Modernist as Fascist exemplifies this tendency. Jameson argues that Lewis's novels are structured by an irresolvable contest between the stylistic productivity of his sentences (the "molecular") and extreme narrative containment (the "molar").[2] This schema aptly describes, for example, the end of *The Apes of God*, where a sprawling, 300-page chapter is followed by a tight, six-page chapter. Jameson almost obsessively describes the molecular, hyperproductive side of Lewis's narration using tropes of machinery: his style is a "veritable self-generating image- and sentence-producing machine," while the "illimitable sentence-producing capacity" of *The Apes of God* becomes "a figure for human productive power in the industrial age."[3] But Jameson describes Lewis's prose style in these terms without devoting much attention to how Lewis himself theorized technology, a move made possible because of long-standing arguments about his technophilia.[4] This chapter argues that Lewis theorized technology in far more complicated terms than merely promoting it. Not only did Lewis offer a theory of technology, but he also theorized what kind of a novel should be understood as machinelike. That question was a matter of urgent importance for him, something with the potential to shape not only modernist aesthetics but modernity's understanding of technology itself.

Jameson's division between the molecular and the molar can be roughly mapped onto a set of terms that structured an important strain of modernist aesthetics as well as Lewis's own critical vocabulary: the tightly controlled molar resembles what Lewis would call the art of the eye, which exists as a contained object that a spectator regards intellectually, from a distance. The productive molecular, ruled by a logic in which one word or sentence is always followed by another one, is an art of the ear, and spreads out through time; such art moves through the spectator and solicits an emotional reaction. Lewis inherited these ideas most directly from French philosopher Julien Benda, who blamed modern music for the contemporary dominance of the aesthetics of the ear. This chapter traces Lewis's specific intervention in modernist anti-musicality: unlike Benda, Lewis identified modern technology, not music, as the dominant factor in the rise of the art of the ear. In *The Art of Being Ruled* (1926) and *Time and Western Man* (1927), he argues that people are addicted to the time-driven art of the ear because they have internalized the organizing principle of modern technology: that everything is in a constant state of change and improvement. That rhythm of modern life, Lewis argues, derives from a certain understanding of technology associated with the epoch he frequently calls the Machine Age.

But Lewis maintained that the progress-driven version was only one way, the modern way, of defining technology. Modern society urgently needed to forge a different understanding, and that philosophical battle would be fought in art, which he saw as the cultural space in which philosophical problems manifest themselves.[5] In *Paleface, or the Philosophy of the "Melting-Pot"* (1929), Lewis attempts to unseat the industrial imperative toward newness by insisting that the modern age is no more high tech than the ancient world, and that the devices modern people like to worship as new are really old. His argument turns on the idea that works of art can be more technological than any more obvious machine, when technology is defined as a highly structured, complete object rather than as a temporal rhythm oriented toward the new. From this perspective, the most technological work of art might be the one that is temporally static and repels a spectator's emotional involvement. Lewis here reprises the familiar vorticist claim that geometric art is machinelike, but he ascribes new consequences to that move, stakes that critics of Lewis have not yet recognized: the art of the ear and the art of the eye are not just two aesthetics, but two competing understandings of technology.[6] To view the molecular or the molar, or the art of the ear or that of the eye, as technological is not merely an exercise in aesthetic description, but a polemical philosophical act. Recently, scholars such as Jessica Burstein and Lisa Siraganian have been interested in tracing the distancing mechanisms Lewis used to create an art of the eye by preventing readers from identifying with characters in novels or from having any involvement in the construction of a work's meaning.[7] Building on this work, my contribution is to show how Lewis's theory about distancing readers is, simultaneously, a theory about technology.[8]

One might expect Lewis to focus his effort to change technology through art on sculpture, painting, or even poetry – types of art that modernists often imagined as contained objects that do not extend in time. But the novel was the key aesthetic form for his rhetorical purpose, because it faces the same problem technology does: like machines as they have been incorporated into modern society, novels seem to require the progression of time. Unlike poems or statues, which can be easily rendered as fully static, imagist objects, whole novels simply cannot be read in a moment. In Lewis's view, no matter how much a writer strives to compose an objective, exterior novel, the very process of reading will bring it back into the logic of the ear: readers get close to novels, emotionally but also through the physical process of reading. The novel extends through the reader's lived, experiential time, so reader and work become intertwined; the reader does not, and cannot, remain a distant, intellectual observer. Because the novel is in a state equally precarious as that of modern technology – because both seem destined to be forms governed by the ear rather than the eye – Lewis saw their fates as linked: he would strive to redefine modern technology by theorizing a fully contained novel of the eye.

To do so, Lewis would have to develop a static, fully exterior mode of novel-reading, something he did in one of his most interesting and least read pieces of aesthetic theory. In "The Taxi-Cab Driver Test of Fiction" (1930), Lewis offers an account of how reading might be rendered atemporal and stripped of any sort of emotional involvement: he asks a taxi-cab driver to "test" a novel by reading a single, random page. In this satiric rewriting of the impressionist move to use a female, child, or working-class character to access pure interiority or the immediacy of the impression, Lewis presents the cab driver as the perfect reader who cannot understand a work, and who is thus uniquely, ironically positioned to treat it only as an emotionless, intellectual object. Such a reading turns the novel into something like a taxi-cab, which does not solicit identification and will not become a reader's friend – how middlebrow readers often behaved toward novels, according to common modernist critiques. The novel as taxi is a machine, in a particular sense: Lewis saw taxis as the most inefficient of modern devices, so slow that they actively seemed to resist the fast rhythm of industry. Imagining the novel as a machine and the reader as its operator, Lewis simultaneously argues for an anti-Machine-Age, atemporal understanding of technology.

Yet Lewis did not allow himself to conquer the problem he spent so many pages diagnosing this easily. The writer cannot compose a novel that will, on its own, remake technology; the taxi-cab driver test itself acknowledges the role of an unknown party, the reader, who must collaborate to make the novel a machine in a positive sense. To place a style of reading at the center of his aesthetic ideal is a risky proposition, and Lewis's recursive critical process focalizes that risk, especially in his fiction. Critics have long noticed that his novels are often structured to meet his vision of geometric containment, only then to flaunt his own theoretical imperatives by aggressively emphasizing narrative flow and progressive time. In such moments of formal contradiction, this chapter argues, we can see Lewis holding his utopian ideas about how the novel might change the social meaning of technology up for scrutiny. Rather than portraying his theory of the novel as a simple solution, he situates it in irresolvable tension with the mammoth social problem to which it responds. Even as he imagines a way the novel might become a new kind of technology, he nonetheless insists on the partial, utopian nature of that project – he forces us to confront the fact that the novel remains embedded in a society driven by modern technological time.

In this context, the out-of-control production of new characters at the end of *Tarr* (1918) looks like Lewis reintegrating his text into the industrial time it has sought to escape from, with satiric resignation. The novel also pits the possibility of containment and stasis against the drive toward progressive production in the scene where Kreisler rapes Bertha. While the novel initially seems to contain the rape by imagining it as a space rather than an event, the rape is then transformed into a series of figures, each providing the energy for the next, generating a new level of sequence. As the attempt at containment fails, the rape becomes a nightmarish version of the art of the ear, in which the beholder is invasively penetrated by the art that passes through her. The end of *The Apes of God* (1930) takes up this same dynamic, on a different scale: Lewis presents the General Strike of 1926 as a powerful image for how novelistic containment works against industrial time, when the novel freezes what Jameson imagined as the productive machinery that generated its massive penultimate chapter with a terse final section about the strike. But the strike proceeds to generate new narrative activity, and even to produce taxi-cab drivers who do not at all behave like the utopian figure of the test: Lewis insists on the novel's inability to redefine technology on its own, and dramatizes the tension between what the machine means now and the possibility of an alternative.

Before moving on, a note on terminology is in order. Of all the writers this study considers, Wyndham Lewis is the one most explicitly concerned with defining technology as a category, but it is important to recognize that Lewis never actually uses the term "technology." Rather, it is the language of the machine that is omnipresent in his work. Lewis was not unusual in using "machine" where we would write "technology," even though "technique" and "technical" are part of his vocabulary; thus the widespread description, in the 1920s and 30s, of modernity as the "Machine Age."[9] "Technology," meaning both empirical machines and the techniques and knowledge systems that inhere in them, was not yet in wide circulation in English. The *OED*'s etymology charts a long development in which the term's meaning moves from a "discourse or treatise on an art or arts," in the seventeenth and eighteenth centuries, to "knowledge dealing with the mechanical arts," in the nineteenth century.[10] The meanings "technical knowledge or know-how" and "machinery, equipment, etc." were only beginning to emerge at the turn of the twentieth century. An Ngram search of the Google Books corpus suggests that "technology" would only become the preferred general term for these meanings later in the century: there is negligible use of the term "technology" in books in English until the 1930s; use of the term grew quickly from 1960 and surpassed use of the term "machine" in the late 1970s.[11] Thus in order to think about technologies not as mere physical devices, but as objects with a way of knowing the world, especially a way of knowing time, embedded within them, Lewis uses the language of the machine. To keep with current usage, however, this chapter will generally use the term "technology," except where it seems accurate to emphasize the physical apparatus itself.

In one sense, this terminological difference is a historical accident. In another sense, though, the fact that English and American writers were using the language of machinery while French and German writers were using the language of technology does imply a subtle difference in connotation that we can see at work in Lewis's thinking. The question of technique – and thus of the relationship between artistic technique and technical know-how associated with science and engineering, between aesthetic and technological form or design – was unavoidable for contemporary German thinkers, the likes of Benjamin, Adorno, and Heidegger. For Lewis, and in English more generally, the association with technique, with ways of knowing and doing, is less immediate. Instead, the terminology of the machine is more closely associated with ideas of volition – a machine is "an apparatus constructed to perform a task" (sense IV), and has meant at various times in history "a structure regarded as functioning as an independent body" (sense I), a "contrivance" (sense II) in literature or theatre, and a "living being considered to move or act automatically or mechanically, rather than of its own volition" (sense V).[12] This indeed has been a crucial question for all of the writers I consider – imagining how the novel can escape from the reader's volition, and thus maintain distance and autonomy from the reader. For Lewis, the question of volition is particularly vital: the rhythm of modern technology leads to the collapse of distance between art object and beholder, such that the art object merges into the beholder and becomes subject to her will. A different conceptualization of technology would be necessary to ensure the possibility of distance between art object and beholder – something Lewis sees as a crucial theoretical and aesthetic project, even if he is unable fully to imagine its success.

The Art of the Ear and the Time of Technology

Lewis's polemic against the art of the ear appears in its most developed form in *Time and Western Man*, where he draws heavily on a key text in modernist social aesthetics, Julien Benda's *Belphégor* (1918). Benda is better known today for his 1927 book *La trahison des clercs*, translated into English by Richard Aldington as *The Treason of the Intellectuals*. In that work, Benda argues that contemporary intellectuals have betrayed their commitment to pure, abstract ideas and have been corrupted by nationalist and racist passions. *La trahison des clercs* develops ideas about the over-emotional nature of modern life that he had applied to aesthetics in his earlier work. It was this earlier work that especially influenced Lewis in the years following World War I: Benda was to Lewis what Remy de Gourmont was to Ezra Pound, as Vincent Sherry puts it.[13] Benda's *Belphégor* is an attack on empathy, the integration of art and life, and Henri Bergson's ideas about the primacy of subjective temporal experience. His overarching argument is that modern culture witnessed the devastating triumph of the sensuous emotion of music, which involved the listener in the work, over the pure intellectual form of plastic art, which the viewer could contemplate as a whole from a distance. Sherry, who situates this discourse of political aesthetics at the center of modernism, describes its central tenet this way: "whereas the democratic ear merges, the aristocratic eye divides."[14]

Two points from *Belphégor* are particularly salient for Lewis's rewriting of Benda's critique. First is that the aural lacks structure. Benda argues that his contemporaries, who have a penchant for "a certain invertebrate modern music," want to reimagine other forms of art to "imitate the pure mobility and indeterminateness" of music.[15] Benda's adjective "invertebrate" implies not only softness and fluidity, but also a sense of regression toward the primordial ooze. He insists that modern music has lost the structural complexity that once made it both intellectual and meaningfully aesthetic, and this is what happens to other arts when they become musical: in what Benda characterizes as a "cult of the indistinct," specific parts are no longer stable or identifiable, but merge together.[16] Second, Lewis emphasizes that the relationship between art object and spectator comes to be structured by sympathy and emotion rather than distanced intellection. Benda writes: "What the majority of men seek, in contemplating a work of art, is an opportunity to indulge in the *emotion of sympathy* ... they derive but little pleasure unless the emotions depicted are of a kind that they can share."[17] Such an emotional connection comes at the expense of intellectual understanding, as art becomes "emotion itself, not the contemplation of it."[18] Contemplation requires distance between spectator and artwork, and it is impossible with musical works, because the spectator "must completely suppress looking in any form (since looking upon anything implies remaining outside of it)."[19]

Lewis largely repeated Benda's ideas, but he made one major change: for him, the cultural dominance of the art of the ear derives not from music but from what he calls the "'revolutionary' tendency" of modern life, a constant desire for and expectation of change.[20] This attitude, which has infected all social and cultural life, has its origins in modern technology. Lewis articulates these claims most clearly in the appendix to Book One of *Time and Western Man*, in a passage that seems particularly important because Lewis kept rewriting it over the course of the 1920s: the version in *Time and Western Man* is a revision of the "Revolution Rooted in the Technique of Industry" chapter already published in *The Art of Being Ruled*. Lewis uses Marx to argue that "the 'progress' of the engineer, the rapid changes and improvements of the technique of industry, make it natural for him to regard everything in terms of change and improvement, and to think that he can apply to himself or to other men the methods proper to machinery."[21] Modern technology is defined, in Lewis's terms, by the revolutionary logic of progress: we constantly seek new advancements, and whatever machine is in place now must be superseded. That industrial vision of time has been generalized, as people internalize the temporal principle of technology: "It is because our lives are so attached to and involved with the evolution of our machines that we have grown to see and feel everything in revolutionary terms, just as once the natural mood was conservative."[22] Modern technology, here, threatens the western subjects that would claim to have invented it – as Douglas Mao has argued, for Lewis, the threat faced by the western subject in modernity derives not from an other (colonized populations or women, for example) but from "a technological expansion driven by an increasingly powerful instrumental reason."[23] Technology's temporality is one particularly infectious mechanism of that threat.

Machines, thus, set modernity's rhythm. They provide the "music" that determines the shape of western societies, which, Lewis writes, are composed of "emotionally-excited, closely-packed, heavily-standardized mass-units, acting in a blind, ecstatic unison, as though in response to the throbbing of some unseen music."[24] The "unseen music" in question is precisely the "insistent, hypnotic rhythm" of what Lewis calls "fortuitous technical discoveries" or "the frenzied evolutionary war of the machines."[25] As people internalize the temporality of modern machines – this system, he tells us, is "machine-made" – they begin to act just like the works and spectators that are victims of Benda's art of the ear, in two ways.[26] First, people are physically and emotionally moved from without rather than by their own minds. Second, people lose their individuating differences and merge into a "closely-packed, heavily-standardized" crowd; the individual is no longer a meaningful structure.[27] Modern technology is at the heart of what Lewis sees as a profound social shift toward the "suppressing of *differences*" between subjects and objects, self and other.[28] Across Lewis's voluminous writing, he links this phenomenon to the behavior of crowds, fascism and communism, capitalist economics, contemporary philosophy and science, and, of course, most modern art.[29]

What results is an anti-intellectual need for speed, as subjects live by the rhythm of modernity:

> Everything in our life to-day conspires to thrust most people into prescribed tracks, in what can be called a sort of *trance of action*. Hurrying, without any significant reason, from spot to spot at the maximum speed obtainable, drugged in that mechanical activity, how is the typical individual of this epoch to do some detached thinking for himself? All his life is disposed with a view to banishing reflection.[30]

The human subject becomes a machine, where that means being moved by an external will to engage in "that mechanical activity." He has no reason for his actions and cannot think; instead he follows along a "track" that is "prescribed" in advance, moving from place to homogeneous place ("spot to spot") with concern only for "maximum speed obtainable." Here we are in terrain familiar from Heidegger but also Ford, both of whom diagnose the homogenization of thought and the impossibility of any new thinking, as subjects cycle through a menu of predetermined choices.

In Lewis's first version of this material, in *The Art of Being Ruled*, the argument is not without hope for the future. Even though true social revolution seems to become less likely once the very idea of revolution is redefined in purely technical terms, Lewis sees some possibilities emerging from industrial time's emphasis on superseding what exists with something better: it leads us "to be dissatisfied at … sloth, untidiness, and lack of definition" and give us "the itch to improve."[31] But when he re-presents this material, as an appendix to *Time and Western Man*'s notorious critique of modernity as a "time cult," the mechanical experience of time as revolution no longer seems so innocuous. The appendix begins with the thesis that "the technique of industry, then, the engineer and his machine, is the true source of the inevitably 'revolutionary' conditions subsisting to-day."[32] He proceeds to factor out the implications of the revolutionary rhythm of technology, concluding finally that it will result in the catastrophic "merging of the spectator and the performer" by promoting amateurism in artistic production.[33] Through its revolutionary temporality, modern technology creates historical circumstances that demand the time-driven art of the ear, and amateur art is the pinnacle of that progression: it represents a situation in which the spectator merges so fully with the artwork that she becomes an (inevitably bad) artist.[34] Thus, the phenomenon of amateur art can be traced back to machine rhythm: the "revolutionary rich" are used to identifying with works of art and constantly want something new.[35] Becoming an amateur – a "gifted eternal-child, their naïveté never blemished by that odious 'power' that knowledge brings" – is a way to live in perpetual newness: the amateur is so stupid and inexperienced that everything is new and wonderful, and she gets to feel like a Henry Ford, one of that "very small number of inventive, creative men [who] are responsible for the entire spectacular ferment of the modern world," despite being just one of the herd.[36]

Modernism is thoroughly complicit in modernity's revolutionary time, in Lewis's view. Indeed, its investment in the new exemplifies the deep irony of modern temporality. In an essay about Auden and his associates, Lewis argued that their generation "still have that eager air" of running so as not "to *miss the train* – the every five-minute *Rapide*."[37] Writing as the grizzled voice of experience, Lewis mocks the new modernists of the 1930s for trying so hard to make it new. This train, it turns out, runs on a circular track: the travelers on this "chronologic merry-go-round," egged on by "my dear old friend Ezra Pound," are always rushing to get where they've already been.[38] Modern technology has created a temporality of belatedness: the modern subject feels herself to be permanently late, because she can never get anywhere new while obsessively desiring newness. The train metaphor to which Lewis frequently returns perfectly describes this relationship: one runs to catch the train, that great technology of the nineteenth century, itself already an old story, nothing more impressive than a "merry-go-round."

Modernists who look for an alternative in premodern cultural influences are stuck on the same merry-go-round. Lewis directs much of *Paleface* toward arguing that seeking solace in an era before the modern only reinscribes the temporality of modern technology. That was exactly the strategy pursued by the modern primitivists, who romanticize the emotional, collective, authentic behavior they see in societies before they have been exposed to modern industry. But in the very shape of such an argument, Lewis argues, his two exemplary primitivists, Sherwood Anderson and D. H. Lawrence, reveal that they themselves have been infected by the mechanized industry they claim to despise. In imagining a moment before modern technology to which they would like to return, these writers show that they have bought into its most essential principle: the idea that technological progress drives history. Even if Anderson and Lawrence dislike this logic, they are also moved by it when they imagine capitalist industry as the fall of civilization: they cannot help thinking that technological development is the engine of historical change. Thus, modernist primitivists fetishize the new even when they idealize a time before the new.

Lewis begins to articulate an alternative point of view by arguing that what Lawrence and Anderson see as new is actually old. What they envision as preindustrial behavior is precisely what Lewis sees as an effect of industrialization. His analysis turns on Anderson's novel *Poor White*, in particular one quotation which exemplifies pre-machine authenticity for Anderson and the most debased mechanical behavior for Lewis: "The bodies of all the men running up and down the landing-stage were one body. One could not be distinguished from another."[39] In Lewis's view, Anderson here mistakes the aftermath of industry for what preceded it. Lewis argues "that admiration for savages ... is really an expression of the worst side of the Machine Age – that Machine-Age Man is effusive about them *because they are machines* like himself."[40] What appears to be primitive and, ultimately, a source of renewal for over-technologized modern man is actually already technological, and if this seems like an utterly defeatist point of view that leaves no hope for the future, it is actually the only way to avoid giving in to the rhythm of modernity.

One implication of Lewis's argument is that if there is no time before modern technology, then no one can take the credit or the blame for being its owner or inventor. Lewis thinks his way into a difficult and racist corner as he works out the logic of this proposition. In *Paleface*, he argues that technology cannot be understood as a white or western phenomenon. To think of technology as white is a primitivist mistake, because there is nothing new about the Machine Age, an era that for Lewis existed long before Europe dominated the globe. In *Paleface*, he argues that white European culture has been sucked into a dangerous guilt spiral surrounding technology. The white subject feels guilty for having conquered the Native American, in particular, because "[h]e knew that he had been able to do it only because he possessed his 'longue carabine,'" because he had technology that the Native American did not rather than any inherent racial superiority.[41] Lewis's response is at least not the most obviously racist position – he does not insist that technology is indeed white, a product of the white man's hard work, and thus that the white man deserved to conquer the pretechnological Native American. Rather, he claims that technology is not, in fact, really "white Magic" after all: the "primitive races" had technology all along, the implication being that white people should not feel guilty about their conquest of Native Americans.

Instead, Lewis argues, contemporary western cultures must recuperate the version of technology he finds exemplified in those indigenous cultures – a technology that can be defined by the art of the eye. He looks at premodern, indigenous artworks as technologies, not because they are old, but because they are examples of the art of the eye:

> An alaskan totem-pole, a Soloman Island canoe, a siamese or indian temple, is a *machine*, inasmuch as it is, in its concatenated parts, composed of very mechanically definite units, and is built up according to a rigid geometric plan. The bunch of cylinders of a petrol engine has very much the same structural appeal as a totem-pole or the column of a mayan divinity.[42]

These works are structured, they extend in space rather than time, and they do not solicit the spectator to be their friend. If the artworks are machinelike, then machines themselves must be defined by their spatial structure – "rigid," "definite," and "concatenated" – rather than through their relation to time. The argument works by redefining technology in terms of the art of the eye, by insisting that the art of the eye is technological. If such works are examples of technology, then, as he insists in a section title in *Paleface*, "Every Age has been 'a Machine Age.'"[43] There is no before: Lewis removes technology from sequential thinking, from history, and from time. While Anderson and Lawrence want to resist the pull of the Machine Age by promoting preindustrial culture, Lewis's method is the opposite: he denies the possibility that there was any era before modern technology, and thus invalidates the claim that white Europeans invented it.

Certainly, Lewis's description of abstract art as static, geometric, and rigidly formal would have struck a reader in the late 1920s as familiar, if not substantially derivative. T. E. Hulme had already done the work of bringing this theory of abstraction to England, via Wilhelm Worringer's expressionist art history. Michael Levenson dates the heyday of these positions to 1911 and 1912, not 1929, when Lewis pronounced that every age is a Machine Age.[44] But this sense of derivativeness feeds back into Lewis's argument – he is trying to imagine a way out of modern technology's fetishizing of the new, after all.

The Novel as Machine and the Reader as Operator

In *Paleface*'s list of artworks that should be considered machines in this powerfully positive, static way, literature of any sort is notably absent. In the age of imagism, Lewis could have made a Hulmian classicist argument on behalf of modern poetry as intellectual object. Hulme had opposed poetry and prose in these terms: "while one [poetry] arrests your mind all the time with a picture, the other [prose] allows the mind to run along with the least possible effort to a conclusion."[45] But Lewis was much more interested in the possibility of imagining how fiction – the literary form that most clearly seems to require temporal extension and thus to be governed by the ear – might be an art of the eye. Situating Lewis's analysis of the novel in the context of his polemic about technology provides a new reason why he took on such a task: fiction is the form of art that most closely faces the same plight as the machine in modernity. If the novel can be theorized as an art of the eye, despite its inherent tendency toward temporal extension, then it can be a machine in the classical sense Lewis opposes to time-driven modern industry. In the process, he opens a chink in the Machine Age and suggests a utopian possibility. The novel might be able to change the nature of the machine – not by single-handedly renovating society's relationship to technology, but by making visible something beyond the totalizing experience of technology as time.

Like technology, fiction relies on forward temporal momentum. In his chapter on Hemingway in *Men Without Art* (1934), Lewis describes how specific pages are swept up by the pull of novelistic sequence:

> When I read *Farewell to Arms* doubtless I read this page as I came to it, just as I should watch scenes unfolding on the screen in the cinema, without pictorial criticism; and it, page eighty-three, contributed its fraction to the general effect: and when I had finished the book I thought it a very good book. By that I meant that the cumulative effect was impressive, as *the events themselves* would be. Or it is like reading a newspaper, day by day, about some matter of absorbing interest – say the reports of a divorce, murder, or libel action.[46]

Lewis seems to be arguing here that Hemingway is a good novelist. His dissatisfaction is not with Hemingway but with the novel as a form.

When he compares reading the novel to watching "scenes unfolding" in a movie or following a story in the newspaper, "day by day," Lewis emphasizes the continuous forward motion of reading.[47] As we read we are continually looking ahead, waiting for the next scene or the resolution of a scandalous case.

Because of fiction's forward temporal motion, it lacks the structure Lewis finds in the totem-pole or the Mayan temple. We cannot isolate the particular borders of the work – we cannot identify what particular role page eighty-three of *A Farewell to Arms* plays in the whole any more than we can identify one individual in the crowd. Instead, readers can access only the "cumulative" or "general effect"; "it is *the whole* that counts."[48] Fiction is "a sprawling jelly of the vulgarest sentiment" rather than an intellectual object.[49] We cannot isolate the definite contours of the work as an object, or determine even where it begins or ends: when Lewis compares reading fiction to reading a newspaper in *Men Without Art*, he suggests it becomes difficult to tell the difference between "*the events themselves*" and their literary representation, because both unfold in the same way, through continuous, experiential time.[50]

The most crucial effect of fiction's reliance on temporal momentum is that readers cannot maintain distance from the work. Fiction needs to unfold through time, but the work cannot do that on its own: it borrows the reader's experiential time to achieve its temporal extension. In *Time and Western Man*, Lewis pursues this argument with respect to music:

> there is no concrete shape existing altogether, once and for all, or *spatially*. There is a shape, an organic completion, but it is a pure creation of *time*. It cannot spatialize itself. The representation goes on inside your mind, in making use of your memory. Its concreteness is not objective but subjective.[51]

Because music must extend in time, it vampirically borrows the experience of the listener in order to realize itself: "You have to live the music."[52] In Worringer's terms, music requires progressive perception, in which the spectator gradually gathers sensory experience, unlike sculpture, which is able "to reproduce … a whole for the imagination" all at once.[53] Fiction functions more like music than like sculpture, in *Men Without Art*: the reader and the work merge together, and *A Farewell to Arms* becomes a span of the reader's existence rather than an independent object.[54]

In this respect, Lewis was more pessimistic about fiction specifically than was Benda, because he interpreted the spectator's integration into a work of art in a literal, physical way.[55] While Benda imagines that individual artworks can invite or repel emotion and sympathy – and thus that even works of fiction can be visual rather than aural – Lewis emphasizes the physical dimensions of the reading and listening processes, which require that the spectator experience the work regardless of the content of that work. In Lewis's exacting logic, any work that must borrow the experiential time of its spectator, any work that does not exist "in its totality" at once, will create a too-close bond with its spectator and prevent her from staying on the outside of the work.[56] Benda seems to be making a similar point when he criticizes what he calls music's "pure mobility," but for him that temporal movement is more a metaphor for indeterminateness than an incontrovertible literal reality that prevents music from achieving classical structure.[57]

When readers "live" the work of fiction, their relation to it is primarily emotional rather than intellectual. Fiction, like technology, facilitates the transformation of thinking individuals into the overemotional, mechanized crowds of *Time and Western Man*. Here, Lewis's thought dovetails with the strain of modernist novel theory, best exemplified by Q. D. Leavis, that criticizes modern readers for wanting books to be emotional companions, even friends. Novels seemed to be getting emotionally closer and closer to their readers all the time, and for Benda and Lewis, emotion and sympathy can only be had at the expense of intellectual comprehension. In Benda's less-warm picture of the predicament Leavis diagnoses, readers (the plural has emphasis, implying that this sort of behavior derives from crowds, not individuals) "enjoy, with half-closed eyes, and mouths agape, the eternal unintelligibility of the universe."[58]

One of Lewis's responses to the troubling aesthetic situation of fiction is his well-known external method. Promoting the exteriority of *The Apes of God*, Lewis explained his mode of characterization: characters' "shells, or pelts, or the language of their bodily movements, come first, not last."[59] He theorizes how to write characters that "do not live" but are instead "congealed and frozen into logic," characters that are "complete cyphers, ... monuments of dead imperfection."[60] His external method positions Lewis firmly on the form side of the form-versus-life debates of the 1920s, as characters become formal devices, "creaking men machines" and "not living beings."[61] Lewis's characters do not imitate real people and will not be the reader's best friend – they are thus machines in the abstract sense, comparable to totem poles or ancient canoes, because they block a reader's empathy. They are bodies, mere physical apparatuses, not living beings with interiority.[62] His is an extreme version of more familiar positions taken against E. M. Forster's *Aspects of the Novel*, which argued for the novel's continuity with life and for characters that are more real and convincing than actual people. Critiquing Forster, Edwin Muir, for example, argued that it is disingenuous to favor round characters over flat since all characters are necessarily mechanical constructions.[63] In the larger context of modernist novel theory, Lewis, along with Muir and Leavis, comes down on the side of form over life, distance over empathy, stasis over sequence.

In his fiction, there is ample evidence of Lewis executing his external method, writing novels with mechanical characters who lack insides and reject a reader's empathy. But the particular challenge of Lewis's novel theory can be found in his attempt to change not writing but reading. If fiction is phenomenologically tied to forward temporal movement, if it requires the experiential time of the reader in order to realize itself, then even the most externally written of texts can or even must still be lived by a reader. As he remarks in *Men Without Art*, sounding ironically like Wolfgang Iser, "it takes two to make a 'classic' work of art: the artist alone is not enough."[64] It seems much more straightforward to write with the external method – to isolate the individual word in an attempt to stall linguistic momentum, to focus on contained settings and the outsides of characters – than it is to *read* with the external method, because reading would seem necessarily to involve taking sequential words into one's mind.[65]

Lewis tackles this issue in the "Taxi-Cab Driver Test of Fiction," a series of paragraphs that form part of *Satire and Fiction* (1930), a pamphlet defending *The Apes of God*, and were later included as an appendix to *Men Without Art*. The test is an attempt to read a novel, any novel, in an instant, to remove it from time and radically contain it as a concrete, intellectual object.

> I believe that you should be able to request a taxi-cab driver to step into your house, and (just as you might ask him to cut a pack of cards) invite him to open a given work of fiction, which you had placed in readiness for this experiment upon your table; and that then *at whatever page he happened to open it*, it should be, in its texture, something more than, and something different from, the usual thing that such an operation would reveal.[66]

On one level, Lewis's vision of the taxi-cab driver test is fairly reasonable: reading a short bit of a novel may reveal its quality quite quickly. At the same time, the taxi-cab driver test is an early gesture toward New Criticism, a way to "judg[e] writing without reference to author or title … to see that the text stands on its own terms," as one critic puts it.[67]

But this moment of novel theory is both stranger and more daring than can be appreciated by assimilating it either to the quick evaluation one might do by flipping through a book in a bookstore or to the general New Critical interest in isolating texts from historical or biographical context: Lewis is suggesting a radical way to remove both time and emotion from the reading process. Rather than developing over a period of time, the way a story does over a series of minutes in the cinema or days in the newspaper, the work of fiction is made to exist only in the single moment it takes to open a book.[68] Lewis equates this process of reading to looking at a card after one cuts the deck: the inevitable temporality of reading even a page is shrunk to an absolute minimum, transformed into a mere glance. Yes, that glance must occupy an expanse of time, but Lewis attempts to shrink duration to a vanishing point. The driver turns no pages, and does not lend his experiential time to the novel in order for it to unfold its story. The cab driver is simultaneously stripped of any emotional relation to the novel – he is not allowed to see enough of the story to feel anything or to identify with a character. The resulting page must then be apprehended not for meaning but "texture": it becomes a physical object, rather than a semantic one, and would seem to repel the involvement and depth of reading. The taxi-cab driver is not asked to *read* the book, per se; he *tests* it. Instead of penetrating the interior of the text, he assesses its exterior. The result is difficult to take seriously as a critical method – but here Lewis really tackles the difficulty of making reading atemporal.

Lewis's solution to the problem of reading is idiosyncratic, but the problem to which he responds was well-recognized in mainstream modernist novel theory. Lewis just went much further than other theorists in imagining an alternative to sequential reading. In *The Craft of Fiction*, the book that was widely thought to exemplify the form side of the form-versus-life debate, Percy Lubbock certainly concurred that reading interfered with the reader's ability to treat the novel intellectually. That is the defeatist note on which Lubbock's book begins, with the idea that the novel fades away and disappears as we read it, due to the necessary temporality of reading: "the book, the thing he made, lies imprisoned in the volume, and our glimpse of it was too fleeting, it seems, to leave us with a lasting knowledge of its form."[69] The reader, he argues, must strive to maintain an attitude of critical, even clinical distance from the novel, although the very process of reading makes that task all but impossible. Over the course of his volume, Lubbock never really solves this problem, never deals with the issue of reading in all of its scope, as Lewis would.

Lubbock would reimagine reading as seeing, with his emphasis on the category of point of view, linking the novel to the art of the eye and distancing it from the ear. But ultimately, even that strategy cannot solve the problem of reading: the critic must still watch the book disappear as she reads, and no critical method is fully adequate to solving the problem of reading, which dooms literary criticism to an unscientific fuzziness. Thus, the book ends, as it began, on a note of "helplessness": "after all, it is impossible – that is certain: the book vanishes as we lay hands on it."[70] His entire critical method, Lubbock concludes, is but "a spark of light" among these impenetrable shadows.[71]

Even Virginia Woolf, whom we would usually situate on the life side of the form-versus-life debates, thought that sequential reading made it difficult to see the novel as a whole. In her 1926 essay "How Should One Read a Book?," she tells us that novels "are an attempt to make something as formed and controlled as a building," the only problem being that "words are more impalpable than bricks; reading is a longer and more complicated process than seeing."[72] Narrative expands in time, not just in space, and that temporal dimension of reading makes it hard to figure out how a novel might be as whole, complete, and palpable as a building. Her response was to divide the reading process into two distinct parts. The first part involves collaboration between writer and reader, where good readers, anyway, will be the friend, "fellow-worker and accomplice" of the writer – Lewis would be horrified.[73] But there is a second stage, Woolf continues, where "the cat is out of the bag, and the true complexity of reading is admitted": the reader is called on to judge the text, a procedure that interrupts her sympathy with the writer.[74] The reader must, at this point, "make of these fleeting shapes one that is hard and lasting."[75] Woolf here enters into territory occupied by Lubbock and Lewis, in imagining how to transform the ever-disappearing text into a solid, durable object. In this second stage of reading, which takes place after sequential, fleeting reading is over, the reader simply stops and backs off: "suddenly, without our willing it, for it is thus that Nature undertakes these transitions, the book will return, but differently. It will float to the top of the mind as a whole."[76] This version of the text is totally different from the one that emerges slowly, sequentially, as the reader reads. "We see the shape from start to finish; it is a barn, a pig-sty, or a cathedral": the reader can see around its edges, to where it starts and stops.[77] This is the opposite of the kind of immersion she describes as the first part of reading. The novel can emerge as a solid object only when a reader can be convinced to stop actively reading.

Writing in the 1940s, Joseph Frank would take Woolf's solution one step further, arguing that some novels can be written to avoid that first stage of reading altogether. For him, a novel can be written spatially, to avoid temporal succession, and such books can somehow manage to avoid the progressive experience of reading. James Joyce's *Ulysses* and Djuna Barnes's *Nightwood*, in particular, exemplify this to him. That is to say, a writer can solve the problem of the temporality of reading: "Joyce cannot be read – he can only be re-read."[78] Certainly, Frank's critics would later take him to task for this suggestion. Walter Sutton found Frank's theory of rereading to be nonsensical: "How can the idea of the image as an instantaneously-apprehended phenomenon be reconciled with the fact that the whole work, as an image, is read consecutively through a period of time?"[79] He went back to Frank's key primary text, T. S. Eliot's introduction to *Nightwood*, for evidence that Eliot in fact had to read the novel sequentially: "What is noteworthy is that the conception of the form of the work as a whole developed *during* the reading of novel."[80] For Sutton, it is simply ridiculous to imagine that one can do away with time in reading: "I would deny that the apprehension of this unity could ever be – for more than a one-image or *hokku* [sic]-like poem – instantaneous."[81] It is one thing to see such a disregard for physical reality in Ezra Pound, Sutton protests, but another thing in a professor of literature. Frank responded to Sutton in a 1977 essay, admitting that it is impossible to read a novel in an instant but arguing that the basic physical requirements of reading do not stop the novelists from aiming for the impossible.[82] Even though it is a contentious, ultimately untenable position, Frank persists in claiming that spatial novels cannot not be read sequentially. Woolf, Lubbock, and Frank approach Lewis's territory by identifying the losses associated with sequential reading and then attempting to imagine an alternative process that would make it possible to avoid the temporal progression that merges the reader into the text, instead allowing that reader to see the novel as a whole.

When Lewis attempts to solve this problem, he does not imagine that a reader can actually read a whole novel in an instant, as Frank did. Rather, Lewis aims to restore intellectual distance to the act of novel-reading by invoking a figure from beyond the literary intelligentsia – a cab driver – as his exemplary reader. He makes this point by structuring the taxi-cab driver test as an explicit, satiric inversion of a well-established impressionist trope for how an intellectual or artist can capture raw sensation: in what Jesse Matz calls "collaboration," the writer borrows the point of view of someone who seems to have a more embodied, limited point of view – this is how Henry James uses Maisie, how Virginia Woolf uses Mrs. Brown.[83] By "collaborating" with a woman, a child, or a working-class character, the impressionist writer claims to access the sensory immediacy of experience before it is assimilated to intellection, without thereby giving up intellectual mastery. Certainly, such impressionist experiments fell squarely into the "internal model" that Lewis critiques, promoting narration that centers on an individual's interiority, in explicit contrast to intellection. James uses Maisie as a center of consciousness because she cannot understand what she sees and he finds that lack of mastery aesthetically compelling.[84] Lewis chooses a cab driver because Lewis sees him as a figure that lacks intellectual understanding, much like Maisie. But because the cab driver seems to be someone who cannot understand the novel, he is exactly the character who can best treat it as an intellectual object, in Lewis's idiosyncratic terms: the driver only sees the outside of the novel and cannot penetrate within. In James's world, intellectuals have lost the ability to feel and sense, to take in the world immediately, without the interference of intellectual distance. In Lewis's world, the opposite is true: intellectuals can only feel and sense, and cannot keep critical distance. Offering the taxi-cab driver as his ideal reader, Lewis externalizes the interior method through reading.

The satire of impressionist collaboration has one more key layer: the taxi-cab driver is useful to Lewis not because he can feel or sense more deeply or immediately than the writer, the way Maisie can, but because he knows how to operate a machine, where operating a machine is the polar opposite of feeling. The cab driver, that is, treats the novel not as his friend, but as he does his cab, which does not provoke feelings and cannot make him feel less alone in the world. The cab does not need to borrow his experience of time because it already exists, on its own, as a physical object in space. The cab is not an amorphous whole but has distinct, identifiable, replaceable parts that work together to make it run. In "The Meaning of the Wild Body" (1927), Lewis presents the taxi-cab driver as a particularly good figure for such "detachment": "He did not identify himself with his machine."[85] The reasoning behind this claim is that the cab is most often "a very slow and ineffective conveyance," and the cab driver cannot help but realize how bad his cab is, how far removed it is from "what a taxi ought to be."[86] Because cabs are usually terrible – because they do not fit into the fast-paced industrial temporality we expect to apply to technology, because they resist the rhythm of modern life – the cab driver's critical intelligence is activated. Thus, the driver's body might merge with the cab during his long hours on the job, but his actual mind, which knows what an incompetent machine his taxi is, cannot help but maintain critical distance from it. He is a machine-operator, more than the conventional reader who merges with the text and emotionally bonds with the characters. Transforming reading into the operating of a machine, the taxi-cab driver models a mechanical vision of the reading process, where "machine" is defined in a utopian way, as a structured, static object with which one cannot identify.

As a strategy, impressionist collaboration has much in common with modernist primitivism, another discourse Lewis satirizes in the few dense pages of the "Taxi-Cab Driver Test." Like impressionists, modernist primitivists laud the perspective of a population they see as diametrically opposed to their own: people who are in touch with the unconscious and the deeply organic world of bodily instinct, who belong to an older culture that existed before modern technology restructured the world. Lewis flattens the historical and geographical hierarchies of primitivism, finding his primitive informant in the contemporary moment of his own city. He also reverses the attitude he so thoroughly critiqued in *Paleface*, of imagining the primitive as pretechnological. Rather, he performs his argument that "Every Age has been 'a Machine Age'": the primitive subject he calls in is a thoroughly technologized one.

Certainly, Lewis does not ordinarily think of machine operators as intellectual heroes. For the most part, he sees them as the willing victims of the modern, time-driven understanding of technology, the workers in Henry Ford's automobile factories who "want to feed and sleep – and mechanical work is a sort of sleep – and be told what to do, nothing more."[87] They are the "machine-minder" Lewis lampoons in *The Apes of God*, "[t]he little oiler feeder and keeper of the machines of the Mechanical Age" with no mind outside of the machine whose orders they passively follow.[88] But, of course, ordinary reading, in Lewis's view, is not very different from minding a Machine-Age machine: we let a succession of images pass without differentiation, and feel emotions rather than thinking – it is a mode of reading that depends upon the hurried temporality of modern technology. So here Lewis performs the rhetorical polemic he promised in the "Every Age has been 'a Machine Age'" section of *Paleface*: he uses novel-reading to reinvent the mechanical worker and the mechanical worker to reinvent novel-reading, mutually redefining art and machine. If machines can be understood as highly structured objects without insides, rather than time-driven hypnotic action generators, then the machine operator would be exactly the right person to read a novel as though it were an object without an inside, space without time.

With its utopian view of the machine-minder, the taxi-cab driver test challenges a long-standing critical view: that Lewis envisions technology as a force that will strengthen the elite by hardening them, while simultaneously hypnotizing the idiot masses.[89] Such a position led Hal Foster to describe Lewis as a British version of Ernst Jünger, the German soldier-philosopher whose nihilistic view of technology inspired Heidegger and exemplified the "reconciliation of technology and unreason" that Jeffrey Herf theorizes as the heart of Nazi ideology.[90] Jünger saw modern technologies as a manifestation of man's will to power, and celebrated the soldier as an *Übermensch* who "combined human passion with technical precision, hot flesh with cold steel," in Michael Zimmerman's terms.[91] While there certainly are continuities between Lewis's theory of technology and the "reactionary modernism" of fascist Germany, it would be inaccurate to describe Lewis's thinking, as Foster does, as "a protofascist desire to *elevate* this self-alienation into an absolute value (for a select few)."[92] Lewis was ultimately not interested in imagining the artist as technological *Übermensch*, the hardened individual who can oppose the masses. While the bright line distinction between artist and common machine-minder might generally describe life in the Machine Age, for Lewis, the artist cannot meaningfully escape the hypnosis of machines without redefining the machine altogether. With the taxi-cab driver test, Lewis speculates about what Ford's machine-minders would be like if machines were entirely different than they are in modern reality. Lewis's argument does not therefore present the taxi-cab driver as a figure for the artist – but for what readers, the debased group that prefers Anita Loos or even Gertrude Stein to Wyndham Lewis, could be.[93] What we have here is a vivid example of a tension Andrzej Gąsiorek diagnoses between Lewis's satirical mocking of the general population and his utopian cultural criticism, which aimed to teach and improve those same people.[94] Indeed, it is the doubleness of Lewis's thinking about technology – his satire of the machine-minder and his simultaneously utopian reimagining of what the machine could be – that makes it difficult to categorize his thinking as protofascist. There is no stable, deep belief in any romantic concept such as *Volk*, blood, myth, or will that can be rendered compatible with modern technology, in Lewis's thinking. Instead, he mercilessly mocks machine-minders while positioning them at the core of a new vision of the machine.

Satire Meets Utopia

With the taxi-cab driver test, Lewis opens up the possibility of a fully external novel, one that gets out of the pull of progressive time and models a new vision of what technology means. But the novel cannot become a static, geometric technology on its own – it needs a reader who is willing to treat it as such, who refuses to be absorbed in the flow of narration. The reader's necessary collaboration is both a source of hopeful possibility and a troubling example of the novel's inadequacy for the task Lewis has set out for it. If readers would really act like the taxi-cab driver, then perhaps the novel could profoundly influence society, and reimagine society's relationship to technology as Lewis hopes. But Lewis keeps his attention on the extraordinary difficulty of that task: on its own, how can a novel forge a new social understanding of technology, in a culture ruled so completely by the logic of modern technology and its rhythm of industrial time? This tension – between Lewis's utopian vision of technology and his satiric diagnosis that the problem overwhelms his solution for it – helps to explain a structure that critics have diagnosed at the heart of Lewis's fictional practice: his novels strive to achieve containment and forestall sequence, only then to undercut their own attempts.[95] In the most notorious examples of this structure – the end of *Tarr* and the rape of Bertha in that novel, as well as the last chapter of *The Apes of God* – Lewis stalls industrial time only then finally to reinforce it. Lewis leaves the emphasis on how inescapable modern technological time is, and cedes the last move to the reader he cannot control, who may or may not choose to read as the taxi-cab driver does.

Jameson reads the conclusion of *Tarr* as bald evidence that "the narrative has failed" in its own terms.[96] But in the context of Lewis's critique of his society's industrial rhythm, *Tarr*'s final undoing of containment might be understood as a dramatic staging of the novel's relationship to social forces that outweigh it: Lewis embeds his own novel back into industrial time, foregrounding the insufficiency of the novel to complete its task. At the start of the last chapter, the novel seems to drive toward a formal, geometric stasis that rejects the absorbing pull of progressive time: Tarr marries Bertha, in a classic gesture of closure that is amplified by a suggestion that the novel's end is a return to its beginning and an undoing of all the events that have transpired. "Things are exactly the same as before," Tarr explains, alleging that "I have merely gone back a year into the past and fulfilled a pledge ... All is in perfect order."[97] Here the novel lends itself to the taxi-cab driver test: a reader need only examine these last pages to see the perfectly ordered shape of the whole, which did not need hundreds of pages for its contours to emerge, after all. But against this gesture toward stasis and containment, the last paragraphs undo the marriage along with Tarr's affair with Anastasia, and then create two new characters, future lovers of Tarr: Rose Fawcett and Prism Dirkes. It is not coincidental that critics have often seen this final act of creation as evidence that the novel has devolved into a technological nightmare of out-of-control production, as the text itself self-consciously imagines the creation of these characters in terms of progressive, industrial time with the image of a clock: Prism "represents the swing back of the pendulum once more."[98] Once the novel has created Rose and Prism, there is no reason to stop there; the novel's form, its sense of completion, is undone, and the pendulum threatens to simply keep swinging. Here, Lewis emphasizes the novel's necessary existence within the context of Machine-Age time, and refuses to pretend that the novel alone can change that. He violently exposes the novel to technological time, rather than protecting it.

The creation of Rose and Prism in the final paragraph is an extreme manifestation of a double structure of productivity and containment, the "*molecular* and … *molar* impulses" identified by Jameson.[99] This structure, constituted by tension between the revolutionary time of the Machine Age and the temporal stasis of the art of the eye, is at work across the novel, as one more example – the scene in which Kreisler rapes Bertha – will suggest. The rape first appears in the novel as a bounded, spatial structure, rather than an event taking place in linear, progressive time. The novel spatializes the rape in the way it introduces the scene: rather than describing the event or the characters that take part in it, the text fixates on the windows, "incandescent with steady saffron rays," that form the boundary lines of Kreisler's apartment, his "small shell of a room" where the rape occurs.[100] The rape is imagined as an event that restricts the progression of time: destiny "snapped down upon Bertha" and "[a]n iron curtain rushed down" on the event.[101] The apartment almost physically delimits this temporal confinement, as "unreasonable limitations gave its specific colour to thin glass" in the windows.[102] The novel explicitly takes this scene out of a continuous, sequential narrative: as the chapter begins, Bertha curses Kreisler for having raped her, before the reader has any idea that a rape has occurred at all. The rape has already concluded before it happens; it is a complete thing, rather than an event that will unfold gradually over the course of the chapter. The text marks this disjuncture in sequence when Bertha speculates that "[a] separate framework of time had been arranged for it to happen in, this last disrespectful attack."[103]

However, against this containment that attempts to mitigate the event's duration through time, the novel proliferates narrative sequences. The novel's initial attempt to explain why Bertha is cursing Kreisler replaces the rape with a series of figures. While the rape itself is isolated within a "separate framework of time" behind an "iron curtain," the novel gets caught up in spinning out replacement figures to describe Bertha's reaction. As the passage careens from description to description, each providing some kernel that motivates the next, it becomes an example of the "sheerly additive sentence production" that Jameson describes as the "mechanistic enterprise" of Lewis's writing.[104]

> All the repulsion of her being … pumped up in spasms and hissing on her lips as she spat out the usual epithets for the occasion. The deepening sing-song of the "hässlicher Mensch!" was accompanied by a disgusting sound like the brutal relishing and gobbling of food. The appetite of hatred spat and gobbled while it lasted. Her attitude was reminiscent of the way people are seen to stand, bent awkwardly forward, neck craned out, slowly wiping the dirt off their clothes, or spitting out the remains of the polluted drink, cursing the person who has victimized them, after the successful execution of some practical joke.[105]

Rather than describing the specific source of Bertha's repulsion, the passage transforms the rape into a completely ordinary incident, which generates the "usual epithets for the occasion." Next, this spitting out of clichéd responses to an everyday scene turns into an episode of gluttonous eating. In turn, this meal provides the premise of another figure, in which Bertha's food is poisoned, as she "spit[s] out the remains of the polluted drink." The final figure diffuses the violence of the "execution" into a mere practical joke. This series of descriptions expands the rape by initiating several new scenes of narrative action: a meal, an attempted poisoning, and a prank. While the novel encloses and objectifies the rape scene by taking it out of the narrative progression, here it expands into another succession of narrative events. The rape won't stop, despite the novel's attempts at containment: this is the productive temporality that governs novel-reading.[106]

It is fitting that the novel would launch an attempt at molar containment and then undercut it with the molecular generation of new narrative in this particular scene, whose content resonates with Lewis's aesthetic critique of time-driven art. Both the rape and the metaphoric poisoning that replaces it are examples of the body being forced to take in an alien substance that violently disrupts its integrity. This is indeed what happens in the art of the ear, in Lewis's account: the art object parasitically enters, even takes control of, the spectator or reader's body. Here, at this moment when the novel is mechanically "pump[ing] out" figure after figure, giving into the molecular impulse of continuous productivity, the novel comes close to thematizing Lewis's theory of the art of the ear: Bertha's victimization, the violent penetration of her body, figures the invasion of the reader as she reads and the novel moves through her. To contain the scene, to fully seal it off, would be to make the novel more like an art of the eye that stays outside of the reader who can contemplate it at a distance without being penetrated by it. But while the novel attempts that containment, Lewis does not let it succeed. The penetration keeps happening, as Lewis reintegrates the scene into the continuous, revolutionary, technological time that requires machines and art objects to merge into the subjects that use or observe them.

The Apes of God more explicitly imagines narrative containment as a specific corrective for industrial time, before then, like Tarr, undoing its hard-won containment, in a moment that comes close to a satire of the taxi-cab driver test. Lewis would almost certainly consider the penultimate chapter of the novel, "Lord Osmund's Lenten Party," to be "mechanical" in the debased modern sense – at 255 pages, it is the ultimate satire of the shapeless "molecular" novel, driven by the mechanical logic of ceaseless revolution, where another sentence is always sure to follow. The short final chapter on the General Strike of 1926 heroically intervenes, terminating the interminable. The General Strike is a figure for stillness, for stopping mechanical work and the repetitive progressive temporality that work entails – but it is also a powerful image for the novel's own formal shift from hyperproductivity to containment: the novel also stops, associating the strike with what Scott Klein calls "a falling away of textuality."[107] In containing the novel with the figure of the strike, the last chapter self-consciously redefines what it means for the novel to be a machine: the mechanical production of the previous chapter, driven by the revolutionary temporality of the Machine Age in which one sentence, or one machine, must inevitably follow another, is replaced by Paleface's atemporal, highly structured machine.

The General Strike of May 1926 is a particularly apt figure for the novel as static machine. Not only did this strike produce large scale, multi-industry work stoppage, and thus a momentary stalling of industrial time, but the strike was also widely imagined as an anticlimax, even though its failure had profound effects on British politics.[108]

Commentators noted the peacefulness and unexciting atmosphere of the strike, a consequence both of orderly behavior by strikers and the "general spirit of renewal, fun, and licence" engendered by the multitudes of people who volunteered to drive ambulances and print newspapers.[109] Strikers, volunteers, and police staged football games, billiard matches, and concerts – and the end of *Apes* mocks just this kind of holiday-making.[110] The anticlimax of the event is particularly vivid because of the actual violence of general strikes elsewhere in Europe in the early twentieth century as well as the rhetoric of violence in syndicalist political theories like those of Georges Sorel.[111] A passage from Virginia Woolf's diary suggests the implication of the strike's anticlimactic nature for its future in narration: "I suppose all pages devoted to the Strike will be skipped, when I read over this book. O that dull old chapter, I shall say."[112] Thus the General Strike of 1926 was the perfect subject for precisely the sort of narrative that might resist the pull of forward momentum – one might read it with the "amused boredom" Beatrice Webb saw on the faces of bystanders, rather than with the pull of "absorbing interest" that makes one want to watch events unfold, to turn page after page.[113]

But even within the confined boundaries of the final chapter, Lewis stages the tension between his two ideas of what it might mean for the novel to be a machine.[114] The novel transforms even the strike as nonevent into new material that extends the novel for several more paragraphs beyond the protagonist's exit and the death of several of the apes – two occurrences that had seemed to conclude the novel's action. Rather than simply bringing all narrative action to a halt, that is, the strike also generates a new level of narrative activity. Initially, the strike promises to still mechanical movement, to provide the first moment of peace since the death of Queen Victoria: "it was a death of life – the throbbing circulation of incessant machines, in thunderous rotation, in the arteries of London was stopped."[115] But in a devastating reversal, the apes, "the embattled Motorist-Middleclass" of amateur artists, become taxi-cab drivers to fill the void left by striking transportation workers.[116] This moment seems to satirically co-opt the taxi-cab driver test of fiction: the taxi-cab driver, that ideal reader, might actually turn out to be everything Lewis hated about his society, and is certainly not within the novel's control.[117] Then, a series of plays on the word "strike" in the last pages make the term indicate not only an ending but also an unstoppable wellspring of more versions of that ending: the silence of the strike gives Lady Fredigonde's husband a "stroke," thus prompting her immediate engagement to Horace Zagreus, and a jazz band "struck up" in the penultimate paragraph.[118]

The striking up of the jazz band is a particularly daunting sign of the strike's resignification as the continuation of mechanical movement and the triumph of revolutionary industrial time. For Lewis, jazz explicitly follows the temporality of mechanical production, with its hurried tempo that never leads anywhere new: "The band manufactured its melodic treacle, thumped in imitation of abrupt machinery – a titanic treacle-can factory. Shock after shock – then more sad sickly sugar."[119] Horace Zagreus tells us that jazz is the music of the factory, beloved by the "machine-hind," "[t]he little oiler feeder and keeper of the machines of the Mechanical Age."[120] The machine-minders love jazz because it is music with an "official stamp": "Jazz is the folk-music of the metropolitan mass – slum-peasant, machine-minder – the heart-cry of the city-serf. His masters sing his songs – they even write them for him!"[121] Zagreus invokes jazz as the ironic opposite of folk culture, what would be an at least partly original creation of the underclass itself. Jazz constitutes a rejection of all forms of originality and authenticity, making it a natural fit both for the actual machine-minders and the more well-off class of amateur artists who, after all, merely "ape" the work of real artists. In the place of actual creative innovation or thought, there is constant movement, as exemplified by Dick Whittington, Lady Fredigonde's nephew: "His legs kept turning to the massed gramophoning of his slowly revolving eardrums, like the disks of records."[122] Dick's body ceaselessly plays the already recorded music of the jazz record; like the machine-minders, his mind is a machine, powerless to produce critical or original thought but entirely capable of continuing the rhythm of mechanical motion.

In the novel's final chapter, Lewis returns to this set of associations with jazz, only to emphasize its complicity with the unending forward movement of industrial time. In a satire of *The Waste Land*, a thunderstorm erupts as a jazz band simultaneously explodes into a rendition of an Irving Berlin song:

> Whoddle ah *doo*
> Wen *yoo*
> Are *far*
> Away
> An *I*
> am *bloo*
> Whoddle ah *doo*
> Whoddlah DOOOO!"[123]

Eliot's rejuvenating Sanskrit "Da" becomes a command for further mechanical action: "DOOOO!" The jazz song is followed by yet one more paragraph. Dan is on his way home, having been rejected by Zagreus, but his successor, Archie Margolin, emerges in a virtuoso performance of the revolutionary temporality of industry: "In the great reception-room immediately beneath Archie Margolin, as he heard the first notes of the street-instrumentalists, stiffened, and, with elf-like nigger-bottom-wagging, he traversed the oppressive spaces of this monster apartment ... smiling at himself as he advanced (with his St. Vitus puppet-shiver) in the mighty victorian looking-glasses."[124] Despite all of the novel's heroic gestures toward closure – two deaths, a marriage, and a strike – this final paragraph is a scene of the triumphant continuation of the apes' production into another generation. The novel performs this reproduction on multiple levels: Archie's very appearance after Dan's rejection, his mindless "St. Vitus puppet shiver" dancing, and his literal multiplication as he watches himself in not one but several mirrors. In this final image of multiple Archies jazz dancing, against the "oppressive" closure of the apartment and the looming final page, the novel stages its desire for containment, stillness, and the geometric machinery of the Totem pole, against the incessantly moving, technological time of industry. Lewis, thus, ends the novel by insisting on what society's love of technological time might do to the novel, not how the novel might be able to change the meaning of technology.

The end of *The Apes of God* performs the full complexity of Lewis's theory of the novel as machine. He wants to imagine the novel as a machine at the moment it stops being read, at the moment where a reader can gaze upon a contained, clearly defined visual object without being involved, feeling empathy, or otherwise experiencing a text. If that kind of a novel is a machine, and someone like the taxi-cab driver is its operator, then a machine, in turn, is a contained, geometric work. But the novel cannot reshape society's understanding of technology on its own. Even the novel as static machine necessarily remains embedded in the Machine Age, whose denizens cannot help but understand technology as a rhythm rather than a spatial object, a revolutionary attitude that leads us to expect and want the next machine, the next sentence, and the next moment. Like the machine, the novel, too, is caught between the ear and the eye, between what seems to be a natural, necessary extension in time – new machines replace old, one page follows the last – and the possibility that every age has been a Machine Age, and that a taxi-cab driver who glances at a page in a moment might be the best reader of a novel.

To understand the novel as a machine is a polemical, not a descriptive act. The effort to reimagine the machine is significant not because it will succeed – after all, he is trying to define both novel and machine against their most stable contemporary characteristics – but because of the possibility it opens. So, the strike strikes up, the novel is read, the machine works again.

CHAPTER 4

From Empathy to the Super-Cortex
Rebecca West's Technics of the Novel

This final chapter turns toward a writer who would not ordinarily be situated in the trajectory of novel theory traced by this book thus far. Rebecca West's reputation as a prolific and influential literary critic and aesthetic theorist was recuperated in the 1990s through the efforts of Jane Marcus, Bonnie Kime Scott, Margaret Stetz, and other feminist scholars, after a long period during which her political journalism and travel writing dominated her reception.[1] To this point, our critical accounts have largely described West's literary criticism as anti-formalist, arguing that she theorized the novel as firmly grounded in its reader's personal experience and embedded in life. As a critic, West has been imagined as the polar opposite of the writers this study has examined, who struggled to theorize how the novel might repel the instrumentalizing grasp of readers and avoid being merged into their experience.

West's most complex and extended work of criticism – a long essay that is, in some ways, a review of *Ulysses* – would seem to confirm these views. When it first appeared, "The Strange Necessity" (1928) quickly emerged as a significant but controversial theory of the modernist novel. Samuel Beckett, William Carlos Williams, and Virginia Woolf all responded explicitly to West in their own essays at the time, and her criticism of *Ulysses* earned her a cameo in *Finnegans Wake*.[2] "The Strange Necessity" is a meditation on West's personal experience of reading Joyce in Paris, the role of art in human life, and the relationship of the novel to Pavlov's experiments in behaviorism. The essay's narrative is structured around a meandering walk through Paris, and West's account of *Ulysses* is juxtaposed with her thoughts about dresses, hats, paintings, and letters from friends. It is thus not surprising that critics have understood the essay as positing the work of art's essential connectedness to its beholder's personal experience – her affective and physical states as well as the communities she inhabits. As Laura Heffernan has recently put it, literary value seems to derive from outside of the text for West.[3] Such a position

seems consistent with the feminist version of modernism usually associated with West, one that rejects aesthetic autonomy and the "hard" or
"external" values of classicism, promoted by T. E. Hulme, Wyndham
Lewis, and T. S. Eliot (for whom West reserved particular ire).[4] Indeed,
Francesca Frigerio idealizes West's essay as the kind of embodied criticism
that Molly Bloom herself would write.[5]

West's "soft," feminist aesthetics have also been understood as particularly organic: "Underlying all of her writing on the arts was a philosophy
of organicism," writes Stetz.[6] From this view, West critiques the cold,
mechanistic, masculinist abstraction of classicism, instead theorizing
the art object as deeply connected to the body, to nature, and to the
feminine. West's most modernist novel, *Harriet Hume* (1929), can be
easily read in such terms: the eponymous heroine is a pianist who plays
nature as an instrument, transforming a flower into "a phrase in a sonata
by Mozart" and producing a particularly organic art.[7] Arnold Condorex,
the novel's antagonist, is finally recuperated in the novel's final pages,
after attempting to murder Harriet, when he agrees to "learn that
which shall reconcile me to nature."[8] Based on her critical reputation,
West surely seems an unlikely candidate for thinking about the novel
as deeply connected to technology and antagonistic to or autonomous
from its reader.

But this chapter recuperates a neglected side of West's aesthetics,
one that shows her actively participating in the shift within modernist novel theory that this book has traced. She dismisses reading as a
central critical category in order to situate the novel in the domain of
technology, as a device for gathering and organizing knowledge. In "The
Strange Necessity" and her other essays on the novel from the late 1920s,
West defines the novel as a form of scientific experiment that produces
research, not an experience to be completed by an engaged reader. As
West re-envisions the novel as a tool for information collection, she
emphasizes how it develops human experience into knowledge, not how
it affects readers. Her associative account of wandering around Paris,
thinking about Joyce, looks quite different if we take seriously her explicit
account of the novel as research tool. She is performing, in criticism, the
work of analysis and synthesis of experience that is the task of any artistic
text, transforming experience into usable knowledge.

West's theory most fully exemplifies the specifically modernist intervention in novel theory that this book has traced. Modernist novel theory's investment in point of view and attempts to imagine a static novel
outside of temporal progression are all aspects of how it reconceived the

novel's primary effect as epistemological rather than affective. James and Lubbock may not have explicitly theorized the novel as an information tool, but as Dames has argued, in prioritizing point of view, they shifted critical methods toward extracting data from the novel and theorized moments where knowledge is revealed as the most significant and defining part of a text.[9] West's "The Strange Necessity" performs this shift from affect to epistemology: it envisions the novel as an experimental form of art that is useful and important precisely because, like a scientific experiment, it yields information about the world. She is not driven by a desire to take control of the work from the reader, to pedagogically train the reader, or to separate the novel from mass culture, as the other writers I have examined were, but nonetheless she imagines the meaning of the novel as deriving not from its effects on a reader but from the information it provides about the world. West's work allows us to see the depth and scope of the transition away from the reader as the focus of novel theory. Thus, it is surprising that Dames does not mention Rebecca West in his account of modernist novel theory's turn from reading. He focuses instead on James, Lubbock, and I. A. Richards, and mentions several more minor figures such as Carl Grabo and Edwin Muir.[10] Perhaps West's reputation for opposing aesthetic autonomy and favoring an organic, anti-hierarchical vision of the novel and a feminist, personal, autobiographical approach to criticism has made it difficult to see her connection with this discourse, which has certainly been associated primarily with male writers promoting masculine-coded aesthetic values.[11]

West's reputation has also hidden a layer of her theory of the novel that is particularly significant to this book's narrative: for her, because the novel is an experimental tool for gathering information, it belongs to the field of technics. The novel is part of what she describes, in a repurposing of Pavlovian terms, as a collective "super-cortex" that stores and coordinates knowledge. The super-cortex is the center of human efforts to better adapt to their environment through technology – by learning to fly through designing an airplane instead of trying to grow wings. Though she does not use the term technics herself – it would have been unlikely for an English writer to use this word in 1928 – she is describing precisely what French philosopher Bernard Siegert would define as technics, seventy years later: man's extra-genetic interventions into the process of evolution, a process that is at the center of what it means to be human, in Siegert's terms. West's theory of the super-cortex surprisingly anticipates Siegert's twenty-first century thinking, but also adds another, crucial component: she situates the novel at the heart of technics, as one of humanity's most effective and necessary means of adapting itself better to the environment. West ultimately offers a strategy for envisioning the novel's significance even in a world increasingly dominated by science and technology.

This book has traced, thus, a gradual deepening of links between the novel and technology. James and Ford found in contemporary devices models for a novel that can move and unfold in time, on its own terms, and without the intervention of a reader; they ultimately imagined how the novel might be constructed as a homology to film projectors and telephone connections. Lewis went further, conceptualizing the novel as a genre bound up with the machine as a category, because they share a relationship to time. West similarly connects the novel to technology as a category, focusing not on its temporality but its epistemology: for her, the novel and technics share a relationship to knowledge. Technics is at the origin of technologies, generating the kinds of technical knowledge that enable any specific technological advancement.

At the same time, West's work makes clear the specifically modernist character of this link between technics and the novel. On one historical side, she positions herself in the tradition of late Victorian thinking about empathy, but then makes a clear and significant departure from that tradition by radically redefining empathy in terms linked to modernist formalism. On the other side, West differentiated her position from arguments about media and technology that emerged later in the century, arguments we could now call postmodern. In a 1969 lecture about Marshall McLuhan, West ruefully admitted that she thought "The Strange Necessity" anticipated the arguments McLuhan makes in *Understanding Media* (1964), in particular the idea that media such as the novel are "extensions of man." But in the same lecture, West launches into a deep critique of McLuhan for where he takes that idea – his argument that new media inherently encourage participation. The electronic extensions of man would increasingly replace specialization and depth of knowledge with an economy of participation, where everyone is able to participate in everything and only the medium – whether and how it allows participation, not what it communicates – matters. West argues against the ideology of participation and interactivity, and in doing so reveals a particularly modernist vision of the novel's relationship to technology: the novel as a prosthesis that creates knowledge itself, without concern for its reader and without encouraging or requiring participation.

From Empathy to Experiment

As early as the author's note that precedes "The Strange Necessity," West locates her essay in an ambivalent relationship to late Victorian novel theory, with its focus on the reader. The note invokes this context through a defensive claim about the word "empathy," the English translation of a concept from German psychology. Empathy had been integrated into the mainstream of novel theory by Vernon Lee, who was deeply associated with the tradition of physiological aesthetics that informed late Victorian ideas about reading.[12] The note reads as follows:

> Certain persons concerned with the preparation of my manuscript have accused me of using in 'empathy' a word that is absent from most dictionaries. I imagine, however, that it is familiar to most people, as a term to express our power of entering into the experience of objects outside ourselves, through its presence in the pages of Lipps (as *Einfühlung*) and Vernon Lee; and though I have modified it to suit my own purposes I hope those modifications are justified by the context.[13]

While claiming this particular intellectual heritage, West also promises to manipulate it, to repurpose empathy to mean something else.

For Lee and her partner, Clementina Anstrusther-Thomson, aesthetic response by definition works through a process of empathy. In *Beauty and Ugliness* (1912), they associate the term with a deep conflation of beholder and aesthetic object, a response in which one "transport[s] oneself into something in feeling."[14] Empathy involves "the projection of our own dynamical and emotional experience into the seen form" and "attribution of our life to seen shapes": the viewer feels something, and then projects it onto the work.[15] When we behold an art object, we imagine what we would feel if we inhabited its form, and then displace our own feeling onto the work: "in looking at the Doric column, for instance, and its entablature, we are attributing to the lines and surfaces, to the spatial forms, those dynamic experiences which we should have were we to put our bodies into similar conditions."[16] The viewer never sees the work itself as an external, distant object to contemplate; instead, she is immediately embroiled in "dynamic experiences." The qualities attributed to the work itself ultimately originate in and belong to the viewing subject – thus the work does not mean on its own, but only after a beholder projects her own experience onto it. Empathy describes the disappearance of the work behind the beholder – exactly what terrified so many of the critics this book has analyzed – as the basis of all aesthetic response.

Our major accounts of West's aesthetics present her ideas in terms that are often associated with Lee: embodied, personal, organic. Shafquat Towheed describes Lee's aesthetic theory with language that might be found in an account of West: her method "values empathy and personal association, 'not the oracular *we* of the printed book' but 'an art-philosophy entirely unabstract, unsystematic, essentially personal' that had developed organically in order 'to serve the requirements of personal tendencies.'"[17] Initially, "The Strange Necessity" seems to exemplify Lee's concept of empathy, because it appears to analyze *Ulysses* by recounting what Joyce's work makes Rebecca West feel. West purchases Joyce's *Pomes Penyeach* from Sylvia Beach's bookstore, and then observes similarities between the feelings generated by his texts and by other objects – a black lace dress, for instance, and a painting by Ingres. But despite these connections, West's essay reconceptualizes empathy dramatically, shifting it from an affective and experiential register to an epistemological one. Rather than naming how a beholder merges with a work through feeling, empathy instead comes to signify the way a work of art mines usable knowledge out of the real world.

Throughout "The Strange Necessity," West repeats one central claim, the thesis of the essay: that "art is at least in part a way of collecting information about the universe."[18] She develops this argument by referencing the work of the Russian physiologist Ivan Petrovich Pavlov, whose volume of lectures, *Conditioned Reflexes*, had just appeared in English translation. Pavlov observed dogs under the administration of various stimuli, and West argues that works of art do the same thing. According to this line of thinking, both novels and experiments work by exposing subjects to certain stimuli and observing how they react:

> at the end of it [the novelist] has established just how certain kinds of people act in certain circumstances that uncover their attitudes to recurring and fundamental factors of life, just as Professor Pavlov has established how a certain kind of dog behaved when it was given meat powder under certain conditions. An experiment has been conducted, an observation has been made, bearing on a principle, it has been faithfully reported.[19]

The novelist becomes an experimenter, and the novel is a scientific record of human behavior under specific conditions.

West certainly could have invoked Pavlov in the service of the aesthetics of empathy. He argues for the behaviorist proposition that there is no difference between psychology and physiology – that the mind should be studied through objective physiological observation, rather than through attempting to understand subjective mental states.[20] Such a position is entirely compatible with Lee's aesthetics and with the main-stream of Victorian novel theory. Lee was centrally interested in what the "dynamic experience" of art did to the human body. She understood the reader's body as a mechanical instrument that was moved, some-times literally, by the work of art: words are "made to vibrate" in the reader's mind, for instance.[21] G. H. Lewes, similarly, was so convinced that aesthetic response was a physical reflex that he thought there was no significant difference between conscious and unconscious responses to a novel.[22] Pavlov would be the perfect 1920s scientist to continue this train of thought – to de-intellectualize aesthetic response, to theorize it as an automatic physiological reaction. Indeed, several critics have recently situated I. A. Richards in this tradition, reading him as an heir to Victorian aesthetic theory who mixed its concepts with behaviorism.[23] Thus, in *Practical Criticism*, Richards gives his students decontextualized poems without telling them who the author is, in order to record their most automatic and immediate responses to poetic language.

It is tempting to link West to this tradition, in part because doing so would seem to confirm the long-standing view that she promoted an aesthetics focused on the reader's embodied response. But "The Strange Necessity" does not pursue a behaviorist, physiological aesthet-ics. Instead, what she takes from Pavlov is the structure of his scientific experiments. In order to study conditioning, or the way animals learn to adapt to their environment, Pavlov observed dogs under the influence of particular stimuli. In *Lectures on Conditioned Responses*, he devotes sub-stantial attention to the scientist's behavior, what she must do in order to generate scientific knowledge from such experiments. He warns that scientists must be careful to "abandon entirely the natural inclination to transpose our own subjective condition upon the mechanism of the reaction of the experimental animal."[24] In order to produce objective sci-entific knowledge, an observer must refrain from a response that sounds much like empathy, as Lee theorized it: the observer must preserve distance from the animal, and cannot project her own feelings onto the experimental subject.

"The Strange Necessity" insists that art, to be art, cannot be merely the meat powder that makes the dog salivate in Pavlov's experiment. Rather, "[t]he experiments themselves form close parallels to imaginative works of art."[25] Pavlov studied how dogs developed reflex responses to a variety of stimuli; for West, the work of art is defined as such by the fact that it similarly studies how humans respond to stimuli. Art is the experi-ment, not the stimulus. At the same time, art is not merely the record of experiences. As she puts it in a formulation that appears throughout her literary criticism from the late 1920s and early 30s, the work of art engages in the "analysis and synthesis of experience."[26] Art thus translates direct experience into knowledge through analysis. Lee's version of empathy has the potential to disrupt this process of analysis – a scientist must be objective and analyze the facts as they are rather than letting her feelings interfere. For a reader, this means finding a way to avoid projecting her own experience onto a work.

How, then, do we understand the structure of "The Strange Necessity," which would seem to displace *Ulysses* with West's reading experience? The problem resolves if we recognize that for West, "The Strange Necessity" is itself a work of art. It analyzes and synthesizes experience, performing the task that defines art as such. Criticism and theory function the same way that works of art do. This is possible because the work of art, in her theory, is intellectual and analytical, so the distance between a creative and critical work is vanishingly small.[27] From this perspective it is not surprising that the essay discusses *Ulysses* so little, and hardly at all in its last two-thirds: "The Strange Necessity" is, ultimately, not about *Ulysses*, or about West's reaction to it. The essay is, rather, a work of art on its own terms, and Rebecca West is the subject of its experiment.

West did not simply discard empathy as a concept. Rather, she imagined a new version of empathy – one that departs significantly from Lee's affect-focused use of the concept and that centers on the writer, not the reader. For a writer, a certain version of empathy turns out to be necessary for generating knowledge. To produce a work that qualifies as art, the writer "is under an obligation to analyze his experience in the light of all the other analyses of experience that are accessible to his age," as she puts it in another essay.[28] Thus, in order for the novel to analyze and synthesize experience the way art must, it cannot merely be self-expression, a record of an individual's own life. A work that "seems to have no other body of knowledge concerning the universe which he [the artist] can use as a basis for comparison" cannot rise to the level of art.[29] This is the role played by *Ulysses* in "The Strange Necessity": it is a point of analytical comparison that enables West to turn her experience into knowledge. Thus, West writes: "I have among my experiences one that bears a strong resemblance to James Joyce's experience which made him write *Ulysses*."[30] When she reads the novel, she is able to "see what was peculiar to myself and what was universal in the form in which this common experience presented itself to me."[31] True artists must ultimately perform a certain kind of empathy: they must constantly compare their own experience to that of others, stepping outside of themselves and generalizing or objectifying themselves to think about how other people respond. Artists must still "transport" themselves "into something," as Lee argues – but that transport operates through analysis, not feeling. Empathy is transformed into analytical comparison.

This retooled version of empathy helps to explain how novels in particular are able to produce knowledge about the real world and real people, despite the fact that they are fictional. West insists that fiction reveals information about the real world precisely because we can compare ourselves to other people: "On the foundation of our experience we are able to penetrate imaginatively into the experience of others."[32] Art in fact has an advantage over science, West argues, because it allows us to gather information about emotions and mental states, which are inaccessible to physiological science (Pavlov, of course, would disagree). Because of empathy, the novel becomes a tool for gathering information about the real world:

> we have no excuse for denying that there is a process by which a man can use in fantasy psychological mechanisms which he does not use in real life, and since these are common to all other human beings he is thereby reconstructing the experience of other real people; so that the record by a person using this process, of the behaviour of imaginary people in a book is as sound a guide to the understanding of real people in the real world outside that book as the record of the behaviour of real dogs in a laboratory is to the understanding of real dogs outside a laboratory.[33]

The work of fiction becomes a laboratory in which experiments are performed on real people. The artifice of the novel is no greater than that of the lab, and does not impede the novelistic experiment's bearing on reality. Empathy is no longer about the reader projecting herself onto the work, but is instead the mechanism that allows writers to analyze real reflexes in fictional works. Empathy, redefined, enables the novel to create information about the world, and transforms it into a research technique.

The Experiment as Modernist Form

West goes even further in moving novel theory away from the reader and toward knowledge. The reader should avoid projecting her feelings onto a text, but beyond that, the novel should not strive to inspire any sort of feeling at all in a reader. She directly opposes the novel's scientific, information-gathering role from any effect it might have on a reader, arguing that if a novelist so much as cares about a reader's experience, the novel in question will fail to be a scientific experiment and therefore will not rise to the level of art. Such a novel is nothing but a document of sentimentality. With this position, she aligns "The Strange Necessity" with modernism's various kinds of formalism, though not without simultaneously shifting their direction. Her argument that art reveals knowledge about the world – that art is indeed a crucial way to know and understand the world we inhabit – connects her tightly to Wilhelm Worringer's vision of formalist abstraction, which inspired T. E. Hulme.[34] However, at the same time, West insisted on redefining modernist formalism, represented for her by T. S. Eliot and Clive Bell, to ensure the novel's relevance to a world dominated by science and technology. For her, Eliot and Bell failed on just this count, by isolating art from contemporary life and situating it instead in the realms of myth or pure, anti-representational form. Much as it did with Lee's concept of empathy, "The Strange Necessity" offers a corrective: a version of form rooted in, rather than distant from, contemporary life, and defined by, rather than opposed to, the capacity to provide information about the world.

West explicitly differentiates the scientific, information-producing function of the novel from any experience it might generate in a reader. The latter, she argues, defines beauty, something that has nothing to do with the novel-as-art, its ability to develop new knowledge about the world: "beauty is that other factor which creates that other emotion, that ecstasy which is surely different from this brisk consciousness of stimulation. Beauty may be present in a novel, but on the other hand it may not, and still the novel may be valuable, because of the presence of this first factor which seems to bear this close resemblance to Science."[35] Beauty is erotic, affective, experiential. Scientific information, on the other hand, is a matter of "brisk consciousness" – cold intellectualism that seems compatible with the "chill" and "dry hardness" of Hulme's classicism.[36]

In West's terms, the writer who constructs a scientific, "investigatory" novel – a work of art – cannot actually be concerned about the reader.[37] To think self-consciously about the reader is to be sentimental. This is West's main critique of Joyce: "he is playing a game, he is moving certain objects according to certain rules in front of spectators."[38] Rather than attempting "to please others," the novelist-as-artist will be focused on running an experiment, and the reader will come across the results naturally:

> To communicate one's experience to an audience is no trouble to an artist, since in point of fact giving formal expression to a work of art is to interpret one's experience to oneself, so that one merely permits the audience to look over one's shoulder. But to condition the expression of one's experience out of regard for the effect on one's audience's mind is to bring into the artistic process a factor so little of a constant, since that mind is perpetually changing according to the social and intellectual movements of the time, and one's understanding of it is as unstable, that it is comparable to playing bowls on a highroad.[39]

Letting into the reader's mind a set of variables that cannot be controlled in the laboratory threatens the novel's scientific status. This is the problem with sentiment: the writer is tempted into "falsifying" her material in order "to make an impression on the audience."[40] In an essay on Bruckner, West similarly argues that creating truthful knowledge about the world and affecting an audience are opposed goals: "what he cares for is not discovering the truth about his material but creating with it the greatest possible emotional effect on the audience."[41] Ultimately, then, such sentimentality "prevents a performance from being a work of art."[42]

West develops the opposition between understanding the novel as a conveyer of information and as a work designed to produce an effect on a reader in a 1931 essay on the controversy over the censorship of Radclyffe Hall's *The Well of Loneliness*. One wants to defend this novel by arguing that as a work of art, its emphasis is epistemological rather than affective:

> When a book of great literary merit is denounced the first line of defence always is to point out that that kind of book, which conscientiously analyzes a human experience and gives its findings honestly, cannot do those who read it any harm, since it adds to the knowledge of reality by which man lives. It has always been emphasized that far more harmful are books written sentimentally, that is to say written by persons who do not pass their subject matter through their imaginations and report on the results, but who describe their subject matter without investigation in terms they think likely to cause certain emotions in their readers.[43]

If the job of a work of art is to provide knowledge, then it really cannot affect a reader negatively – because that reader's emotional reactions are irrelevant when the novel functions epistemologically. Affect and epistemology are opposed, and one can divide works of literature into categories based on whether they are aimed toward one or the other.

The situation with Radclyffe Hall was complicated, however, by the fact that *The Well of Loneliness* is sentimental, not a work of art, for West. Rather than creating knowledge, it attempts to influence the reader. This is particularly unfortunate, in West's view, because of Hall's reputation as an amateur scientist, one of "the old admirals and generals and squires who use their leisure in solving the problem of perpetual motion."[44] West here alludes to Hall's work on spiritualism: she presented a scientific paper on her attempts to reach her dead lover through séances to the Society for Psychical Research in 1918, and later attempted to join the organization's governing council, though her application caused disagreement and resulted in a lawsuit for slander.[45] West wanted to defend Hall, whose scientific interests seemed to make her laudable in West's terms, but she found the book itself to be scientifically – and thus artistically – insignificant. Thus, West argues, literary luminaries signed petitions on Hall's behalf, but failed to make persuasive arguments on behalf of the novel's artistic merit. The result was "an imbroglio in which nobody can play a comfortable part."[46]

In opposing the novel's capacity for providing knowledge about the world to any effect it might have on a reader, West links herself to the context of modernist formalism. In particular, she develops Worringer's idea that man was drawn to formal, abstract art because it showed the "absolute value" of an object, something like its Platonic form.[47] In *Abstraction and Empathy*, he posits that art can only accomplish this by freeing the object from the arbitrary contingencies of material reality, from life. Art must strive "to tear [the object] out of the flux of happening, to free it from all contingency and caprice, to raise it up into the realm of the necessary."[48] The less comfortable man feels in the world, the happier he is to be reminded of "absolute value," of "the necessary," and the more he is drawn toward abstract art, which visualizes the laws behind the accidents. The beholder of the abstract work wants not to merge with the artwork through feeling but rather to observe the "necessity" it reveals: the work must be "as far as possible independent both of the ambient external world and of the subject – the spectator – who desires to enjoy in it not the cognate-organic, but the necessity and regularity in which, with his attachment to life, he can rest as in the abstraction for which he has yearned and which is alone accessible to him."[49] Abstraction purifies the world, and enables the spectator to "rest" in tranquility by showing the essential laws of the world.

"The Strange Necessity" follows the path of Worringer's argument in describing art's scientific function. "Art is not a luxury, but a necessity" to humanity, she argues, because of its particular ability to transform experience into knowledge that we can use: "there is no profitable way of dealing with one's experience except by analysis and synthesis into an excitatory complex; that is why man has to tolerate the maintenance of this monstrous organ known as art, which is apparently so completely useless to all his other organs."[50] Art thus cuts through all the accidents and contingencies we encounter in daily life, analyzing experience to reduce the unnecessary and turn the rest into usable knowledge, West's "excitatory complex."

For both Worringer and West, art has this capacity to let us see the useful knowledge behind contingent accidents only because it is disconnected from the natural world – because art is not merely trying to imitate nature but instead sees through it to its basic structures. Worringer argues that "the work of art, as an autonomous organism, stands beside nature on equal terms and, in its deepest and innermost essence, devoid of any connection with it."[51] Art is defined by its own internal form, Worringer insists, something that is discontinuous with and unrelated to the forms found in nature. West relies upon similar logic. For her, the novel can analyze and synthesize experience because it is an experiment performed on experience in controlled conditions, not experience itself. She opposes the novel that rises to the condition of work of art to "the formless novel of character which most living citizens of Great Britain and the United States can now write as easily as they can breathe."[52] The novel of character – exactly the sort of book Forster promotes as reducing the distance between the novel and life and that Q. D. Leavis criticizes for the same reason – is, West suggests, akin to a badly designed experiment that observes dogs in uncontrolled situations and, therefore, cannot provide any legitimate scientific information. Such a novel is more like direct experience than an analysis and synthesis of that direct experience; it is, indeed, like breathing. The novel must be separated from life – moved into a laboratory where an experiment can be conducted under specific conditions. The novel is something done to direct experience, and simply to record life as it happens is radically insufficient.

The novel – as work of art that produces scientific knowledge – must be formally autonomous and distinct from the contemporary organic life that surrounds it. But at the same time, West insists, the novel must be directed at life: it must shape life into knowledge. She takes aim at two versions of modernist formalism that get too far away from the contingencies and ephemera that constitute life. Her efforts in this regard are concentrated in a dense passage in "The Strange Necessity" that explains why the novel cannot simply record direct experience, why it needs to be designed as an experiment. The observed experiences must be shaped, just as an experiment shapes life into a form that can produce knowledge: "the prophetic sense of the author invents a story which when enacted by these particular characters traces a significant pattern. The novel must have a theme. Its story must be a myth, in which bodies which are embodiments enact an event which is a type of event."[53] West's weighty language reaches toward that of another, rather more influential essay on *Ulysses*, T. S. Eliot's "*Ulysses*, Order, and Myth" (1923), as well as toward Clive Bell's theory of "significant form" in *Art* (1914). West will proceed to redefine "myth" as form that must emerge from the analysis of modern life, rather than being imposed from without, and to complicate Bell's opposition between form and representation in order to define form as something that provides information about the world.

In the essay to which she alludes, Eliot argues that the significance of *Ulysses* is its use of a mythic method, "a way of controlling, of ordering, of giving a shape and a significance to the immense panorama of futility and anarchy which is contemporary history."[54] West thoroughly dismisses such a view of *Ulysses* in "The Strange Necessity," which claims that the Greek parallel is useless and penetrates only shallowly into the novel, whose structure is more Manichean than Greek.[55] For West, the mythicness of *Ulysses* has a different locus. A theme or myth, West writes, is "a typical pattern traced out by human reflexes; an interesting pattern because it is so immensely at variance with the way that humanity claims it behaves."[56] For her, "myth" is a matter of discovering typical reflexes in human behavior. Rather than imposing order on debased modern materials from without, through the juxtaposition of "contemporaneity and antiquity," in Eliot's words, West's writer-scientist instead discovers order within the modern world itself.[57] In the same essay, Eliot famously describes Joyce's method as a sort of "scientific discovery," and in defining the novel as a scientific experiment, West builds on Eliot's argument.[58] But for myth to be a form of scientific research, in West's terms, the writer cannot apply ancient models to describe modern life, but must analyze patterns in the world as it is.

For West, the mythic method of the novel must analyze even personal experience: rather than creating distance from contemporary life, mythic order must emerge out of its everyday building blocks.[59] Thus, in the frame of "The Strange Necessity," West tells the story of herself walking around Paris: this is West running experiments on herself and producing experiences, the shape and order of which will be discovered in the work of criticism. Indeed, the mythic order that West will find is the link between her letters from her friends, her dress, walking through Paris, and *Ulysses* – that is life shaped and analyzed into an order. In the essay's conclusion, she argues that all of these personal experiences "form a pattern in my mind, a harmony," and that she can "preserve them for ever either by apprehending some work of art with nearly the same theme ... or by doing what I can to create a work of art on that theme."[60] The pattern, theme, or myth that West analyzes involves the personal and is rooted in the contemporary, in direct and explicit opposition to Eliot. In a letter to Richard Ellman in 1958, West writes that "The Strange Necessity" "copied the form, killed stone dead since by T. S. Eliot, of criticism in a personal and almost fictional framework, such as Remy de Gourmont and several other French writers had used."[61] In describing her own critical essay as "almost fictional," West again reduces the distance between fiction and criticism. The two do not operate on different planes of existence, one provoking aesthetic experience and the other not. For West, the two are involved, ultimately, in the same project of analyzing and synthesizing experience – not just recording experience but ordering and shaping and investigating it. The personal form of "The Strange Necessity" is significant because it reveals that art and other thinking or writing about direct experience do the same thing – they analyze and synthesize experience into patterns, transforming Eliot's "mythical method" into something more prosaic, contemporary, and scientific.

West's term "significant pattern" makes an equally pointed adjustment to Bell's concept of "significant form." For Bell, significant form is what defines a work of art and distinguishes it from works that are not art – a distinction with which "The Strange Necessity" is deeply concerned. In Bell's terms, works with significant form generate emotion out of the form itself, the lines and colors of the work as opposed to what that work represents. Works which do not rise to the level of art are concerned instead with affecting their beholder through "the ideas or information suggested or conveyed by their forms."[62] In Bell's view, conveying information is the opposite of art. West directly reverses this formulation, defining as art works that analyze contemporary experience in order to research information about it. For West, the pattern or form is not opposed to information but itself conveys that information.

West is not promoting representational art; instead, she is redefining form in terms of the patterns and order that art discovers in the world. She criticizes Bell for his rejection of primitive art, for instance, as too representational – instead, she argues, a cave-painting of a bison cannot be understood as mere decoration, amusement, or even self-expression. Rather, cave paintings are "an early attempt at the analysis of experience, which, since it was unsuccessful, never led to the stage of synthesis."[63] If art is defined by its ability to glean information about the world, these paintings are halfway there. At the same time, representational painting can clearly fail to rise to the level of art – if, as in the case of derivative works or "Royal Academy stuff," its entire goal appears to be reproduction of the world for its own sake: "really the makers of it ought to have learned by this time that a copy of the universe is not what is required of art; one of the damned thing is ample."[64] To simply reproduce the world without analyzing and synthesizing experience and thus adding knowledge is to overindulge, as West describes in an unkind analogy: these overly-representational paintings "have a disgusting quality as of a person too grossly fat to move."[65] West thus theorizes a version of formalism that ensures the novel's separation from life as an experiment on it, while insisting that the novel must still convey information about life by finding order within it.

Art and Technics

West defines a modernism in which art transforms raw experience, life itself, into usable, scientific knowledge. Art puts life into the form of an experiment, in order to cut through contingency to find the significant knowledge within experience. In these terms, art becomes a technological apparatus named the super-cortex: a collective, transindividual version of the human's cerebral cortex, a prosthetic brain where knowledge is stored outside the individual. But the super-cortex is not merely one prosthesis, one technology among others. Rather, it is the site of what Lewis Mumford and Bernard Stiegler would call technics – where human knowledge is organized toward adaptation. The super-cortex is where humanity shapes what it means to be human, actively and self-consciously evolving the species through external, prosthetic means, rather than waiting for nature to take its own course.

In West's analysis, art is analogous to the human cortex, because both are organs that select, analyze, and synthesize the external world in the interest of allowing the human subject to adapt to its environment: "So alike are art and the cortex, in their like effort to select out of the whole complexity of the universe these units which are of significance to the organism, and to integrate those units into what excites to further living."[66] Both the cortex and art, West argues, are motivated by the clear goal of promoting survival – "further living." Yet the super-cortex is a prosthesis that is not part of our biology. It is an external structure that exists outside of the mind: "the cortex keeps its findings within the head and art stores them outside."[67] Most importantly, the super-cortex works beyond the individual, as a collective version of the cortex: "art, though the product of individual effort, is virtually the property as of many people as are aware of it."[68] Detached from the individual, the super-cortex is a technology that can be used by anyone.

As the site where knowledges are "integrate[d] ... into what excites to further living" and made useful, the super-cortex becomes a sort of tool shed, "an outhouse at the bottom of the garden" where man "keep[s] as much of himself as possible."[69] This is the first crucial link between the super-cortex and technics: the super-cortex is not just one technology, but the organ that organizes all knowledge toward a specific task. Lewis Mumford defines technics as "that part of human activity wherein, by an energetic organization of the process of work, man controls and directs the forces of nature for his own purposes."[70] The super-cortex's essential job is precisely this "organization": it is the site where knowledge becomes purposeful, where knowledge gains the structure of a tool. For West, the super-cortex promotes "further living" by coordinating all of the different pieces of knowledge in the world. This is the synthesizing function of art, its ability not just to locate pieces of knowledge but to link them into "significant patterns" – to give them form, in other words. West outlines this function by quoting Pavlov on the nervous system, which contains "a definite analysing mechanism, by means of which it selects out of the whole complexity of the environment those units which are of significance," but also "a synthesizing mechanism by means of which individual units can be integrated into an excitatory complex" that spurs the organism's adaptation.[71] For Pavlov, the cortex works as a sort of "switchboard" that coordinates an animal's various reflexes.[72] At the level of the super-cortex, this process of organization moves to the level of the species.

West's concept of the super-cortex was further developed by H. G. Wells in his lecture series on "The World Brain" in the 1930s.[73] Wells, with whom West had a son in 1914, argued that the super-cortex's synthesis of knowledge was a task of world-historical significance in the twentieth century, because it had become apparent that the various branches of science and scholarship and knowledge were deeply fragmented and specialized. Here, Wells's critique dovetails with Ford Madox Ford's account of the failure of the critical attitude in information-overloaded society. But Wells proposes to unify these disparate fragments not with the novel, but with a "World Encyclopaedia," written by experts in every field, published on microfilm so it would be affordable. This "new social organ," the world brain, would reduce conflict, promote unity, and "hold the world together mentally."[74] West does not render the super-cortex as literally as does Wells, but she nonetheless envisions a site of collective synthesis that resembles the World Encyclopaedia.[75] Both of them imagined this collective brain as a site of non-reductive kind of group thinking, in opposition to the kind of stultifying, anti-imaginative uniformity that George Orwell would call "Groupthink."[76]

Wells and West also shared a sense of what was at stake in coordinating knowledge: the future of humanity's ability to adapt to its changing environment. Wells argues that while humanity has more or less stopped evolving biologically, social change has replaced biological change as the site of adaptation: "His social life, his habits, have changed completely, have even undergone reversion and reversal, while his heredity seems to have changed very little if at all, since the late Stone Age."[77] The World Encyclopaedia becomes the key strategy for a new science of "human adaptology" that would focus on enabling humanity to self-consciously control and coordinate all the knowledges and tools man has developed.[78]

In Wells's historical narrative, the interwar years presented new and crucial challenges to human adaptation. The nineteenth century was the age of new knowledge, when man developed new "adaptive ideas" in production, machinery, and other fields.[79] But this new knowledge has not been effectively coordinated, so it cannot be accessed and used efficiently. The first world war, he argues, was ultimately the result of "insufficient mental equipment" and "shallowness of mind" produced by poor coordination of knowledge.[80] What frustrates Wells is that the people in charge of the war "had a very considerable amount of knowledge," but "no common understanding whatever of the processes in which they were obliged to mingle and interfere."[81] The war proved that humanity lacked a site where knowledge can be coordinated, and as a result "[m]ental and moral adaptation is lagging dreadfully behind the change in our conditions."[82] Man's insufficient control over his process of social adaptation, his neglect of coordinating these processes, explains the dictators of the 1930s, Wells proclaims: Hitler, Franco, and Mussolini stepped into the void that could otherwise be more justly, peacefully, and effectively filled by the World Encyclopaedia.[83]

West indicts the political system for rejecting the super-cortex in Wellsian terms in *Harriet Hume*, the novel she was writing as the reviews of "The Strange Necessity" appeared. The novel can be read as an allegory in which the super-cortex is feminized and linked to art, while being excluded from the masculinized political realm. Harriet represents the super-cortex: she has a highly developed ability to access and manage tools and knowledge that exist outside of her. She is a piano player who spends her time "in contemplation of the eternal beauties" but also reads the newspaper carefully.[84] She is so in tune with the super-cortex that she has preternatural access to the world's knowledge: she can read the thoughts of her lover, Arnold Condorex, through what he calls her "high occult kind of eavesdropping," and can play the piano with the force of her mind alone.[85] Arnold represents the rejection of the super-cortex. He makes his political career by capitalizing on a lack of knowledge about what is beyond himself and his nation: he willfully invents false knowledge about a province of British-controlled "Mangostan" called Mondh. Arnold is made Lord Mondh until he is found out, dismissed in disgrace, and attempts to murder Harriet. Before he is recuperated at the end of the novel, Arnold confesses that he has lived his life in accordance with a principle that

> forbids one ever to let the simple essences of things react on each other and so produce a real and inevitable event; it prefers that one should perpetually tamper with the materials of life, picking this way with the fingernail, flattening that with the thumb, and scraping that off with one's knife and stamping it on the ground at one's feet.[86]

Motivated entirely by narcissistic ambition, Arnold rejects reality, Debra Rae Cohen argues, and fails to allow it to shape his life.[87] He refuses the principle of adaptation, choosing instead only to imprint himself on the world rather than to gather information about it and adapt. Arnold's fate suggests that of a political system that undervalues knowledge, rejects art, and promotes a hypermasculine will-to-power in place of evolutionary adaptation.

Like Wells, and indeed like Ford, West found the coordination of knowledge to be the essential problem of interwar life. She thought that contemporary thinkers too often wanted to blame technology for the state of society, thus blinding themselves to what was really a much bigger problem. In her most thorough account of technology as such – a November 1928 review of *Whither Mankind: A Panorama of Modern Civilization*, a collection edited by American historian Charles Beard – she critiques Mumford and others for what we would now call technological determinism, or understanding the machine as the driver of history. The collection featured essays by intellectual luminaries including Bertrand Russell, John Dewey, Havelock Ellis, and Sidney and Beatrice Webb, and was framed as an attempt to "search for the essence of civilization."[88] Beard ultimately concludes there are two kinds of civilization, those based on technology and those based on agriculture.[89] The volume proceeds to pose questions such as the fate of art, the family, and religion in "machine civilization," as well as the ontological differences between west and east.[90] West's review was not favorable, and she objected in particular to the volume's central assumption that western civilization is determined by its relationship to the machine. She argued that "there is no reason to suppose that the life which is governed by the mechanical interests differs in any essential respect from the life which was governed by other interests. There is no evidence for stating that machines cause the people who make, operate or enjoy the benefit of them feel or think in a special way whatsoever, and it is therefore impossible that they can determine the psychic life of an entire civilization."[91]

The cause of the deadening of modern life, West argues, is not machines but an excess of uncoordinated knowledge: "There is too much to do. That, surely, is the stultifying factor in this modern civilization ... we know that we need to know as much of reality as possible to chart our way through life; and there is a convention, born in a day when the sum of knowledge was less, that we ought to be able to master nearly all that is known."[92] As evidence, she presents a shorter version of the narrative of "The Strange Necessity." She read Bertrand Russell's contribution to *Whither Mankind*, and then wanted to read another of his books to understand his position, and that book inspired her to read others on physics and psychology. But then she ran into a book about the painter Ingres in the library, and thinking about her own response to that book made her go read Lipps, Worringer, and Vernon Lee – here she retraces the associative logic of "The Strange Necessity." The anecdote here becomes a "mental misadventure," and West uses it to suggest that information overload, not the machine, drives modernity.[93] From this point of view, the personal narrative of West's reaction to Joyce in the first third of "The Strange Necessity" looks less like a positive model for an embodied feminist criticism and more like a plea for a stronger super-cortex to synthesize the overwhelming quantity of knowledge in the world.

The super-cortex needs to be understood as the site of technics because it is responsible for organizing knowledge. But there is a second connection as well: the synthesis or coordination it undertakes is directed toward "furthering life," as West puts it, by improving human adaptation. West's super-cortex thus matches Bernard Stiegler's definition of technics: "As a 'process of exteriorization,' technics is the pursuit of life by means other than life."[94] Stiegler differentiates technical evolution, what he calls "adoption," from genetic evolution or "adaptation."[95] In doing so, he creates an alternative narrative to that of Darwinian evolution, which ignores humanity's cultural adaptation to the environment, imagining

genetic evolution to proceed by random variation instead. Stiegler's technical evolution is a way to imagine what Gerald Moore calls man's "active
construction of a future."[96] Stiegler insists that humans evolve through
technological means, using tools to enable "the realization of a possibility
that is not determined by a biological program."[97]

West's super-cortex is the site of this self-conscious shaping of humanity. The tools in the shed of the super-cortex are man's shortcuts to adapting to his environment without waiting millennia for genetic evolution
to do it:

> He makes a hammer and uses it when he wants it instead of going
> through life welded with its weight like the lobster and its claw. He makes
> an automobile when he wants to move more quickly through space
> instead of laboring through generations to develop his leg-muscles as was
> the tedious and less efficient method of the racehorse and the greyhound.
> He makes an aeroplane when he wants to fly, instead of embarking on the
> growth of wings that would be bound to disturb his balance at moments
> when he had no need of them.[98]

Hammers, airplanes, and automobiles all reside in the super-cortex
alongside *Ulysses* and the canon of world artistic production. What these
diverse objects share is that they all offer strategies for adapting to the
environment, through external rather than internal, biological means.
The super-cortex is where we "externalize new parts of our stomachs
in the forms of cooking-stoves" rather than trying to evolve our stomachs
themselves.[99]

For both West and Stiegler, this external site of human evolution
constitutes a place of memory beyond the individual, of knowledge storage for the species. Technical evolution relies on what Stiegler calls an
"epiphylogenetic" form of memory, which is differentiated from either
genetics or individual human memory.[100] Epiphylogenesis names the way
knowledge is passed on beyond the individual – what Moore describes as
"a kind of social-technical memory" that is then instantiated in technical objects.[101] Epiphylogenetic memory operates in between the genetic,
which is not affected by the individual's experience, and epigenesis, or
the experience of the individual. Epiphylogenetic memory constitutes,
for Steigler, the "conservation, accumulation, and sedimentation of suc-
cessive epigeneses": it is how the individual's experience is preserved and
not simply lost when the individual dies, and is then able to shape future
generations.[102] West's super-cortex is another version of epiphylogenetic
memory, which must operate on a different timescale than that of the
human individual:

> The need to detach such supercortical activity from the individual so that it should not partake of his death would be felt acutely in view of the fact that in these higher functions man matures with a slowness that is maddening in view of the short span of his life.[103]

Thus, the super-cortex must work as a collective organ in order to translate the knowledge of individuals into the adaptation of the species.

Technical evolution is ultimately what makes humans human, Stiegler argues: "the appearance of the human is the appearance of the technical" and constitutes the moment where we depart from biological destiny and shape our own future.[104] Human interiority "is constituted in exteriorization," by his tools: "man (the interior) is essentially defined by the tool (the exterior)."[105] In Stiegler's historical narrative, this means that "the human did not begin with the brain, but with the feet," which allowed man to walk erect and thus use tools to shape his environment.[106] At the same time, though, the human is then constituted by these prostheses that he constructs, and the very category of the human becomes more fragile and less assured than if it were defined biologically. It becomes something that must be cared for and preserved. West shared Stiegler's sense that technics defines the human. Not to engage with the super-cortex, with art, is to no longer be fully human: "No wonder a human being that cuts itself off from art blunders round the world hitting against things as a decorticated dog blunders round in a laboratory."[107] Writing between the wars, she also shared Stiegler's sense of urgency, his sense that we need to take responsibility for our own humanity by nurturing the super-cortex.

But West also adds a crucial idea to Stiegler's thesis – that art is a part of technics, the essential organ that enables man to adapt. Mankind has never "been without an artistic mechanism with which he treats what stimulus is given him by the higher forms of experience, any more than he goes about without his heart or his lungs or his brain … And if against nature one separates man from this mechanism, he suffers as if his heart or his lungs or his brain had been cut out of him."[108] Reading West through Stiegler, these lines gain added potency: the availability of art ensures the survival of the species itself.

West here offers a powerful argument for art's importance, even in a world increasingly defined by science and technology, a world where it is easy to see the machine as the determining force in history. Unlike F. R. Leavis, in his notorious "two cultures" debate with C. P. Snow in the 1960s, West does not revert to arguing against science and technology to prop up the importance of art.[109] For West, art is part of technics, every bit as much as science is: art helps us to learn about the world and to adapt to it successfully. In defining art as technics, West offers an argument more radical than that offered even by I. A. Richards, who was also deeply concerned about literature's value in modernity. In *Science and Poetry* (1926), he, like West, tackled this issue by arguing that literature – poetry, specifically – contributes to knowledge. Poetry and science used to exist in the same sphere of knowledge, but in modernity, they separated into parallel planes. Poetry is tremendously important, but produces what he calls "pseudo-statements," which operate on the level not of truth but of emotion.[110] Richards makes art parallel to science, but West goes further by not allowing for any separation between the two fields. Art is essential to knowledge generation, and exists in the super-cortex, in technics, which is the wellspring from which science and technology emerge. West's super-cortex is, thus, an argument for the deep significance of art, and especially the novel, to the future of human existence.

Post-Script: Modernist Technics

West's theory of the technics of the novel is quintessentially modernist. Her conception of the novel's status in the toolshed of the super-cortex is carefully poised, in between late-Victorian arguments about empathy and postmodern visions of interactivity. Lee, exemplifying the former, thought that the reader feels an emotional response and then projects that onto the work. West reoriented Lee's concept of empathy away from readers and reading, using the term to explain how the novel can provide information about real human behavior despite being fictional. It is the novel's status as research tool, as information provider, that defines it as art and locates it in the field of technics, as an external container of knowledge that man uses to adapt to his environment. On the other end of the historical spectrum, West carefully differentiated her position from an emerging postmodernism she saw exemplified in Marshall McLuhan. She saw clear connections between McLuhan's theory of media and the technics of the novel she articulated in "The Strange Necessity": McLuhan's media are extensions of man, just as art is an external cortex. But in her view, McLuhan moves toward what we would now see as a recognizably postmodern position that valorizes participation and interaction at the expense of knowledge. The specific modernism of her theory emerges: the novel is part of technics because of its externality, but also because of its epistemological status as analyzer and synthesizer of experience. The novel can produce knowledge only if it ignores its reader, and the knowledge it produces has evolutionary significance only far beyond the level of any individual reader or author. Her theory is modernist in defining the novel's technical status not in terms of the degree of participation that it invites or requires, but the information it gathers and organizes.

West's encounter with McLuhan occurred in a lecture she gave in 1969 to the English Association at the University of Leicester, ten years after she had been named Dame Rebecca West. West's essay, "McLuhan and the Future of Literature," attacks McLuhan in terms that resonate with her treatment of T. S. Eliot forty years earlier. To her, they both represented a pernicious and specifically North American influence on literary studies. Both critics created a reputation by promoting the new, without engaging in the analysis and synthesis she saw as necessary to creating knowledge. Eliot she accuses of polluting English literary criticism at its low ebb during World War I, by encouraging the worship of newness. He "honestly believed ... that Mr. Galsworthy must write better than Chaucer because he was born to enjoy the benefits of electric lights and the automobile."[111] Eliot also irked her because he represented a new trend in criticism toward valorizing authority for authority's sake: "He has made his sense of the need for authority and tradition an excuse from refraining from any work likely to establish where authority truly lies, or to hand on tradition by continuing it in vital creation."[112] For Eliot, the desire to produce authoritativeness and a new capital "t" Tradition outweighs the desire to seek out new information, what she defines as the task of art in "The Strange Necessity." Thus, for her, "[i]t is a relief to turn to writers who care not a fig for claiming authority, but who humbly perform the kind of task of discovery and analysis that continues the tradition of English literature."[113] In 1969, she presents McLuhan in similar terms: he has "been allowed to establish himself as an authority" through the fetishization of the new.[114]

West's essay begins by pointing out that "The Strange Necessity" anticipated McLuhan's argument in *The Medium is the Message* that media are prostheses, external extensions of man. West paraphrases McLuhan's argument:

> we have developed various media of communication, all of which are extensions of our senses: books are extensions of our eyes, tools and paint-brushes and pens are extensions of our fingers, roads and railways and cars are extensions of our feet. This has occurred to other people; I said it myself once in a book about art called *The Strange Necessity*.[115]

Like McLuhan, West claims, she too has analyzed books as technical prostheses that extend man's body. But that thesis, she continues, is not particularly significant on its own: "The sole value of the conception is that it suggests that art and science and labour and exploration of the environment are biological functions and that the person who cannot exercise them will suffer from a deprivation akin to hunger or thirst."[116] Art prolongs the reach of the human body, and thus becomes a necessary organ.

But what McLuhan fundamentally misunderstands, in West's view, is *why* these prostheses become necessary to man. For her, art is an essential organ because it analyzes and synthesizes experience into knowledge that will, in time, allow man to evolve. McLuhan, by contrast, argues that the significance of new media is that they allow universal and absolute participation:

> Because we are living in the electric age, our central nervous systems are so far extended by technological activities, not just our own, everybody's, that we receive an impression of everything that is happening practically as it happens; and as a result of this simultaneity of perception, we are all involved in the whole of human proceedings, and necessarily participate, horizontally and vertically, in the results of every human action.[117]

Our perceptual abilities are so far enhanced by media that everyone can feel themselves to be everywhere – and thus can participate in everything. In West's account of McLuhan's historical narrative of the development of media, participation expands at the expense of depth. The bygone age of print "enabled a man to follow a subject along a logical line of thought as far as he wished, working on it in depth, but he therefore became a specialist and thus fragmented himself."[118] In the new age of electricity, specialization and depth are no longer necessary. Instead, there is a new proliferation of "cool" media that encourage shallow participation by everyone, instead of deep engagement by the few specialists. This cooling down then extends far beyond media themselves, to define culture. People are able to participate fully in everything that happens in society, and no one needs to specialize or to go into depth about anything in particular. For McLuhan, participation is the destiny of media.

To some extent, McLuhan's theory of participatory media resonates with West's theory of the super-cortex, which does, after all, account for how individuals participate in the knowledge that is produced by others. The super-cortex enables people to benefit from the information they themselves did not produce – thus it is exterior, supra-individual. The problem for West is that McLuhan goes too far by radically overemphasizing participation above the thing that people are participating in. The result is Ken Kesey, she argues – a prophet without a prophecy, all the participation without any of the knowledge. What she proposes, instead, is the coordination of specialized knowledge – not sacrificing depth for surface. The aspect of McLuhan's theory that irritates West the most is his idea that the medium is more important than the message: "It is his theory that society has always been shaped more by the nature of the media than by the content of the communications they have made. This is a drastic doctrine."[119] To McLuhan, content – the information gathered and communicated by media – is irrelevant. He thinks that only the shape of the medium – what degree of participation it engenders – matters.[120] His theory resembles Lee's theory of empathy, in this way: both are oriented entirely toward how the medium engages the user or reader or spectator and away from the content of the medium, its message. Thus, she argues, "emptiness ... is the core of McLuhanism."[121]

West emphasizes instead the content – what the novel can tell us about reality. To be a work of art, the novel must analyze and synthesize experience into knowledge. How it does that, what kind of an experiment the work runs, does not matter – but the work must gather knowledge about the world to be art. West goes so far as to argue that the work can only gather knowledge if the artist ignores the reader or beholder who will see the work at the end: knowledge and participation are directly opposed. Yes, art is ultimately how the human subject can participate in the evolution of the species, but that participation is indirect and intensively mediated. This is participation that happens through the super-cortex, which is an extension of the subject, certainly, but is also detached from her. This kind of participation happens beyond the level of the individual.

In her rejection of McLuhan's theory of cool media and the participatory society, West delineates the contours of a modernist technics of the novel. For the writers this book has considered, the novel, as a genre, was at a crossroads. It could, as Forster and many others wanted, become more and more part of life. It could merge into its readers' lives. It could be, before anything else, a direct experience for that audience. Those readers would be part of the work, its meaning, and its value. They would be full participants in the novel, which would itself be a fully cooled-down medium that would be incomplete without them. Alternatively, the novel could separate from its public, impose a mediating distance between itself and them. It could insulate itself from their needs and desires. It could resist the sequential pull of the act of reading, which inevitably melts it into the reader's experience. It could insist on its formal integrity, its wholeness, its autonomy from those readers. The novel could move out of the stream of life and into the contained space of the lab, where – now that it is no longer primarily understood as an experience – it might reveal new knowledge. To Lubbock, James, Ford, Lewis, and West, modernist writers and theorists faced a choice: the novel could not be both an autonomous object and a reader's experience. McLuhan might agree, but to him, the choice had already been made by the predominance of electronic media, which inherently promoted participation, and the future of the novel would therefore be experiential and interactive.

But to the modernists examined in this study, the "temperatures" of both novel and machine were still up for grabs. The choice between form and life was urgent, because it was a choice between two different visions of technology, and would shape humanity's technology-driven future. To choose life was to choose against the super-cortex, against depth of content and analysis, to prefer instead the shallowness of universal participation. To choose life was to choose the hurried temporality of the modern crowd, and the homogeneity of a world of constant communication. To choose form was to choose knowledge, the possibility of synthesizing and organizing the fragments of the world into a meaningful whole. To choose form was to promote Ford's critical attitude, and even, for West and Wells, to enable societies to protect themselves from rising dictators. Whether the novel was a formal, integrated object or an experience was a deeply significant choice that signaled how the novel would shape the social future of humanity. It was only by rejecting the idea that the novel is primarily an experience that it could become part of a new field of technology that promised to change society for the better. What emerges is a specifically modernist moment, where technology and technics offer something other than a model of interactivity to fiction.

Conclusion
Novel Theory and Technology in Late Modernism

This book has traced the strategies developed by a set of modernist writers to transform the novel into an autonomous, distant, intellectual object rather than a reader's experience. To structure the novel as such an object, these writers again and again turned to technologies as models, despite technology's inevitable complicity in the cultural formations that led readers to want novels to be part of their lives – in how readers read for the end; in the homogenization of communication; and in the hurried rhythm of Machine-Age life. But these writers reconceptualized what technologies, and technology itself, could mean in modernity. They thought that technologies also promised strategies to intellectualize novel-reading, forestalling readers' attempts to experience the work and forcing them instead to see the work as an aesthetic whole. The novel, structured along these lines, would not only support the work of criticism such as Percy Lubbock's, but would itself resemble a work of criticism. To go even further, the novel could become a mode of scientific research.

This discourse had its climax in the particular climate of 1920s Britain, the site of the great debate over whether the novel is defined by its form or by its relation to life. By the time high modernism proper began to transition into late modernism, it was far more difficult to argue that the novel should be an intellectual object, rather than an experience for a reader, that form should trump life. By 1932, Q. D. Leavis hopelessly argued that "[t]he reading capacity of the general public, it must be concluded, has never been so low as at the present time."[1] Leavis argued that this was a recent development – that people who were then avid readers of detective stories had been, a generation before, on guard against all such light, instrumentalized reading.[2] However hyperbolic her claims might be, Leavis's sense that modernist formalism in the novel was increasingly out of step with contemporary reading practices and ultimately on the decline was widely shared. In the 1930s even high modernists were much more likely to prioritize accessibility, reacting against the perceived elitism and difficulty of 1920s modernism.[3] Virginia Woolf's transition from *The Waves* to *The Years* might be taken as exemplary. The result was the prominence of a more "readable" strand of modernism that might be associated with Elizabeth Bowen, Christopher Isherwood, or Evelyn Waugh, as well as growing permeability between the "modernist" and the "middlebrow," exemplified by writers such as Storm Jameson and Ivy Compton-Burnett.

At the same time, the British novelists of the 1930s and 40s increasingly rejected aesthetic autonomy and believed the novel to be fully defined by its relationship to life, not form. Consider George Orwell, criticizing Joyce's detachment from the world in a 1940 essay: "a writer nowadays is so hopelessly isolated that the typical modern novel is a novel about a novelist. Even when Joyce, for instance, spends a decade or so in patient efforts to make contact with the 'common man,' his 'common man' finally turns out to be ... a bit of a highbrow."[4] In a 1953 essay, C. P. Snow would put modernism's isolation into starker terms: "the 'experimental' novel ... died from starvation, because its intake of human stuff was so low."[5] David Lodge, writing in 1969, would critique Snow's oversimplification, but nonetheless concurred that modernist experimentalism was no longer sufficient, because "[a]rt can no longer compete with life on equal terms."[6] Contemporary critics have described the turn away from form as a defining feature of late modernism, which, writes Tyrus Miller, "reopens the modernist enclosure of form onto the work's social and political environs, facilitating its more direct, polemical engagement with topical and popular discourses."[7] Jed Esty, similarly, shows that late modernism rejects "the redemptive agency of *art*" itself in favor of the idea that literature was a repository of culture, a category embedded in the nation and linked to ritual and tradition.[8]

For Tyrus Miller, George Orwell's 1940 review of Henry Miller's *Tropic of Cancer* presents a defining theory of the age when he describes the 30s as the era of "serious purpose" in literature.[9] Orwell cites Louis MacNiece – lamenting his correctness – that the 20s were an era when technique mattered, while in the 30s, it is subject matter that counts. Orwell argues that the great writers of the immediate post-World War I era, of the 20s, were too demoralized by the war to be interested in "the urgent problems of the moment."[10] They adopted a passive relationship to life and turned instead to form. The generation of the 30s, having always been comfortable, having not lived through the war as adults, saw itself in activist terms. The result, he argued, was a generation "barren of

imaginative prose."[11] For Orwell, the 30s saw the end of aesthetic autonomy: the new generation of writers, typified by the Auden-Spender "Boy
Scout" poets but extending beyond them, saw their literary writing as an
attempt to intervene in the lives of their readers.[12]

In the context of this cultural trajectory, the discourse this book has
analyzed did not disappear, but changed shape. The theoretical concerns that linked the writers this book has examined no longer seemed
to go together, though they can still be traced separately. This study
will conclude by considering several sites where these threads can still
be found, in the period of late modernism and early postmodernism.
F. R. Leavis would extend Ford's and Lewis's social critique of a mechanized, fragmented world that had disastrous consequences for modern
reading practices, but for him the solution to that problem could absolutely not be found in either formal experimentation or the machines
of modern culture. Joseph Frank recapitulated modernist novel theory's
arguments about how the novel might distance its readers by removing
itself from sequential, experiential time, and even dropped in an occa-
sional technological metaphor to describe these attempts, but stripped
away any sense of the social and cultural issues they sought to address.
Marshall McLuhan would pinpoint technology's role in modernist form.
As the last chapter showed, however, McLuhan would associate modernism with greater reader interactivity, not aesthetic autonomy; here I dig
further into his historical narrative, showing that for him, modernism
promised an "organic" future beyond the Machine Age. Ultimately, by
the height of McLuhan's career in the 1960s, the idea that modernism
incorporated technological strategies would be fully stripped of its relationship to ideas of autonomy and linked instead to postmodern ideas of
openness, participation, and interaction.

Readers and Machines in Leavis, Frank, and McLuhan

F. R. Leavis's aesthetic vision, which would become a dominant force
in British literary studies in the 1940s and 50s, was grounded in a deep
critique of machine culture. The Machine Age had painfully interrupted
the traditions of western life, in Leavis's view, leaving behind a society
with no shared tradition, no common taste, and no moral authority. In
"Mass Civilisation and Minority Culture" (1930), he argues that the
modern machine is directly responsible for the dissolution of cultural tradition: "In support of the belief that the modern phase of human history
is unprecedented it is enough to point to the machine. The machine, in

the first place, has brought about change in habit and the circumstances of life at a rate for which we have no parallel."[13] For him, this new stage began with the industrial revolution and continued with mass production and its attendant move toward standardization. And while some might blame these cultural changes on Americanization, Leavis is clear that the problem is the machine, not America: even "those who are most defiant of America do not propose to reverse the processes consequent upon the machine. We are to have greater efficiency, better salesmanship, and more mass-production and standardisation."[14] America merely led the way, since industrialization was the most entrenched and advanced there. He quotes a review of an Eisenstein film as evidence that the rest of the world should be wary of following America's path:

> One fancies, thinking about these things, that America might well send *The Silent Enemy* to Russia and say, "This is what living too long with too much machinery does to people. Think twice, before you commit yourselves irrevocably to the same course."[15]

But no warning would work against the force of the Machine Age; he continues, "it is vain to resist the triumph of the machine."[16]

The standardization that Leavis diagnoses as the major consequence of the rise of the machine has spread across society, he argues. The Book of the Month Club in the United States and the Book Society and BBC book programs in Britain represent the replacement of a shared sense of taste and tradition by standardization: readers no longer possess a culturally-instilled sense of aesthetic or cultural quality, and instead rely on these organizations to tell them what to read.[17] In Leavis's apocalyptic vision, behaviorism and applied psychology, increasingly used in advertising, represent the regulation of the mind, while with eugenics, even the body can be standardized.[18] It is, again, technology that makes the spread of standardization possible. Quoting Richard Paget, he laments that "[b]roadcasting, long-distance telephony, the talking film, and the gramophone ... will make such standardisation possible, and even comparatively easy to establish."[19]

In many ways, Leavis's social critique resembles that of the writers this study has examined. Like Lewis, Leavis associated the mechanism of mass production with a wide-scale alteration in the very tempo of modern life, a rhythm of constant change that leads people to constantly want and expect the new: modernity is characterized by "cultural disintegration, mechanical organization and constant rapid change."[20] Like Ford, Leavis saw in modern England the lack of any strong, stable moral authority amid the chaos of a too communicative culture. "A reader who grew up with Wordsworth moved among a limited set of signals," Leavis writes; "the variety was not overwhelming ... But the modern is exposed to a concourse of signals so bewildering in their variety and number that, unless he is especially gifted or especially favoured, he can hardly begin to discriminate. Here we have the plight of culture in general."[21] Like James, he mourned the state of the reading public. Modern readers, trained by mass culture, would "surrender, under conditions of hypnotic receptivity, to the cheapest emotional appeals."[22]

But for Leavis, modernist formal experimentation only exacerbated these problems. In a critique of Joyce's *Work in Progress*, originally published in the September 1933 issue of *Scrutiny*, Leavis argues that formal experiments went hand in hand with the spread of machine culture across society. Joyce's technique overemphasizes the medium and proceeds through "mechanical manipulation" because his project was not sufficiently animated by a theme that develops out of an "inner center."[23] Language, the medium, can and should evolve, Leavis insists – indeed, Shakespeare developed it. But for him, the difference is that through Shakespeare, it was the wellspring of English tradition – which he locates in an old, agricultural, rural tradition – that evolved the language: "The strength of English belongs to the very spirit of the language – the spirit that was formed when the English people who formed it was predominantly rural."[24] By contrast, with *Work in Progress*, "even in the best parts, we can never be unaware that the organisation is external and mechanical."[25]

Joyce's vacant language-play for its own sake is the logical outgrowth of a society where those values have been lost. That Joyce is the natural endpoint of the Machine Age is most clearly established, for Leavis, by the fact that G. K. Ogden, the creator of Basic English, had "shown an active interest in the *Work in Progress*": Basic English represented the ultimate standardization of all culture, the moment when language would be evaluated solely by its efficiency, by how well it fit into the norms of industrial culture rather than by how much it expressed deeper values, "inner life."[26] According to Leavis's logic, the fact that Joyce was experimenting with how to change the language without any deeper, "inner" purpose showed him to be paving the way for the manipulations of Basic English, which might, in many respects, seem to be the polar opposite of any of Joyce's complex works. Ultimately, for Leavis, modernism's formal experiments are the logical product of machine culture. They empty out literary content – any significant theme, any substantive concern for "life." The writer is left to tinker with the medium, without any deep purpose, clearing the way for the standardization of language itself.

Formal experimentation was particularly problematic for Leavis because it often, as this study confirms, used techniques and strategies associated with the modern machine. In a 1932 essay on *Manhattan Transfer, The Forty-Second Parallel*, and *1919*, Leavis praised John Dos Passos's ambition and his portrayal of the standardization of American society, its "agonised vacuity."[27] But the problem for Leavis is that the only compensatory hope on offer in the novels is form, which is itself deeply influenced by the machine: "It is more than a superficial analogy when the technique is likened to that of the film. The author might be said to conceive his function as selective photography and 'montage.'"[28] As it draws its aesthetic from the source of what it critiques, *Manhattan Transfer* cannot offer meaningful hope for culture. A literature driven by "machine technique" rejects the only possible source of renewal, which is in the old, pre-machine era: "The memory of the old order, the old ways of life, must be the chief hint for, the directing incitement towards, a new, if ever there is to be a new … Whether, in a world of continually developing machine technique, a new order will ever be able to grow may seem doubtful. But without the faith that one might be achieved there can hardly be hope in revolution."[29]

Dos Passos's "camera-eye" was the highbrow equivalent, for Leavis, of the "increasingly scientific direction" of popular literature that he criticizes in "Mass Civilisation and Minority Culture."[30] Publishing houses and best-selling writers themselves were utilizing "what is called market research to find out the buying motives, as exactly as time and money and opportunity permit, from the public itself."[31] Leavis cites, at length and with great horror, a letter from Edgar Rice Burroughs in which he recounts his creation of "a type of fiction that may be read with the minimum of mental effort" because "[i]t has been discovered through repeated experiments that pictures that require thought for appreciation have invariably been box-office failures."[32] Burroughs's account of fiction to be read without thinking would be bad enough for Leavis, certainly, but even worse is the fact that so much thought and research – so much scientific inquiry – went into producing such works. That is what aligns mass culture so closely with machine culture: it uses science, from applied psychology to market research, to make cultural production more efficient and more profitable.

Leavis insisted that machine culture needed to be rejected as fully as possible: cultural renewal could not be found in the machine. To maintain faith in science and technology was to follow the example of critic Max Eastman, who "lives still in the age of H. G. Wells."[33] For Leavis, Wells exemplified, in an exaggerated form, the position of the debased side of modernism, which aligned itself with machine culture. The turn to technical experimentation and "machine technique" is a capitulation to the values of machine culture. It will mean, eventually, that "the efficiency of the machinery becomes the ultimate value."[34] In a 1932 review of Wells's volume *The Work, Wealth and Happiness of Mankind*, Leavis argued that "he belongs to the past": his faith in technology is old-fashioned and belonged to the era before machine culture had shown its voracious capacity to reset all of society's values.[35] Now that the Machine Age had revealed itself, Leavis asked with trepidation, "can a hundred D. H. Lawrences preserve even the idea of emotional sincerity."[36]

By the early 1960s, Leavis had found a new Wells in the form of C. P. Snow, who argued that scientists needed to read literature, but also that novelists and poets needed science. He calls Snow "the spiritual son of H. G. Wells" – the literary figure and public intellectual who put too much faith in science and technology – and criticizes "his crass Wellsianism."[37] In his notorious 1963 "two cultures" lecture, Leavis aggressively opposed Snow's position that literature and science possessed their own cultures, that the second law of thermodynamics was the scientific equivalent of Shakespeare.[38] He argued instead that the dominance of science and technology was, in no small part, responsible for the lack of a unified cultural tradition – something that was once transmitted by literature.

For Leavis, the best literature, what constitutes the "great tradition" of the novel in England, responds to the pressure of the Machine Age by ultimately rejecting machine form on behalf of "life." In *The Great Tradition* (1948), Leavis defines this concept in terms that resonate with Orwell: even form was endowed with "moral significance" by the writers he most admires, such as Jane Austen.[39] James belonged to the same tradition because he focused on the "human significance" of the novel, at least before he went to the dark side in his late work.[40] D. H. Lawrence was the last of this tradition, and he resisted the "dead end" and "cobwebbiness" of modernist formalism because "his innovations and experiments are dictated by the most serious and urgent kind of interest in life."[41]

With machine culture infiltrating the workings of both high and low literary culture, for Leavis, D. H. Lawrence represented an alternative vision of what literary modernism could have been. Lawrence stood apart because unlike Joyce or Dos Passos, who embedded the very form of the novel within machine culture, Lawrence completely rejected the regime of mechanization and envisioned a return to an older, agrarian, rural set of traditions and values. In Leavis's 1955 book on Lawrence, *Women in Love* dramatizes this central conflict of modernity through Gerald Crich: in his character, "we see the malady of the individual psyche as the essential process of industrial civilization."[42] Leavis almost reiterates his critique of modernism in his account of Gerald, who, like Joyce, had "the sense of an inner lack."[43] This lack of inward purpose drove Joyce to attempt to evolve, and ultimately to rationalize, the English language in *Work in Progress* and drove Gerald to find meaning and purpose in the "great social productive machine" as he attempts to overcome his father's idealism and to rationalize the running of the mines.[44] Leavis quotes a passage from *The Rainbow* that articulates his view of Lawrence's philosophy and provides the language for the title of his collection, *For Continuity*: "One England blots out another. The mines had made the halls wealthy. Now they were blotting them out, as they had already blotted out the cottages. The industrial England blots out the agricultural England. One meaning blots out another. The new England blots out the old England. And the continuity is not organic, but mechanical."[45] Lawrence's major works thus narrate the deepest historical problem faced by the west: the rise of machine culture.

For Leavis, a key element of Lawrence's rejection of the machine is a disavowal of formal experimentation for its own sake. In his analysis of Lawrence, his descriptions of form are vague, and he implies that what is good about Lawrence's works is that one does not notice form because it is only a means to an end. It is the argument – the portrayal of the state of modern England – that is the point, and thus to analyze form in technical terms is something of a dead end, as he suggests in the conclusion to his analysis of the "Water-part" chapter of *Women in Love*: "these effects work subtly in with the whole complex organization of poetic and dramatic means that forms this wonderful chapter, means that, in sum, are no more to be brought helpfully under the limiting suggestion of 'symbolism' than the Shakespearian means in an act of *Macbeth*."[46] Comparing Lawrence to his best example of a writer fully motivated by English tradition, Leavis suggests that naming Lawrence's techniques is a useless exercise. These examples also point toward a hallmark of Leavis's critical method: as René Wellek puts it, Leavis "is also quite uninterested in questions of technique of the novel."[47] In Wellek's key example, Leavis "refers to the 'complex rhythm organizing' *The Rainbow* without even attempting to describe it."[48] Leavis returns to the form-versus-life debates of the 1920s and declares them irrelevant: form is useless decoration if not in the service of life.

While Leavis concurred with the critique of Machine-Age culture that motivated the critics this study has examined, he fully rejected their aesthetic response: the idea that the novel ought to be an intellectual object and a formal whole that is autonomous from its readers and their demands. That side of the discourse I have examined would persist, too, into the late modernism of the 1940s, in Joseph Frank's influential theory of spatial form. Frank is interesting in this context not just as an American New Critic who was more interested in form than were Leavis and his followers on the other side of the Atlantic. Frank also inadvertently picks up on the discourse of the 1920s form-versus-life debates by considering the exact problem of novelistic time that so disturbed Percy Lubbock and Wyndham Lewis: how to extirpate the novel from the experiential time lived by the reader, to distance the reader from the novel, to make the novel hold still so one might analyze it.

Over the course of three essays appearing in *The Sewanee Review* in 1945, Frank recapitulated Lubbock's and Lewis's ideas in the framework of a theory of spatial form. Frank argued that the concept of spatial form was necessary to theorize modern novels that attempted to disrupt the flow of time. This turn away from time was easier to understand in modern poetry – his examples here include Pound's theory of imagism and Eliot's idea that the poet sees a whole. To become spatial was to move away from sequence, Frank claimed, and a novelist writing in spatial form attempts to "break up ... the time-flow of narrative."[49] Djuna Barnes's *Nightwood*, his primary example of spatial form in the novel, strives to "express the essence of character in an image" and to reject the temporal flow of narrative in favor of a "static situation."[50]

In the first essay that articulated his theory, Frank broached the problem of how one might read, over a span of progressive time, a spatialized novel that attempts not to exist in such a timeframe. His example is Joyce's *Ulysses*:

> Joyce cannot be read – he can only be re-read. A knowledge of the whole is essential to an understanding of any part; but unless one is a Dubliner, such knowledge can be obtained only after the book has been read, when all the references are fitted into their proper place and grasped as a unity. Although the burdens placed on the reader by this method of composition may seem insuperable, the fact remains that Joyce, in his unbelievably laborious fragmentation of narrative structure, proceeded on the assumption that a unified spatial apprehension of his work would ultimately be possible.[51]

Frank ultimately proposes a criticism based on re-reading, one that omits the temporal flow of reading all together, thus solving the problem Lubbock had identified twenty years earlier.

While Frank describes Joyce's confrontation of the same problem faced by Lewis and Lubbock, his sense of why Joyce or Barnes would place such "insuperable" burdens on their readers is purely aesthetic. They are attempting to realize Hulme's, and Pound's, and Eliot's vision of poetry in the novel – but they are not attempting to change the nature of the novel-reading process because readers increasingly treat novels like dessert, or because they have lost the ability to connect fragments into meaningful wholes, or because of what mechanization has done to temporality. Frank looks at the formal issues that Leavis ignores, but he is uninterested in the cultural critique that drives Leavis's criticism and motivates the formal experiments of the modernists this study has considered. Why is this mode of "unified spatial apprehension" almost impossible at Joyce's historical moment, and why does Joyce "proceed on the assumption" that such a mode of reading "would ultimately be possible"? Such questions are not part of Frank's inquiry.

Frank does use technological metaphors to describe spatial form in the modernist novel, but those references remain incidental and are never developed. Twice, over the course of the spatial form essays, Frank refers to this production of simultaneity in narrative as a "cinematographic" device. He makes this reference in the first of the original essays, discussing the country fair scene in *Madame Bovary*, where "the time-flow of the narrative is halted: attention is fixed on the interplay of relationships within the limited time-area."[52] This method, he remarks, "we might as well call cinematographic, since this analogy comes immediately to mind."[53] He would return to the idea in a response to critics in 1977, when he would quote a line from Alain Robbe-Grillet about "the lack of time-depth in his novels" as a strategy drawn from cinema.[54] Frank does not pursue the connection to cinema as an opening toward any line of critical thought. He seems to bring in cinema parenthetically, merely as a way to describe spatial form more clearly, as a convenient comparison. Because Frank disconnects spatial form from contemporary social contexts that would be significant to any of the writers I have considered, he has nowhere to go with this connection to cinema.

At the same time, despite the clear connections between his line of thought and British novel theory of the 1920s, Frank mentions neither Lewis, nor Lubbock, nor Leavis. Instead, he chooses to situate his theory in a critical lineage that bypasses British novel theory all together, focusing on Eliot, Pound, Worringer, and Hulme and their arguments about classicism and romanticism. Frank Kermode noted this gap in Joseph Frank's essays, pointing out that the theory of spatial form might not strike an English critic quite as it does an American. To an English critic, Kermode argues, Frank's theory recycles an already old way of thinking that had been fully fleshed out in Wyndham Lewis's *Time and Western Man*, fifteen years before Frank's first essay on the topic.[55] In his response, Frank averred, claiming not to have read Lewis's book.[56] We see evidence here, perhaps, for René Wellek's claim that while a number of American critics spent much time in England and vice versa – Eliot and Richards, for example – English and American criticism developed along quite independent lines in the first half of the twentieth century. Wellek found American and British criticism in the modernist era to be so disparate that he chose to separate his critical history into different volumes: a "separate order of exposition is inevitable even though the contact between the two traditions was intense."[57]

The examples of Leavis and Frank suggest how pieces of the discourse traced by this book – the critique of what the machine had done to culture and the interest in the novel's aesthetic autonomy – survived and persisted into late modernism, even though its elements were now separated from each other. These ideas would resurface most fully in the work of Marshall McLuhan, a fact that will not be surprising given the similarities that even Rebecca West observed between his arguments and her own. McLuhan pursued Frank's interest in the formal strategies by which the modernist novel attempted to change the way it might be read, and, of course, he was deeply interested in what Frank neglected – how the modernist novel considered technology in relation to its own formal strategies.

At the same time, though, McLuhan was deeply, if unexpectedly, influenced by the critique of machine culture pursued by Leavis, with whom he had studied at Cambridge. He certainly did not reject technology the way Leavis did, but nonetheless McLuhan's theory of the coming electric age that would supersede the era of the machine draws on qualities Leavis associated with Lawrence, Shakespeare, and the "organic," agrarian tradition that preceded the industrial revolution. Chief among the characteristics of this new era were universal participation and openness; the novel following this tradition would become increasingly interactive. It was what Leavis denigrated as modernism's "machine technique" that would help to make the novel participate in this new, interactive electric age. Thus, despite recuperating the modernist novel's interest in changing its relationship to its reader and incorporating technologies as formal devices, McLuhan would ultimately imagine that modernism's engagement with technology moved it away from aesthetic autonomy and toward an interactive, electric, post-machine future.

McLuhan diagnosed the modernist novel's machine-inspired formal strategies in some of his earliest work. An essay published in *The Sewanee Review* in 1954 analyzed the work of Dickens, Mallarmé, and Joyce as attempts to remodel literature according to the perspective, impersonality, and temporality of the newspaper, which, as part of a larger media ecology including cinema and other technologies, provided formal resources to novelists:

> Once picturesque art, following the spectroscope, had broken up the continuum of linear art and narrative the possibility of cinematic montage emerged at once. And montage has to be arranged forwards or backwards. Forwards it yields narrative. Backwards it is reconstruction of events. Arrested it consists of the static landscape of the press, the co-existence of all aspects of community life. This is the image of the city presented in *Ulysses*.[58]

This passage is notable for how much it follows the line of analysis laid out by Frank ten years earlier in the same journal. But McLuhan shifts the emphasis: he doesn't care about spatial form itself, as a solution to the kinds of aesthetic problems Frank saw Eliot, Pound, and Hulme describing. Rather, McLuhan prioritizes how spatial form emerges out of an ecology of media and technology – how the novel incorporates strategies drawn from media ranging from the spectroscope, to cinema, to the press. In his reading, writers such as Joyce and Mallarmé are constantly "probing the aesthetic consequences and possibilities of the popular arts of industrial man."[59] In the same essay, he argues that by the time of *Finnegans Wake*, Joyce has turned to a different set of communication technologies: "the techniques of the *Wake* are 'telekinetic' and explicitly specified as those of radio, television, newsreel."[60]

These ideas would become a staple of his theory, and they explicitly inspired his own critical practice – the working title to the book that became *The Gutenberg Galaxy* was *The Road to* Finnegans Wake.[61] McLuhan's modus operandi was to seek out sites where he could see the kinds of connections between cultural forms and technologies that this book has analyzed. The category of "media" was so significant for him precisely because it allowed him to see beyond disciplinary boundaries, to connect popular culture, the high modernist novel, politics, science, and society. He saw his project as connected to that of Snow – he told

Snow that he saw *The Gutenberg Galaxy* as a sequel to his two cultures lecture.[62] In his desire to connect literature and technology, McLuhan was the heir to modernist novel theory's interest in technological models for narrative structure.

But McLuhan would ultimately see the historical place and cultural function of what Leavis called "machine technique" in very different terms from those of the writers I have analyzed. For James, Ford, Lewis, and West, formal techniques drawn from the world of technology would help to keep the novel autonomous from the lives of its readers, who wanted to consume it, to experience it, to be its friend, to project themselves on top of it through empathy. For those writers, the novel would use the resources of technologies to compensate for the state of modern reading, which they often imagined as the outgrowth of the culture of the machine – the same kinds of fragmentation and standardization critiqued by Leavis. In McLuhan's narrative, the modernist novel's technological forms would also help it to break out of its Machine Age – not by protecting the novel from its readers, but rather by more fully opening itself to them.

McLuhan thought that western civilization was in the process of emerging into a new, electric age, out of an era dominated by machinery. In the clearest statement of how these two eras differ, in *The Medium is the Massage* (1967), McLuhan writes that "[t]he alphabet and print technology fostered and encouraged a fragmenting process, a process of specialism and of detachment. Electronic technology fosters and encourages unification and involvement."[63] The printed book was one of the key technologies of the machine era – "the first mechanization of a complex handicraft, and ... the archetype of all subsequent mechanization."[64] It is the printed, alphabetic book, he claims in *Understanding Media* (1964), and not the clock, as Lewis Mumford had earlier suggested, that initiated the Machine Age through standardization and the "uniform fragmentation of processes."[65] Typography enabled "the uniformity and repeatability of the printed page," fully separating the printed word from speech and fragmenting the senses.[66] The logic of homogenous repeatability, he argues, contributed directly to the emergence of mass production. The printed book helped to produce a "hot" Machine-Age culture characterized by "detachment and noninvolvement – the power to act without reacting."[67] The Machine Age culminates in the disinterest expressed in the statement, "[h]e couldn't care less."[68] Curiously, McLuhan associates the late Machine Age with precisely the opposite kind of behavior from that diagnosed by the modernist novelists this study has examined:

books inherently encourage detachment, from his point of view, while for Lewis or James, they problematically seem to merge into their readers. The writers covered in this book would go to great lengths to imagine how to write a novel that would be "hot" enough to repel the involvement of its readers.

The sudden dawn of the electric age would cool the west down, according to the historical narrative of *Understanding Media*. The electric age would be characterized by the instantaneous presentation of information, rather than the sequential pages of a book. The electric era would prioritize automation over mechanization and the assembly line, telephone over telegraph, television over print, highways and airplanes over the railroad. Cool media are characterized by the fact that they convey low-density information, which then requires interaction. Electric media favor simultaneity and instantaneous presentation, and thus work against the fragmentation and specialization of the Machine Age. While "hot media do not leave so much to be filled in or completed by the audience," cool media require participation.[69] The result would be a new kind of large-scale global tribalism in which everyone is involved with everyone else: "[a]s electrically contracted, the globe is no more than a village."[70]

For McLuhan, modernism documents the explosion of the cool, electric age into a hot, mechanized culture, while promoting and participating in the emergence of electric media. The static, spatial form he saw in *Ulysses* would become evidence of this – of the novel attempting to produce an electric effect in a book, that product of the Machine Age. In *Understanding Media*, he would link the cinematic effect he diagnosed in *Ulysses* to cubism, which emerged "at this moment of the movie," "the moment that translated us beyond mechanism into the world of growth and organic interrelation. The movie, by sheer speeding up of the mechanical, carried us from the world of sequence and connections into the world of creative configuration and structure."[71] By "seizing on instant total awareness," cubism similarly removed art from the sequential thinking associated with perspective, in its place "set[ting] up an interplay of planes and contradictions or dramatic conflict of patterns, lights, textures that 'drives home the message' by involvement."[72] In the concluding paragraph of *The Gutenberg Galaxy* (1962), he quotes Joyce's *Finnegans Wake* as evidence that modernism wanted to turn the detached reading of the mechanical age into something else: "'My consumers are they not my producers?' Consistently, the twentieth century has worked to free itself from the conditions of passivity, which is to say, from the

Gutenberg heritage itself."[73] In *Understanding Media,* McLuhan reads *A Passage to India* as "a parable of Western man in the electric age," while *Finnegans Wake* records "the reversal by which Western man enters his tribal, or Finn, cycle once more, following the track of the old Finn, but wide awake this time as we re-enter the tribal night," in which "everybody in the world has to live in the utmost proximity created by our electric involvement in one another's lives."[74] For him, modernism recorded and encouraged western society's move toward the global village of absolute participation.

The electric age that McLuhan associated with modernism closely resembles the status quo critiqued by the writers this study has examined, in which they wanted to intervene. Electric media head toward a future in which "[s]pectator becomes artist ... because he must supply all the connections" – a future of amateur artists that resembles the nightmare vision of Lewis's *The Apes of God,* in which the division between artist and spectator has fully dissolved.[75] In both *Understanding Media* and *The Gutenberg Galaxy,* McLuhan offers the detective story as his best example to explain how electric media require reader interaction. McLuhan's analysis repeats Ford's critique about middlebrow novels that turn themselves over to the reader. McLuhan describes why the detective story is a cool form, for him: "in reading a detective story the reader participates as co-author simply because so much has been left out of the narrative."[76] The detective story's inclusion of the reader exemplifies the larger idea that "the consumer's experience" was more important than the art object itself:

> In a word it became necessary to examine the *effect* of art and literature before producing anything at all ... It was Edgar Allan Poe who first worked out the rationale of this ultimate awareness of the poetic process and who saw that instead of directing the work to the reader, it was necessary to incorporate the reader in the work.[77]

The detective story is "the great popular instance of working backwards from effect to cause" because it is engineered entirely to produce an experience in a reader.[78] For McLuhan, modernism would fully incorporate this principle – it is his interpretation of Eliot's "objective correlative" and is the driving aesthetic of symbolist poetry, "whose completion of effect from moment to moment requires the reader to participate in the poetic process itself."[79]

Analyzing modernism's engagement with media technologies, McLuhan generates a postmodernist version of modernism. His view is fully congruent with Wolfgang Iser's analysis of the modernist novel as the one that most fully includes the reader by not giving her all the answers and requiring her to participate. His modernism is the beginning of Michael Fried's theatrical postmodernism, defined by its inclusion of the reader in the art object. In order to generate such a reading, McLuhan has to de-emphasize modernism's debates about form versus life, its critiques of novel-reading, and its attempts to extirpate the novel from the experience of its reader.

The writers this study has examined saw something like McLuhan's vision of participatory modernism as a real possibility. Lubbock worried that it was difficult for any reader to avoid "living" the novel. Lewis thought Joyce, Woolf, and the "time cult" were actively producing an art that involved its reader fully. Ford thought even Conrad was turning the novel over to the reader. West, again, saw Joyce in these terms. But for these writers, the participatory novel was the product of the Machine Age, which left subjects overwhelmed with disconnected information, made them incapable of seeing beyond their own experiences and appetites, and engaged them in an impatient, mechanical temporality.

For a short period, culminating in the 1920s, there was another possibility as well: modernist theorists attempted to imagine how the novel could avoid being an experience, how it could be its own, independent, intellectual object. The novel that was autonomous from its reader might communicate new information, might be accessible to a deeply critical reading, might contribute to scientific knowledge – it could be more than a passing experience. To get there, these writers thought it was necessary to rethink what technology was. They agreed with Leavis in much of his critique of machine culture – but for this set of writers, a return to an organic, prelapsarian world was not the answer. Rather, these writers reimagined technologies as strategies for making the novel autonomous. They worked from the inside of machine culture to imagine how the novel, and the machine, might become something different.

Notes

Introduction

1 Marshall McLuhan, *Understanding Media: The Extensions of Man* (New York, NY: Signet, 1964), 20.

2 Robert Coover, "The End of Books," *New York Times Book Review*, June 21, 1992, n.p. www.nytimes.com/books/98/09/27/specials/coover-end.html.

3 Ibid.

4 Ibid.

5 G. P. Landow argued that "Barthes's distinction between readerly and writerly texts appears to be essentially a distinction between text based on print technology and electronic hypertext" (*Hypertext 2.0: The Convergence of Contemporary Critical Theory and Technology* [Baltimore, MD: Johns Hopkins University Press, 1997], 5). For an overview of critiques of the "first generation" theories of the interactivity of electronic literature, see Adalaide Morris, "New Media Poetics: As We May Think/How to Write," in *New Media Poetics: Contexts, Technotexts, and Theories*, ed. Morris and Thomas Swiss (Cambridge, MA: MIT Press, 2006), 12–13.

6 See Espen J. Aarseth, *Cybertext: Perspectives on Ergodic Literature* (Baltimore, MD: Johns Hopkins University Press, 1997).

7 Nick Montfort, Foreword, in *Interactive Digital Narrative: History, Theory and Practice*, ed. Hartmut Koenitz, Gabriele Ferri, Mads Haar, Diğdem Sezen, and Tonguç Ibrahim Sezen (New York, NY: Routledge, 2015), x. Montfort's taxonomy is all the more interesting because he is an active producer of noninteractive narrative.

8 Lev Manovich, *The Language of New Media* (Cambridge, MA: MIT Press, 2001), 225. Manovich's theory has been widely debated and reworked. N. Katherine Hayles, for instance, argues that database and narrative should be considered not enemies but "symbionts" that exist in a beneficial and necessary relationship with one another. See Hayles, "Narrative and Database: Natural Symbionts," *PMLA*, vol. 122, no. 5 (October 2007), 1603–8. This issue of *PMLA*, which features six contributors discussing the relationship between narrative and database, encapsulates these debates.

9 Andrew Michael Roberts argues that YHCHI make "us aware of our embodied perceptual processes, through the difficulty of processing and disruption of normal reading" ("Why Digital Literature Has Always Been

'Beyond the Screen,'" in *Beyond the Screen: Transformations of Literary Structures, Interfaces and Genres*, ed. Jörgen Shäfer and Peter Gendolla [Bielefeld: Transcript Verlag, 2010], 169). In *Digital Modernism: Making It New in New Media* (New York, NY: Oxford University Press, 2014), Jessica Pressman similarly argues that YHCHI's works invite a particularly materialist kind of close reading.

10 Rebecca Walkowitz responds to these difficulties by using screenshots, though some of YHCHI's texts scroll at such a quick pace that even taking a screenshot of a specific frame can be difficult. See "Close Reading in an Age of Global Writing," *MLQ*, vol. 74, no. 2 (June 2013), 179. "Operation Nukorea" (www.yhchang.com/OPERATION_NUKOREA.html) is an example of a YHCHI text with a languorous pace, while "Dakota" (www .yhchang.com/DAKOTA.html) and "Royal Crown Super Salon" (www .yhchang.com/ROYAL_CROWN_SUPER_SALON.html) are particularly fast.

11 Warren Liu, "Posthuman Difference: *Traveling to Utopia* with Young-Hae Chang Heavy Industries," *Journal of Transnational American Studies*, vol. 4, no. 1 (2012), 9.

12 Thom Swiss, "Distance, Homelessness, Anonymity, and Insignificance: An Interview with Young-Hae Chang Heavy Industries," n.d. thestudio .uiowa.edu/tirw/TIRW_Archive/tirweb/feature/younghae/interview.html.

13 Petra Heck, interview with YHCHI, *Networked Performance*, 2008 archive .turbulence.org/blog/2008/10/23/interview-with-young-hae-chang-heavy-industries/?author=4.

14 Hyun-Joo Yoo, "Intercultural Medium Literature Digital: Interview with Young-Hae Chang Heavy Industries," 2005 www.dichtung-digital .de/2005/2/Yoo/index-engl.htm.

15 Michael Fried, "Art and Objecthood," in *Art and Objecthood: Essays and Reviews* (Chicago, IL: University of Chicago Press, 1998), 160.

16 Ibid., 155.

17 Ibid., 153.

18 Gertrude Stein, "What Are Master-pieces and Why Are There So Few of Them?," in *Writings and Lectures 1909–1945*, ed. Patricia Meyerowitz (Baltimore, MD: Penguin, 1967), 151.

19 Ibid., 150.

20 Jennifer Ashton, *From Modernism to Postmodernism: American Poetry and Theory in the Twentieth Century* (Cambridge: Cambridge University Press, 2005), 8.

21 Stein, "What are Master-pieces," 149–50.

22 Pressman, *Digital Modernism*, 2.

23 Bob Brown imagined a machine called a "readie" that would speed up the process of reading: "I wanted a reading machine to bring the words of others faster into my mind, I wanted a reading machine to carry my words faster and farther into the minds of others" (*Readies for Bob Brown's Machine* [Cagnes-sur-Mer: Roving Eye Press, 1931], 168). The writers I examine did

not envision reading processed through literal machines, but more deeply imagined how technical structures might shape narrative form itself.

24 As Dorothy J. Hale notes, the "Anglo-American scholarly record is virtually unanimous in crediting James and Lubbock as the forefathers of novel theory" (*Social Formalism: The Novel in Theory from Henry James to the Present* [Stanford, CA: Stanford University Press, 1998], 22n3; see also Dorothy J. Hale, "Henry James and the Invention of Novel Theory," in *The Cambridge Companion to Henry James*, ed. Jonathan Freedman [Cambridge: Cambridge University Press, 1998], 79–101).

25 Nicholas Dames's book *The Physiology of the Novel: Reading, Neural Science, and the Form of Victorian Fiction* (Oxford: Oxford University Press, 2007) extends novel theory further in time, beyond what has often been thought of as its beginning point in James and Lukács; in his conclusion, this expanded history shows surprising continuities between I. A. Richards's practical criticism and Victorian thinking about the novel. Hale shows how James anticipates Bakhtin and later theorists who emphasize the novel's ideological role by insisting that "novels instantiate social relations" (*Social Formalism*, 14).

26 Dames, *The Physiology of the Novel*, 29.

27 Leavis proclaims, "[i]n twentieth-century England not only everyone can read, but it is safe to add that everyone does read" (Q. D. Leavis, *Fiction and the Reading Public* [London: Chatto and Windus, 1939 (1932)], 3). Virginia Woolf and Leonard Woolf similarly diagnosed an overabundance of books in a 1927 BBC interview, "Are Too Many Books Written and Published?" (*PMLA*, vol. 121, no. 1 [January 2006], 239–44). Even the Mass Observation team noted in an undated report on "What do you read and why?" that "[t]here have never been so many people reading as much as now" (Mass Observation Archive, TC Reading Habits 20/42, 1937–47).

28 Leavis, *Fiction and the Reading Public*, 58.

29 Ibid., 59, 60.

30 Ibid., 57.

31 Ibid., 61.

32 Quoted in Vera Brittain, *Testament of Friendship: The Story of Winifred Holtby* (New York, NY: Macmillan, 1940), 131. On the readability of the middlebrow novel, see Kristin Erwins, "'Revolutionizing a Mode of Life': Leftist Middlebrow Fiction by Women in the 1930s," *ELH*, vol. 82, no. 1 (Spring 2015), 251–79; and Nicola Humble, *The Feminine Middlebrow Novel, 1920s to 1950s: Class, Domesticity, and Bohemianism* (Oxford: Oxford University Press, 2001), Chapter 1.

33 Storm Jameson, "The Craft of the Novelist," in *Civil Journey* (London: Cassell, 1939), 60.

34 Leavis, *Fiction and the Reading Public*, 49.

35 Ibid.

36 George Orwell, "Bookshop Memories," in *The Collected Essays, Journalism and Letters of George Orwell: An Age Like This, 1920–1940*, ed. Sonia Orwell and Ian Angus (New York, NY: Harcourt, Brace and World, 1968), 246.

37 Graham Greene, "The Cargo Ship," in *Journey Without Maps* (New York, NY: Penguin, 1981 [1936]), 25.
38 Edwin Muir, *The Structure of the Novel* (London: Hogarth, 1960 [1928]), 10.
39 Ibid., 8.
40 Virginia Woolf, "Middlebrow," in *The Death of the Moth and Other Essays* (London: Hogarth, 1942), 115.
41 E. M. Forster, *Aspects of the Novel* (New York, NY: Harcourt, 1955 [1927]), 13.
42 See ibid., Chapter 3, "People," especially 47.
43 See ibid., 66–7.
44 Virginia Woolf, "On Re-reading Novels," in *Collected Essays, Volume 2* (New York, NY: Harcourt, Brace and World, 1967), 126.
45 Ibid.
46 See Virginia Woolf, "The Patron and the Crocus," in *The Common Reader: First Series*, ed. Andrew McNeillie (New York, NY: Harcourt, 1984 [1925]), 207. The idea that the novel is the reader's friend was a commonplace throughout middlebrow novel criticism in the early twentieth century; see David Ayers, *English Literature of the 1920s* (Edinburgh: Edinburgh University Press, 1999), 117–23. In one example from a lecture series chaired by Hugh Walpole, Sidney Dark declared that "great novels not only make priceless addition to the number of our friends and acquaintances, but they give us friends and acquaintances whom we can know far more thoroughly than we can possibly know our next-door neighbours or even the members of our own households" (*The New Reading Public: A Lecture Delivered under the Auspices of "the Society of Bookmen"* [London: George Allen & Unwin, 1922], 8). In another example, Coulson Kernahan argued that "[g]reat novelists give us characters – the creations of genius – who are our friends for life, and thenceforth part of our life, more real to us than not a few known creatures of flesh and blood" (*The Reading Girl: Saunters in Bookland & Chats on the Choice of Books & Methods of Reading* [London: George G. Harrap & Co, 1925], 81).
47 See Leavis, *Fiction and the Reading Public*, 61.
48 Vernon Lee, "Imagination Penetrative: Apropos of Mr. Lubbock's *Craft of Fiction*," in *The Handling of Words and Other Studies in Literary Psychology* (London: John Lane, the Bodley Head, 1922), 275–86.
49 Ibid., 275, 286.
50 Ibid., 280.
51 Vernon Lee and C. Anstruther-Thomson, "Anthropomorphic Aesthetics," in *Beauty and Ugliness and Other Studies in Psychological Aesthetics* (London: John Lane, the Bodley Head, 1912), 29.
52 Vernon Lee and C. Anstruther-Thomson, "Aesthetic Empathy and Its Organic Accompaniments," in *Beauty and Ugliness and Other Studies in Psychological Aesthetics* (London: John Lane, the Bodley Head, 1912), 59.
53 Percy Lubbock, *The Craft of Fiction* (New York, NY: Peter Smith, 1947 [1921]), 2.

54 Ibid., 1.
55 Ibid.
56 Hugh Walpole, *Reading: An Essay* (London: Harper, 1927), 3–4.
57 Forster, *Aspects of the Novel*, 42.
58 Ibid., 160–1.
59 Ibid., 162.
60 Ibid., 164.
61 Hulme addresses the political valence of this opposition in "Romanticism and Classicism," in *Speculations*, ed. Herbert Read (London: Kegan Paul, Trench, Trubner, & Co., 1936), 114–15.
62 See Wyndham Lewis, *Time and Western Man* (Boston, MA: Beacon, 1957 [1927]), 174–6.
63 Music has the "power of seeming to hold an audience or crowd together into an organism," Hulme writes ("Notes on Language and Style," in *Further Speculations*, ed. Sam Hynes [Minneapolis, MN: University of Minnesota Press, 1955], 96).
64 T. E. Hulme, "A Lecture on Modern Poetry," in *Further Speculations*, ed. Sam Hynes [Minneapolis, MN: University of Minnesota Press, 1955], 74.
65 Ibid.
66 Ibid.
67 Hulme, "Romanticism and Classicism," 135.
68 Lewis, *Time and Western Man*, 174–5.
69 Wyndham Lewis, *Men Without Art*, ed. Seamus Cooney (Santa Barbara, CA: Black Sparrow, 1987 [1934]), 237.
70 In a 1920 letter to M. D. Forbes, Richards promises to "send you the introductory chapter of the book on 'The Novel' which I was writing" (*Selected Letters of I. A. Richards*, ed. John Constable [Oxford: Clarendon, 1990)], 20).
71 See Joseph North, "What's 'New Critical' about 'Close Reading?' I. A. Richards and His New Critical Reception," *New Literary History*, vol. 44, no. 1 (Winter 2013), 143–4.
72 I. A. Richards, *Principles of Literary Criticism* (San Diego, CA: Harcourt Brace Jovanovich, 1985 [1925]), 1.
73 See Dames, *The Physiology of the Novel*, 251–2.
74 Richards, *Selected Letters*, 16.
75 Key studies in this regard include the collection edited by Kevin J. H. Dettmar and Stephen Watt, *Marketing Modernisms: Self-Promotion, Canonization, Rereading* (Ann Arbor, MI: University of Michigan Press, 1996); Lawrence S. Rainey's *Institutions of Modernism: Literary Elites and Public Culture* (New Haven, CT: Yale University Press, 1998); and Mark S. Morrisson's *The Public Face of Modernism: Little Magazines, Audiences, and Reception, 1905–1920* (Madison, WI: University of Wisconsin Press, 2000). These studies led the way toward a materialist criticism focused on institutional context as a key site for understanding modernism's relationship to its readers. Another set of influential studies – Jennifer Wicke's *Advertising Fictions: Literature, Advertising, and Social Fictions* (New York, NY: Columbia University Press, 1988); Thomas F. Strychacz's *Modernism, Mass Culture, and Professionalism* (Cambridge: Cambridge University Press, 1993); and, most recently, Elizabeth

Outka's *Consuming Traditions: Modernity, Modernism, and the Commodified Authentic* (Oxford: Oxford University Press, 2009) – show that modernism incorporated mass cultural materials in order to achieve cultural authority with readers. Yet another set of recent studies has focused on the category of celebrity as a goal and strategy that linked modernist and mass cultural productions and shaped modernism's particular relationship to its readers – see Aaron Jaffe's *Modernism and the Culture of Celebrity* (Cambridge: Cambridge University Press, 2005), and Jonathan Goldman's *Modernism Is the Literature of Celebrity* (Austin, TX: University of Texas Press, 2011).

76 See, for example, Mary Grover, *The Ordeal of Warwick Deeping: Middlebrow Authorship and Cultural Embarrassment* (Madison, NJ: Farleigh Dickinson University Press, 2009); Nicola Humble, *The Feminine Middlebrow Novel*; and Phyllis Lassner, "Reading Sideways: Middlebrow into Modernism," the introduction to a special issue of *Space Between: Literature and Culture, 1914–1945*, vol. 9, issue 1 (2013), 7–10.

77 Andreas Huyssen, *After the Great Divide: Modernism, Mass Culture, Postmodernism* (Bloomington, IN: Indiana University Press, 1986).

78 Ashton, *From Modernism to Postmodernism*, 2. There is a strong tradition of such "postmodernizing" in studies of modernism and technology, especially with regard to James Joyce. This tradition can be traced back as far as McLuhan, as I will show in the conclusion. Donald F. Theall's book, *James Joyce's Techno-Poetics* (Toronto: University of Toronto Press, 1997), extends this tradition, explicitly considering *Ulysses* and *Finnegans Wake* as key documents in postmodernism that anticipate aspects of computer culture.

79 Lisa Siraganian, *Modernism's Other Work: The Art Object's Political Life* (New York, NY: Oxford University Press, 2012), 4. Other studies that rethink aesthetic autonomy include Jessica Burstein, *Cold Modernism: Literature, Fashion, Art* (University Park, PA: Pennsylvania State University Press, 2012) and Michael Szalay, *New Deal Modernism: American Literature and the Invention of the Welfare State* (Durham, NC: Duke University Press, 2000).

80 Andrew Goldstone, *Fictions of Autonomy: Modernism from Wilde to de Man* (New York, NY: Oxford University Press, 2013), 5.

81 Ibid., 7.

82 Leavis, *Fiction and the Reading Public*, 157.

83 Ibid. Max Horkheimer and Theodor W. Adorno would argue that "[t]he development of the culture industry has led to the predominance of the effect, the obvious touch, and the technical detail over the work itself" ("The Culture Industry: Enlightenment as Mass Deception," in *Dialectic of Enlightenment*, trans. John Cumming [New York, NY: Continuum, 2002 (1944)], 125).

84 Leavis, *Fiction and the Reading Public*, 226.

85 Modern technology "is always directed from the beginning toward furthering something else, i.e., toward driving on to the maximum yield at the minimum expense" (Martin Heidegger, "The Question Concerning Technology," in *Basic Writings of Martin Heidegger*, revised and expanded edition, ed. David Farrell Krell [New York, NY: Harper Collins, 1993 (1977)], 321).

86 Ibid., 322. Heidegger continues, "[s]een in terms of the standing-reserve, the machine is completely nonautonomous, for it has its standing only on the basis of the ordering of the orderable" (ibid., 322–3).

87 Lewis Mumford, *Technics and Civilization* (San Diego, CA: Harcourt Brace and Co., 1963 [1934]), 72, 84; Wyndham Lewis, *The Apes of God* (Santa Rosa, CA: Black Sparrow Press, 1992 [1930]), 404. Siegfried Giedeon's *Mechanization Takes Command: A Contribution to Anonymous History* (New York, NY: Oxford University Press, 1970 [1948]) would cover similar ground fourteen years after Mumford.

88 Lewis Mumford, "The Drama of the Machines," *Scribners*, vol. 88, no. 2 (August 1930), 150.

89 Modern *technē* still "reveals," but not "into a bringing-forth in the sense of *poiēsis*," and thus it cannot create anything new and heterogeneous (Heidegger, "The Question Concerning Technology," 320). Instead, "[t]he revealing that rules in modern technology is a challenging [*Herausfordern*], which puts to nature the unreasonable demand that it supply energy which cannot be extracted and stored as such" (ibid.). This "challenging" omits a basic component of true poetic revealing, where the human subject must "take care of and maintain" what she brings forth (ibid.).

90 Leavis, *Fiction and the Reading Public*, 61.

91 These claims will be more fully explored in Chapter 3.

92 Mumford, *Technics and Civilization*, 14.

93 Heidegger, "The Question Concerning Technology," 339.

94 "Because the essence of technology is nothing technological, essential reflection upon technology and decisive confrontation with it must happen in a realm that is, on the one hand, akin to the essence of technology, and, on the other, fundamentally different from it. Such a realm is art" (ibid., 340).

95 Wilhelm Worringer, *Abstraction and Empathy: A Contribution to the Psychology of Style*, trans. Michael Bullock (New York, NY: International University Press, 1953 [1908]), 18.

96 See ibid., 11.

97 Ibid., 21.

98 Ibid., 17.

99 Ibid., 16.

100 The most prominent thinkers to follow up on this connection are Gilles Deleuze and Felix Guattari, in *A Thousand Plateaus: Capitalism and Schizophrenia*, trans. Brian Massumi (Minneapolis, MN: University of Minnesota Press, 1987), 498–500. See Joshua Dittrich, "A Life of Matter and Death: Inorganic Life in Worringer, Deleuze, and Guattari," *Discourse*, vol. 33, no. 2 (Spring 2011), 242–62.

101 Wyndham Lewis, *Paleface: The Philosophy of the "Melting-Pot"* (London: Chatto & Windus, 1929), 249.

102 See Jay David Bolter and Richard Grusin, *Remediation: Understanding New Media* (Cambridge, MA: MIT Press, 1999). Remediation describes the way media reproduce other media. New media, in particular, gain authority by remediating older media.

103 Grover, *The Ordeal of Warwick Deeping*, 35–9.
104 Wyndham Lewis, "Manifesto," *BLAST: Review of the Great English Vortex*, no. 1 (1914), 38.
105 Ibid., 41.
106 Wyndham Lewis, "Shropshire Lads or Robots Again," in *Creatures of Habit and Creatures of Change: Essays on Art, Literature and Society, 1914–1956*, ed. Paul Edwards (Santa Rosa, CA: Black Sparrow Press, 1989), 191.
107 William Carlos Williams, "A Point for American Criticism," in *Our Examgination Round His Factification for Incamination of* Work in Progress (New York, NY: New Directions, 1972 [1929]), 178.
108 Ibid., 182.
109 Ibid., 185, 178.
110 Ibid., 180.
111 Lubbock, *The Craft of Fiction*, 172.
112 Ibid.
113 Friedrich Kittler, *Discourse Networks 1800/1900*, trans. Michael Metteer with Chris Cullens (Stanford, CA: Stanford University Press, 1990 [1985]), 212.
114 Sara Danius, *The Senses of Modernism: Technology, Perception, and Aesthetics* (Ithaca, NY: Cornell University Press, 2002), 3.
115 Mark Goble, *Beautiful Circuits: Modernism and the Mediated Life* (New York, NY: Columbia University Press, 2010), 16.

Chapter 1

1 Henry James, "The Art of Fiction," in *The Art of Criticism: Henry James on the Theory and the Practice of Fiction*, ed. William Veeder and Susan M. Griffin (Chicago, IL: University of Chicago Press, 1986), 168.
2 Ibid., 168–9.
3 Ibid., 169.
4 Ibid., 168 (first quotation), 169.
5 Walter Besant, *The Art of Fiction* (London: Chatto and Windus, 1902 [1884]), 78.
6 G. H. Lewes, "Causes of Success and Failure in Literature, and Division of the Subject," in *Principles of Success in Literature*, third edition, ed. Fred N. Scott (Boston, MA: Allyn and Bacon, 1894 [1865]), 26.
7 Ibid., 28.
8 Fredric Jameson, "Reification and Utopia in Mass Culture," *Social Text*, vol. 1 (Winter 1979), 132.
9 Ibid., 131.
10 Theodor W. Adorno, "On the Fetish Character in Music and the Regression of Listening," in *The Culture Industry: Selected Essays on Mass Culture*, ed. J. M. Bernstein (New York, NY and London: Routledge, 1991), 47.
11 Ibid., 36.
12 Ibid., 53.

13 Max Horkheimer and Theodor W. Adorno, "The Culture Industry," in *Dialectic of Enlightenment*, trans. John Cumming (New York, NY: Continuum, 2002 [1944]), 125.

14 Timothy P. Martin elaborates the argument that Lubbock nudges James toward a formalism that is not present in James's own criticism in "Henry James and Percy Lubbock: From Mimesis to Formalism" (*NOVEL: A Forum on Fiction*, vol. 14, no. 1 [Fall 1980], 20–9). Lubbock has largely fallen out of critical interest, especially in modernist studies, probably due to his long-standing, self-cultivated critical reputation as James's "disciple" (for a fascinating account of Lubbock's relationship to James, see Michael Anesko, *Monopolizing the Master: Henry James and the Politics of Modern Literary Scholarship* [Stanford, CA: Stanford University Press, 2012], 73–108). Indeed, contemporary critics have often wanted to free James from Lubbock's systematizing influence. To cite just one of myriad examples, David Herman critiques Lubbock's "invidious" influence on James's reputation: "Lubbock appropriated James's ideas to produce a markedly prescriptive framework" that dumbs down Jamesian complexity ("Histories of Narrative Theory (I): A Genealogy of Early Developments," in *A Companion to Narrative Theory*, ed. James Phelan and Peter J. Rabinowitz [Malden, MA: Blackwell, 2005], 27).

15 Percy Lubbock, *The Craft of Fiction* (New York, NY: Peter Smith, 1947 [1921]), 3.

16 Ibid., 12.

17 Ibid., 66.

18 Ibid., 67.

19 Nicholas Dames has analyzed Lubbock's theory in similar terms: "Lubbock is interested in how we *know*, not how we *react*" (*The Physiology of the Novel: Reading, Neural Science, and the Form of Victorian Fiction* [Oxford: Oxford University Press, 2007], 35).

20 Richard Menke argues that in the novella "In the Cage," James uses the figure of the telegraphist to "highlight problems of subjectivism, discontinuity, and mediation" in realist narrative conventions (*Telegraphic Realism: Victorian Fiction and Other Information Systems* [Stanford, CA: Stanford University Press, 2008], 214). Pamela Thurschwell reads a "model of exteriorization" of consciousness, enabled by technologies such as the telegraph, in James's late work (*Literature, Technology and Magical Thinking, 1880–1920* [Cambridge: Cambridge University Press, 2004], 97). These readings, like mine, are indebted to Sharon Cameron's influential *Thinking in Henry James* (Chicago, IL: University of Chicago Press, 1989), which argues that James's novels cannot be understood within the framework of psychological realism. Cameron claims that consciousness in James is portable, external, mediated, and systemic, rather than a quality localized in a centered, individual subjectivity.

21 Mark Goble, by contrast, analyzes technological mediation and indirect communication as sources of pleasure that inspired James to reimagine intimacy in terms of indirect mediation. Goble writes: "What sets James apart . . . is his interest in the intimate effects of media, his sense that the same technologies that make it possible to extend language and consciousness over geographic distance also make it possible to distend and disfigure the idea of proximity

itself, to imagine that 'connexion' – whether conceived in social, psychologi-cal, sexual, or artistic terms – is best achieved, and most intensely registered, when as mediated and 'circuitous' as possible" (*Beautiful Circuits: Modernism and the Mediated Life* [New York, NY: Columbia University Press, 2010], 79).

22 This understanding of the prefaces as a site where James can "attempt to control the reading of his work without entering that work as an interloper who would invalidate the aesthetic he seeks to promote" is elaborated more fully by John H. Pearson (*The Prefaces of Henry James: Framing the Modern Reader* [University Park, PA: Pennsylvania State University Press, 1997], 17).

23 James, "The Art of Fiction," 165.

24 Henry James, "The New Novel," in *Notes on Novelists with Some Other Notes* (New York, NY: Scribner's, 1914), 325.

25 Ibid., 341 (first two quotations), 342.

26 Ibid., 341.

27 On the trope of reading as eating, a common site where nineteenth-century novel theory argued that mass culture turns works of art into instruments for satisfying the basic, animal needs of readers, see Steven Mailloux, "The Rhetorical Use and Abuse of Fiction: Eating Books in Late Nineteenth-Century America," *boundary 2*, vol. 17, no. 1 (Spring 1990), 133–57.

28 Lubbock, *The Craft of Fiction*, 6.

29 Ibid.

30 Ibid., 8.

31 Ibid., 9. Throughout, Lubbock uses the term "rounding" to describe this activity of making the novel real. This term is significant because it prepared the ground for E. M. Forster, who famously argued for the superiority of "round" characters, as opposed to flat ones (*Aspects of the Novel* [New York, NY: Harcourt, 1955 (1927)], 67–77). The idea of the round character would become a key issue in the form-versus-life debates of the 1920s, with Lubbock and Edwin Muir defending against the need for characters to become round (see *The Structure of the Novel* [London: Hogarth, 1960 (1928)], 25–6). To be round, Lubbock implies, is to gain three-dimensional reality off the page. It is an effect that merges the novel into life, making characters real.

32 Henry James, "The Future of the Novel," in *The Art of Criticism: Henry James on the Theory and the Practice of Fiction*, ed. William Veeder and Susan M. Griffin (Chicago, IL: University of Chicago Press, 1986), 245.

33 Ibid.

34 Ibid., 247.

35 James, "The New Novel," 315.

36 Ibid.

37 Lubbock, *The Craft of Fiction*, 17.

38 Ibid., 6, 17, 15.

39 Ibid., 5.

40 Ibid., 19.

41 James, "The New Novel," 348.

42 James notes with surprise that Conrad's popular success shows that the common reader can actually appreciate form. See "The New Novel," 349.

43 Ibid., 347.
44 Ibid., 346.
45 Henry James, "*The Portrait of a Lady*," in *The Art of Criticism: Henry James on the Theory and the Practice of Fiction*, ed. William Veeder and Susan M. Griffin (Chicago, IL: University of Chicago Press, 1986), 290.
46 Henry James, *What Maisie Knew* (Chicago, IL: Herbert S. Stone and Co., 1897), 9–10.
47 Henry James, "*What Maisie Knew*," in *The Art of Criticism: Henry James on the Theory and the Practice of Fiction*, ed. William Veeder and Susan M. Griffin (Chicago, IL: University of Chicago Press, 1986), 319–20.
48 Christina Britzolakis, "Technologies of Vision in Henry James's *What Maisie Knew*," *NOVEL: A Forum on Fiction*, vol. 34, no. 3 (Summer 2001), 369.
49 Henry James, "*The Ambassadors*," in *The Art of Criticism: Henry James on the Theory and the Practice of Fiction*, ed. William Veeder and Susan M. Griffin (Chicago, IL: University of Chicago Press, 1986), 364. The term "projection" appears with great frequency in James's criticism, as a way to describe the relationship of a variety of figures to the fictional scene: the character's ("how much too scantly projected and suggested a field poor Roderick and his large capacity for ruin are made to turn round"), the author's (James's "projection of memory" of composition upon his novels), or even life's (life "retains its power of projecting itself upon [man's] imagination") ("*Roderick Hudson*," in *The Art of Criticism: Henry James on the Theory and the Practice of Fiction*, ed. William Veeder and Susan M. Griffin [Chicago, IL: University of Chicago Press, 1986], 266; "*The Portrait of a Lady*," 287; "The Future of the Novel," 250). This confusing flexibility of the term is a key part of James's arsenal for precisely describing points of view – how any variety of figures are "placed" in relation to a fictional scene. On one of these uses of the term – to describe the author's contribution to the novel – see Dorothy J. Hale, *Social Formalism: The Novel in Theory from Henry James to the Present* (Stanford, CA: Stanford University Press, 1998), 26–30.
50 James, "*The Ambassadors*," 364.
51 Ibid.
52 Ibid., 368–9.
53 Lubbock, *The Craft of Fiction*, 162.
54 James, "*The Ambassadors*," 365.
55 Ibid.
56 Ibid., 373.
57 Ibid., 374.
58 Ibid., 370.
59 Ibid., 372.
60 James, "The New Novel," 348.
61 James, *What Maisie Knew*, 10.
62 "The Future of the Aeroplane," *Times of London*, June 25, 1913, p. 24.
63 James, "The New Novel," 348.

64 Ibid., 349.

65 Ibid.

66 Vernon Lee and C. Anstruther-Thomson, "Anthropomorphic Aesthetics," in *Beauty and Ugliness and Other Studies in Psychological Aesthetics* (London: John Lane, the Bodley Head, 1912), 29.

67 Ibid., 34.

68 Ibid., 30.

69 Adalaide Morris, "The Concept of Projection: H. D.'s Visionary Powers," *Contemporary Literature*, vol. 25, no. 4 (Winter 1984), 429; H. D., "The Dream," *Contemporary Literature* vol. 10, no. 4 (Autumn 1969): 605.

70 H. D., "The Dream," 606.

71 Ibid.

72 On the material and erotic dimensions of this spectator-writer relationship, see chapter 4 of Susan McCabe's *Cinematic Modernism: Modernist Poetry and Film* (Cambridge: Cambridge University Press, 2005).

73 José Ortega y Gasset, "The Dehumanization of Art," in *The Dehumanization of Art and Other Essays on Art, Culture, and Literature*, trans. Helene Weyl (Princeton, NJ: Princeton University Press, 1972 [1925]), 28.

74 Ibid., 10.

75 Ibid.

76 James, *What Maisie Knew*, 10; James, "*The Ambassadors*," 364.

77 Stuart Burrows, *A Familiar Strangeness: American Fiction and the Language of Photography, 1839–1945* (Athens, GA: University of Georgia Press, 2008), 85, 88.

78 Henry James, "The Golden Bowl," in *The Art of Criticism: Henry James on the Theory and the Practice of Fiction*, ed. William Veeder and Susan M. Griffin (Chicago, IL: University of Chicago Press, 1986) 380.

79 Ibid., 381.

80 James, "*The Ambassadors*," 364.

81 Virginia Woolf, "'Anon' and 'The Reader': Virginia Woolf's Last Essays," ed. Brenda R. Silver, *Twentieth Century Literature*, vol. 25, no. 3–4 (Autumn-Winter 1979), 429; Virginia Woolf, "The 'Movie' Novel," in *The Essays of Virginia Woolf Volume 2, 1912–1918*, ed. Andrew McNeillie (New York, NY: Harcourt Brace Jovanovich, 1987), 290. The latter essay is a 1918 review of Compton Mackenzie's *Sylvia Scarlett*, which Woolf criticizes as a "book of cinema" that does not rise to the status of literature ("The 'Movie' Novel," 291). For Woolf, the novel that resembles film is, necessarily, a popular one. In her reading of this essay, Laura Marcus suggests that Woolf conceptualizes film as "locomotive" but emotionless – quite similar to how James understands projection, though valorized in the opposite way (*The Tenth Muse: Writing about Cinema in the Modernist Period* [New York, NY: Oxford University Press, 2007], 104).

82 Christopher Isherwood, *Prater Violet* (New York, NY: Farrar, Strauss and Giroux, 1996 [1945]), 30–1.

83 Ibid., 32.
84 David Trotter, "T. S. Eliot and Cinema," *Modernism/Modernity*, vol. 13, no. 2 (April 2006), 241. See also Maria DiBattista, "This is Not a Movie: *Ulysses* and Cinema," *Modernism/Modernity*, vol. 13, no. 2 (April 2006), 219–35. Laura Marcus also explores how modernist writers used the figure of the automata, the robot, and the doll to describe film's ability to move (*The Tenth Muse*, 27–43).
85 Garrett Stewart, like James, reads automaticity as being precisely what these two media have in common. Stewart argues that the opposition between literature and film that modernist writers often posit is untenable because the "breaks" that the reader can induce in the reading experience are themselves generated by a more fundamental automatism. For Stewart, modernism remakes language into an incessant procession of discontinuous units of language, while film's essential characteristic is the movement of "photogrammic" units that disappear in seriality. Modernism becomes "an *automatism* of language beneath the intentionalities of inscription, a writing always in flux beneath the written, undoing what it funds in utterances, unraveling the lexical discreteness it both requires and provides" (*Between Film and Screen: Modernism's Photo/Synthesis* [Chicago, IL: University of Chicago Press, 1999], 283).
86 Lubbock, *The Craft of Fiction*, 1.
87 Ibid., 143.
88 Ibid., 157.
89 My reading challenges one of the only recent critical accounts of *The Craft of Fiction*. Dorothy Hale attributes to Lubbock a "noetic materialism" in which the reader recreates the novel in her mind; a similar reading of Lubbock provides key evidence for John Carlos Rowe's position that James's prefaces theorize a formalism that requires a "constitutive role of the reader" (Hale, *Social Formalism*, 62; John Carlos Rowe, *The Theoretical Dimensions of Henry James* [Madison, WI: University of Wisconsin Press, 1984], 250). But these readings impose a kind of postmodern, constructive reading onto Lubbock's text and underestimate how deeply problematic Lubbock found reading to be. As Nicholas Dames has pointed out, Lubbock posited a reader who is incapable of remembering what happens from page to page (*The Physiology of the Novel*, 33–6). The only way to compensate for this "disability," as Lubbock calls it, is to maintain distance from the novel, to see its form, rather than to become immersed in it (*The Craft of Fiction*, 3). From a wider view of Lubbock's work, then, when he writes that "[t]he reader of a novel – by which I mean the critical reader – is himself a novelist," he is not imagining that the active reader co-writes the novel (Ibid., 17). The forgetful reader would certainly not be able to do a very good job. The end of the book clarifies Lubbock's meaning here: "The author of the book was a craftsman, the critic must overtake him at his work and see how the book was made" (Ibid., 274). The reader, to maintain distance, must attempt not to become involved with the book's characters and fictional scene, and instead take on a workmanlike focus on craft, on form.

90 Lubbock, *The Craft of Fiction*, 178.

91 Ibid., 14.

92 This is the main argument of Jonathan Crary's *Techniques of the Observer: On Vision and Modernity in the Nineteenth Century* (Cambridge, MA: MIT Press, 1992).

93 Ibid., 47–8.

94 Ibid., 113.

95 Ibid., 77–8.

96 Jonathan Crary, *Suspensions of Perception: Attention, Spectacle, and Modern Culture* (Cambridge, MA: MIT Press, 2001), 13.

97 Certainly, this strategy runs the risk of returning to the long period following R. P. Blackmur's collection of the prefaces into the volume *The Art of the Novel*, when the prefaces "tyrannized over criticism on Henry James" (Herschel Parker, "Deconstructing *The Art of the Novel* and Liberating James's Prefaces," *Henry James Review*, vol. 14, no. 3 [Fall 1993], 285). Since my project is to excavate James's strategies for controlling reading, though, that seems a risk worth taking.

98 Henry James, *The Ambassadors*, ed. R. W. Stallman (New York, NY: Signet, 1979 [1903]), 326.

99 Ibid., 330, 331.

100 Ibid., 112.

101 Ibid., 333.

102 Ibid.

103 Ibid., 360.

104 Jonathan Freedman, "*The Ambassadors* and the Culture of Optical Illusion," *Raritan*, vol. 34, no. 3 (Winter 2015), 153.

105 Freedman has elsewhere made a similar argument for the cinematic qualities of James's late style by linking it to G.A. Smith's point-of-view shots. See Jonathan Freedman, "Henry James and Early Film," *The Henry James Review*, vol. 33, no. 3 (Fall 2012), 255–64.

106 Freedman, "*The Ambassadors* and the Culture of Optical Illusion," 154–5.

107 James, *The Ambassadors*, 332.

108 Ibid., 75.

109 Ibid., 232.

110 Ibid., 53.

111 James, "*The Ambassadors*," 364

112 James, *The Ambassadors*, 54.

113 Ibid., 333.

114 Ian Watt describes such moments in James's late style as part of "the general Jamesian tendency to present characters and actions on a plane of abstract categorisation" ("The First Paragraph of *The Ambassadors*: An Explication," *Essays in Criticism*, vol. 10, no. 3 [1960], 259).

115 Megan Quigley has recently analyzed *The Ambassadors* in these terms, arguing that Strether's vague language, deferred referents, and abstractions reflect the fact that "Strether would like to be distanced from the intimacy upon which he has intruded" (*Modernist Fiction and Vagueness: Philosophy,*

Form, and Language [New York, NY: Cambridge University Press, 2015], 59).

116 My analysis builds on a long critical tradition that sees the moment on the river as a site where the representational economy associated with Mme. de Vionnet and Paris wins out over that associated with Mrs. Newsome and Woollett. While Mrs. Newsome is the absent referent that aims to govern her delegates, in Paris Strether learns that signifiers are not fully controlled by their referents. Instead, representations turn out to be embedded in an economy of loss and lack and never fulfill the promise of full presence in representation. For instance, Maud Ellman argues that in the countryside Strether sees that "[b]ecause every picture represents a loss, it functions as a trap to catch the gaze," and ensnares him in the lovers' desires ("'The Intimate Difference': Power and Representation in The Ambassadors," in *Henry James: Fiction as History*, ed. Ian F. A. Bell [London: Vision, 1984], 108). Similarly, Julie Rivkin argues that at this moment, Strether does not learn some deep and ultimate truth about Chad, but instead what he "discover[s] as he replaces one truth about experience with another is that there is no stopping point in this logic of revision, no superlative that will stand beyond all comparison, no originating intention that can hold its meaning fixed to the ultimate referent" ("The Logic of Delegation in The Ambassadors," *PMLA*, vol. 101, no. 5 [October 1986], 829).

117 James, "*The Ambassadors*," 367.
118 James, *The Ambassadors*, 114.
119 Ibid., 39.
120 Ibid., 7.
121 Ibid., 77.
122 Ibid., 72.
123 Maud Ellman, "'The Intimate Difference,'" 107.
124 James, *The Ambassadors*, 64, 65.
125 Ibid., 85, 180.
126 Ibid., 95.
127 Ibid., 96.
128 Ibid., 97.
129 Ibid., 102.
130 Henry James, "Crapy Cornelia," in *The Finer Grain* (New York, NY: Scribner's, 1910), 201.
131 Ibid.
132 It is plausible to associate this 1909 metaphor with the complex of images from James's earlier texts – the magic lantern from the prefaces, the moving painting from *The Ambassadors* – in part because James was probably not imagining the most up-to-date developments. David Trotter notes that James's cinema metaphor is self-consciously dated, referring to a cinematic effect that could be more easily associated with a film from 1895, not 1909 – but "the literature of cinema continued to dwell on its original effect" (*Cinema and Modernism* [New York, NY: Wiley, 2007], 20).
133 Crary, *Suspensions of Perception*, 200.
134 Ibid., 188.
135 James, *The Ambassadors*, 39.

136 Ibid., 372.

137 Ibid., 373.

138 Ibid., 372.

139 Ibid.

140 H. G. Wells, *Boon: The Mind of the Race, the Wild Asses of the Devil, and the Last Trump* (New York, NY: George H. Doran, 1915), 109.

Chapter 2

1 T. S. Eliot, "The Perfect Critic," in *The Sacred Wood: Essays on Poetry and Criticism* (New York, NY: Knopf, 1921), 9.

2 Ford Madox Ford, "The Passing of the Great Figure," in *The Critical Attitude* (London: Duckworth, 1911), 111–30.

3 Ford Madox Ford, *The Good Soldier* (New York, NY: Vintage, 1983 [1915]), 13.

4 Ford Madox Ford, "On the Functions of the Arts in the Republic," in *The Critical Attitude* (London: Duckworth, 1911), 28.

5 Mark S. Morrisson, *The Public Face of Modernism: Little Magazines, Audiences, and Reception, 1905–1920* (Madison, WI: University of Wisconsin Press, 2001), 46. Morrisson argues that *The English Review* is characterized by an "optimism about entering the public sphere" that seems unexpected, given a long-standing interpretation of Ford as a hopeless skeptic who retreated into a childlike rejection of social responsibility (ibid., 22). Morrisson shows that in the era of his editing of *The English Review*, Ford, like Habermas, idealized "a coherent public sphere – one stabilized not by strong party structures, but by an imaginative and cohesive culture" (ibid., 19–20). On the irony and sarcasm generated by Ford's mixture of pessimism about cultural decline and the journal's "project to embody disinterestedness," see Simon Grimble, "'A Few Inches above the Moral Atmosphere of these Islands': The Perspectives of the *English Review*," in *Ford Madox Ford, Modernist Magazines and Editing*, ed. Jason Harding (New York, NY: Rodopi, 2010), 160.

6 Mark Wollaeger, *Modernism, Media, and Propaganda: British Narrative from 1900 to 1945* (Princeton, NJ: Princeton University Press, 2006), 142.

7 Ibid., 144, 142. Wollaeger builds on the work of Jesse Matz, who shows that impressionism involves mediation between part and whole or fragment and totality – not just rendering immediacy (see *Literary Impressionism and Modernist Aesthetics* [Cambridge: Cambridge University Press, 2001], 16–17).

8 Ford Madox Ford, *Joseph Conrad: A Personal Remembrance* (Boston, MA: Little, Brown, and Company, 1924), 203.

9 Gérard Genette, *Narrative Discourse: An Essay in Method*, trans. Jane E. Lewin (Ithaca, NY: Cornell University Press, 1980 [1972]), 45.

10 Quoted in Wolfgang Iser, *The Implied Reader: Patterns of Communication in Prose Fiction from Bunyan to Beckett* (Baltimore, MD: Johns Hopkins University Press, 1987 [1974]), 101.

11 Ibid., 290. As Iser puts it, "reading causes the literary work to unfold its inherently dynamic character" (ibid., 275).

12 Ibid., 120.

13 One influential version is that of Michael H. Levenson, who thinks Ford retreated into subjectivism and uncertainty. In this view, Ford's

impressionism is fully exemplified by John Dowell's "refusal of 'adult' morality and . . . embrace of childhood insignificance and irresponsibility" (*A Genealogy of Modernism: A Study of English Literary Doctrine, 1908–1922* [Cambridge: Cambridge University Press, 1984], 57).

14 Ian Watt, *Conrad in the Nineteenth Century* (Berkeley, CA: University of California Press, 1979), 197. Dorothy J. Hale describes the basic difference between their theories of the novel this way: Watt assumes the "plentitude of novelistic mimesis," while Iser assumes its poverty, and the reader must fill in what the novel cannot provide (Hale, "Introduction to Part IX: Novel Readers," in *The Novel: An Anthology of Criticism and Theory, 1900–2000* [Malden, MA: Blackwell, 2006], 754). Impressionism thus epitomizes the novel in general, for Iser; for Watt it is something of an exception.

15 One important example, from the scholarship of *Parade's End* in particular, is Paul B. Armstrong's *The Challenge of Bewilderment: Understanding and Representation in James, Conrad, and Ford* (Ithaca, NY: Cornell University Press, 1987). Armstrong argues that *Parade's End* is ultimately about "the reader's quest for coherence": the temporal gaps in the novels, for instance, "serve the epistemological purpose of foregrounding our need for hypotheses if we are to achieve hermeneutic syntheses – to discover patterns and connections that link up what was separate. The eradication of some of these gaps requires not only synthesis, however, but also imaginative amplification. This is the correlative in the reading experience to the role of belief in filling out hidden sides" (ibid., 244). For Armstrong, the goal of *Parade's End* is for the reader to recognize her own labor in making the novel coherent.

16 Robert Green, *Ford Madox Ford: Prose and Politics* (Cambridge: Cambridge University Press, 1981), 69.

17 Ford Madox Ford, "Modern Poetry," in *The Critical Attitude* (London: Duckworth, 1911), 178.

18 Ford, "The Passing of the Great Figure," 123, 121.

19 Ford, "Modern Poetry," 186.

20 Ford, "The Passing of the Great Figure," 119.

21 Ford, "Modern Poetry," 178.

22 Ford Madox Ford, "English Literature of To-Day – I," in *The Critical Attitude* (London: Duckworth, 1911), 60.

23 Ibid., 64.

24 Ford, "The Passing of the Great Figure," 125. As Elena Lamberti puts it, "Ford perceives the newly reformed mass-society as a by-product of its cultural attitude, and as the result of a much broader crisis, both of which are linked to . . . the acquisition of a new, appealing style of life fomented by new forms of communication which turn original thinking into subliminally controlled commonplaces" ("Real Cities and Virtual Communities: Ford and the International Republic of Letters," in *Ford Madox Ford and the City*, ed. Sara Haslam [Amsterdam: Rodopi, 2005], 146).

25 Ford, "The Passing of the Great Figure," 124–5.

26 Walter Benjamin, "The Storyteller: Reflections on the Works of Nikolai Leskov," in *Illuminations*, trans. Harry Zohn (New York, NY: Schocken, 1968), 89.

27 Ford, "The Passing of the Great Figure," 125–6.

28 Ibid., 125.

29 Ford, "On the Functions of the Arts in the Republic," 33.

30 Ford, *Joseph Conrad*, 222.

31 Ford Madox Ford, *The Last Post*, in *Parade's End* (New York, NY: Penguin, 2001 [1924–8]), 692.

32 Ford Madox Ford, *A Man Could Stand Up–*, in *Parade's End* (New York, NY: Penguin, 2001 [1924–8]), 617.

33 Ibid.

34 Ford Madox Ford, *Some Do Not . . .*, in *Parade's End* (New York, NY: Penguin, 2001 [1924–8]), 281.

35 Ford, *A Man Could Stand Up–*, 607.

36 Ibid., 629.

37 Ibid.

38 Ibid., 629 (first two quotations), 651.

39 Ford, *The Good Soldier*, 40.

40 Charles Dickens, *Charles Dickens' Book of Memoranda: A Photographic and Typographic Facsimile of the Notebook Begun in January 1855* (New York, NY: New York Public Library, 1981), entry 89 (1862).

41 Richard Menke argues that the telegraph functions as an image for "a coherent structure of unseen connections," the common threads that link human communities (*Telegraphic Realism: Victorian Fiction and Other Information Systems* [Stanford, CA: Stanford University Press, 2008], 90). See also Elizabeth Deeds Ermarth, *Realism and Consensus in the English Novel: Time, Space and Narrative* (Edinburgh: Edinburgh University Press, 1998), 194–7.

42 Kate McLoughlin has recently analyzed this side of the telephone's function – "extreme and chaotic interruption" – in the third volume of *Parade's End* ("Interruption Overload: Telephones in Ford Madox Ford's '4692 Padd,' *A Call*, and *A Man Could Stand Up–*," *Journal of Modern Literature*, vol. 36, no. 3 [Spring 2013], 64).

43 Ford, *A Man Could Stand Up–*, 652, 518, 551.

44 Ibid., 575.

45 Ibid., 519.

46 Ibid., 528.

47 Ford, *The Last Post*, 778.

48 Ford Madox Ford, *A Call: The Tale of Two Passions* (New York, NY: Ecco, 1985 [1910]), 75.

49 Ibid., 189, 191.

50 Walter Benjamin, *Berlin Childhood Around 1900*, trans. Howard Eiland (Cambridge, MA: Harvard University Press, 2006 [1932–1938]), 49.

51 Ibid.

52 Paul K. Saint-Amour, *Tense Future: Modernism, Total War, Encyclopedic Form* (New York, NY: Oxford University Press, 2015), 284.

53 Ibid.

54 Ford Madox Ford, *No More Parades*, in *Parade's End*, (New York, NY: Penguin, 2001 [1924–8]), 330.

55 Ibid., 356.

56 The telephone's socially connective force would be noted by many writers in the fiction of the 1930s, when, as David Trotter has shown, the telephone was often associated with the dissemination of new kinds of intimacy and "mediated promiscuity" into domestic spaces for young women ("e-Modernism: Telephony in British Fiction, 1925–1940," *Critical Quarterly*, vol. 51, no. 1 [April 2009], 18).

57 Ford, *Some Do Not . . .* 18, 281.

58 Ibid., 281.

59 Ibid., 166.

60 Ibid., 272.

61 Ford, *Joseph Conrad*, 225. Critical accounts of *progression d'effet* have not tended to take this precise formulation very seriously. Ian Watt, for example, describes the term as "technical jargon" that hides the simplicity of the concept, "a planned sequence of effects on the reader" (*Conrad in the Nineteenth Century*, 305, 306).

62 Ford, *Joseph Conrad*, 204.

63 Ibid., 200–1, 203.

64 Tim Armstrong, *Modernism: A Cultural History* (Cambridge: Polity, 2005), 13.

65 Ford, *Joseph Conrad*, 203.

66 Ford, *Some Do Not . . .*, 3.

67 Ibid., 12.

68 Thomas Moser, *The Life in the Fiction of Ford Madox Ford* (Princeton, NJ: Princeton University Press, 1980), 217.

69 Tietjens is initially a figure for omniscience, something the series proceeds to break down by confronting his point of view with those of a multitude of other competing perspectives that render his relative and unstable. Rob Hawkes, for example, makes this diagnosis in *Ford Madox Ford and the Misfit Moderns: Edwardian Fiction and the First World War* (New York, NY: Palgrave Macmillan, 2012), 152, 156–62.

70 Ford, *Joseph Conrad*, 203.

71 Shierry Weber Nicholsen, *Exact Imagination, Late Work: On Adorno's Aesthetics* (Cambridge, MA: MIT Press, 1997), 83–4.

72 Sara Danius, *The Senses of Modernism: Technology, Perception, and Aesthetics* (Ithaca, NY: Cornell University Press, 2002), 180.

73 James Joyce, *Ulysses*, ed. Hans Walter Gabler (New York, NY: Vintage, 1993 [1922]), 189.

74 Tom Gunning, "Heard over the Phone: *The Lonely Villa* and the de Lorde Tradition of the Terrors of Technology," *Screen*, vol. 32, no 2 (Summer 1991), 184–96.

75 Eileen Bowser dates parallel editing as a way to show telephone calls to 1908; by 1911 it was the "normal way to show any telephone conversation" for many directors (*The Transformation of Cinema, 1907–1915* [Berkeley, CA: University of California Press, 1990], 68).

76 Gunning, "Heard over the Phone," 193.

77 Avital Ronell, *The Telephone Book: Technology, Schizophrenia, Electric Speech* (Lincoln, NE: University of Nebraska Press, 1989), 252.

78 Ibid., 4, 20.

79 Matz, *Literary Impressionism and Modernist Aesthetics*, 1.

80 Ford, *Joseph Conrad*, 184.

81 Ibid., 204.

82 Genette, Narrative Discourse, 42, 48.

83 Ibid., 45.

84 Roland Barthes, "An Introduction to the Structural Analysis of Narrative," trans. Lionel Duisit, *New Literary History*, vol. 6, no. 2 (Winter 1975 [1966]), 248.

85 Ibid.

86 Ford, *A Man Could Stand Up–*, 503.

87 Ibid., 654. Even Christopher imagines destiny as a device that calls, to which one answers: he would "pass thirty months in the frozen circle of hell, for the chance of thirty seconds in which to tell Valentine Wannop what he had answered back . . . to Destiny!" (Ford, *No More Parades*, 339).

88 Ford, *Joseph Conrad*, 203.

89 Michael J. Reddy, "The Conduit Metaphor – A Case of Frame Conflict in Our Language About Language," in *Metaphor and Thought*, ed. Andrew Ortony (Cambridge: Cambridge University Press, 1979), 290.

90 Ibid., 313.

91 Ford Madox Ford, "Thus to Revisit," *Picadilly Review* (1919), rptd. in *Critical Essays*, ed. Max Saunders and Richard Stang (New York, NY: New York University Press, 2004), 187.

92 Ford, *Joseph Conrad*, 225.

93 Ibid., 221, 219.

94 Ford Madox Ford, "English Literature of To-Day – II," in *The Critical Attitude* (London: Duckworth, 1911), 91–2.

95 Ford, *Joseph Conrad*, 221.

96 Ibid., 199.

97 Ibid.

98 See, for instance, Anders Pettersson, *The Concept of Literary Application: Readers' Analogies from Text to Life* (New York, NY: Palgrave Macmillan, 2012), 153.

99 Iser, *The Implied Reader*, 275.

100 Ibid., 277. To be more precise, for Iser this conduit is an ideal reader constructed by a real reader out of the gaps in a text.

101 Jacques Derrida, "Ulysses Gramophone: Hear Say Yes in Joyce," trans. Tina Kendall and Shari Benstock, in *Acts of Literature*, ed. Derek Attridge (New York, NY: Routledge, 1992), 288.

102 Ibid., 276.

103 Ford, *Some Do Not . . .*, 221.

104 Ibid., 274.

105 Ibid., 167.

106 Ibid., 168.

107 Ibid., 167.

108 Ibid., 272.
109 Genette, *Narrative Discourse*, 56.
110 Vincent Sherry, *The Great War and the Language of Modernism* (New York, NY: Oxford University Press, 2003), 228–9.
111 Ford, *A Man Could Stand Up–*, 503.
112 Ibid., 504.
113 Ibid., 506, 505.
114 Ibid., 661.
115 Ibid., 662–3.
116 Ibid., 663.

Chapter 3

 1 Hal Foster, "Prosthetic Gods," *Modernism/Modernity*, vol. 4, no. 2 (1997), 4.
 2 Fredric Jameson, *Fables of Aggression: Wyndham Lewis, the Modernist as Fascist* (Berkeley, CA: University of California Press, 1979), 7.
 3 Ibid., 28 (first quotation), 32.
 4 Jameson does point out that Lewis does not oppose the mechanical and the organic (see *Fables of Aggression*, 25–7), but his primary methodology is to apply the term to Lewis's work rather than to examine Lewis's explicit arguments about technology.
 5 Wyndham Lewis, *Time and Western Man* (Boston, MA: Beacon Press, 1957 [1927]), x.
 6 On the machine in vorticism, see Miranda B. Hickman, who explores how vorticists were inspired by the "precision and dynamism" of machinery (*The Geometry of Modernism: The Vorticist Idiom in Lewis, Pound, H. D., and Yeats* [Austin, TX: University of Texas Press, 2005], 23).
 7 See Jessica Burstein, *Cold Modernism: Literature, Fashion, Art* (University Park, PA: Pennsylvania State University Press, 2012), Chapter 2; and Lisa Siraganian, *Modernism's Other Work: The Art Object's Political Life* (New York, NY: Oxford University Press, 2012), Chapter 2.
 8 To argue that Lewis has a stable theory is also to read against the grain of another strain of criticism, which sees the doubleness in his thinking about technology as inconsistency (for example, see Michael North, *Machine-Age Comedy* [New York, NY: Oxford University Press, 2009], 117).
 9 The OED dates the term "Machine Age" to Lewis Mumford's essay in the 1922 collection *Civilization in the United States: An Enquiry by Thirty Americans* ("machine, n," OED Online, April 2017, Oxford University Press www.oed.com/view/Entry/111850).
10 "technology, n," OED Online, April 2017, Oxford University Press www.oed.com/view/Entry/198469.
11 "machine, technology," Google Books ngram viewer books.google.com/ngrams.
12 "machine, n," OED Online, April 2017, Oxford University Press www.oed.com/view/Entry/111850.

13 Vincent Sherry, *Ezra Pound, Wyndham Lewis, and Radical Modernism* (New York, NY: Oxford University Press, 1993), 5.

14 Ibid.

15 Julien Benda, *Belphégor*, trans. S. J. I. Lawson (New York, NY: Payson and Clarke, 1929 [1918]), 27.

16 Ibid., 18.

17 Ibid., 40.

18 Ibid., 58.

19 Ibid., 7.

20 Lewis, *Time and Western Man*, 35. Vincent Sherry, in *Ezra Pound, Wyndham Lewis, and Radical Modernism*, 17–20, provides the clearest account of Benda's contribution to Lewis's aesthetics and to modernism's theory of the eye versus the ear.

21 Lewis, *Time and Western Man*, 122.

22 Wyndham Lewis, *The Art of Being Ruled*, ed. Reed Way Dasenbrock (Santa Rosa, CA: Black Sparrow Press, 1989 [1926]), 23.

23 Douglas Mao, *Solid Objects: Modernism and the Test of Production* (Princeton, NJ: Princeton University Press, 1998), 99.

24 Lewis, *Time and Western Man*, 26.

25 Ibid., 26 (first two quotations); ibid., 23; Lewis, *The Art of Being Ruled*, 23.

26 Lewis, *Time and Western Man*, 26.

27 Ibid.

28 Lewis, *The Art of Being Ruled*, 30.

29 See Peter Nicholls, "Apes and Familiars: Modernism, Mimesis and the Work of Wyndham Lewis," *Textual Practice*, vol. 6, no. 3 (1992), 421–38.

30 Lewis, *Time and Western Man*, vii.

31 Lewis, *The Art of Being Ruled*, 24.

32 Lewis, *Time and Western Man*, 122.

33 Ibid., 129.

34 In Lewis's most extended nonfictional critique of amateur art, "The Dithyrambic Spectator," he attributes the rise of the amateur to machines for another reason as well. Modern industry has fulfilled all of society's needs so well that art has been rendered useless: "So the fine arts, corresponding to no present need that a variety of industries cannot answer more effectively, the last survivals of the *hand* against the *machine*, but beaten by the machine in every contest involving a practical issue, must, if they survive at all, survive as a sport, as a privilege of the wealthy, negligently indulged in – not any longer as an object of serious devotion" ("The Dithyrambic Spectator: An Essay on the Origins and Survivals of Art," in *The Diabolical Principle and the Dithyrambic Spectator* [London: Chatto & Windus, 1931], 163).

35 Lewis, *Time and Western Man*, 127.

36 Ibid., 128, 124. For an extended analysis of Lewis's critique of amateur art, see Mao's *Solid Objects*, which links Lewis's distaste for amateur art to his queasiness about the overproduction in modern industry made possible by technology (110–15, 135).

37 Wyndham Lewis, "Shropshire Lads or Robots Again," in *Creatures of Habit and Creatures of Change: Essays on Art, Literature and Society, 1914–1956*, ed. Paul Edwards (Santa Rosa, CA: Black Sparrow Press, 1989), 191.

38 Ibid.

39 Quoted in Wyndham Lewis, *Paleface: The Philosophy of the "Melting-Pot"* (London: Chatto & Windus, 1929), 221.

40 Ibid., 195.

41 Ibid., 235.

42 Ibid., 250–1.

43 Ibid., 249.

44 Michael H. Levenson, *A Genealogy of Modernism: A Study of English Literary Doctrine, 1908–1922* (Cambridge: Cambridge University Press, 1984), 92–6.

45 T. E. Hulme, "A Lecture on Modern Poetry," *Further Speculations*, ed. Sam Hynes (Minneapolis, MN: University of Minnesota Press, 1955), 74.

46 Wyndham Lewis, *Men Without Art*, ed. Seamus Cooney (Santa Barbara, CA: Black Sparrow, 1987 [1934]), 33.

47 Anthony Paraskeva notes that in *The Childermass*, Lewis uses cinematic techniques precisely to forestall sequence, as a way to emphasize the discrete image against the flow of language – the opposite of how cinema works in this analogy in *Men Without Art* ("Wyndham Lewis vs Charlie Chaplin," *Forum for Modern Language Studies*, vol. 43, no. 3 [2007], 230–1). The duality of Lewis's theory of technology repeats in his understanding of cinema, which sometimes epitomizes the debasement of modern culture and sometimes seems to have redemptive aesthetic qualities.

48 Lewis, *Men Without Art*, 33 (first two quotations), 237.

49 Ibid.

50 Ibid., 33.

51 Lewis, *Time and Western Man*, 175.

52 Ibid.

53 Wilhelm Worringer, *Abstraction and Empathy: A Contribution to the Psychology of Style*, trans. Michael Bullock (New York, NY: International University Press, 1953 [1908]), 40.

54 For a discussion of how important it was for Lewis that the spectator stay distinct from the work, with particular focus on art, see Siraganian, *Modernism's Other Work*, especially 55–63.

55 Benda argues that a particularly good artist might be able "to impose the plastic form on the fluid material with which he liked to work"; he then offers a passage from Chateaubriand as a not very convincing example (*Belphégor*, 33). David Ayers notes another distinction between Benda and Lewis: "Benda always offers his arguments in full seriousness, while Lewis constantly ironises his own position" (*Wyndham Lewis and Western Man* [New York, NY: St. Martin's, 1992], 192).

56 Lewis, *Time and Western Man*, 174.

57 Benda, *Belphégor*, 27.

58 Ibid., 90.

59 Wyndham Lewis, *Satire and Fiction: Enemy Pamphlets No. 1* (London: Arthur Press, 1930), 46.

60 Wyndham Lewis, "Inferior Religions," in *The Wild Body: A Soldier of Humour and Other Stories* (New York, NY: Harcourt, Brace, and Company, 1928), 236.

61 Ibid., 233, 236.

62 On Lewis's conception of the body and its relationship to his external method, see Jessica Burstein, *Cold Modernism*, esp. 75–81.

63 See Edwin Muir, *Structure of the Novel* (London: Hogarth, 1960 [1928]), 140–9.

64 Lewis, *Men Without Art*, 155.

65 On Lewis's linguistic strategies for containment, see Sherry, *Ezra Pound, Wyndham Lewis, and Radical Modernism*, 105ff. On his narrative strategies for containment, see Jameson, *Fables of Aggression*, 42–6; and Scott W. Klein, *The Fictions of James Joyce and Wyndham Lewis: Monsters of Nature and Design* (Cambridge: Cambridge University Press, 1994), 118–22.

66 Lewis, *Men Without Art*, 237.

67 Frederick K. Sanders, "The Poet and the Taxi-Cab Driver Test," *The Sewanee Review*, vol. 78, no. 2 (Spring 1970), 358. See also, for example, Seamus Cooney's brief note to his afterword to *Men Without Art*, where he describes the taxi-cab driver test as "that early gesture towards a sort of 'new criticism' approach to prose" (316n2).

68 Critics have also tended to interpret the taxi-cab driver test as a general statement about the need for "a certain level of excellence and verbal precision" (Ravendra Prakash, *The Literary Criticism of Wyndham Lewis* [Jaipur: Pointer, 1989], 89–90). This is how Sanders, for example, justifies applying the taxi-cab driver test to contemporary poetry. Such an interpretation misses that Lewis's argument here is directed toward the specific aesthetic problems of fiction, including the fact that fiction extends in time.

69 Percy Lubbock, *The Craft of Fiction* (New York, NY: Peter Smith, 1947 [1921]), 5.

70 Ibid., 274, 273.

71 Ibid., 274.

72 Virginia Woolf, "How Should One Read a Book?", in *The Second Common Reader*, ed. Andrew McNeillie (San Diego, CA: Harcourt, 1986 [1932]), 259.

73 Ibid.

74 Ibid., 266.

75 Ibid.

76 Ibid., 266–7.

77 Ibid., 267.

78 Joseph Frank, "Spatial Form in Modern Literature: An Essay in Two Parts, Part I," *The Sewanee Review*, vol. 53, no. 2 (Spring 1945), 234–5.

79 Walter Sutton, "The Literary Image and the Reader: A Consideration of the Theory of Spatial Form," *The Journal of Aesthetics and Art Criticism*, vol. 16, no. 1 (September 1957), 115.

80 Ibid., 117.

81 Ibid., 116–17.

82 Joseph Frank, "Spatial Form: An Answer to Critics," *Critical Inquiry*, vol. 4, no. 2 (Winter 1977), 235.

83 Jesse Matz, *Literary Impressionism and Modernist Aesthetics* (Cambridge: Cambridge University Press, 2001), 40. One of Matz's primary examples of collaboration is the "peasant cabman" described in Ford Madox Ford's 1914 essay "On Impressionism" (see 155–64).

84 See Henry James, "*What Maisie Knew*," in *The Art of Criticism: Henry James on the Theory and the Practice of Fiction*, ed. William Veeder and Susan M. Griffin (Chicago, IL: University of Chicago Press, 1986), 319–20.

85 Wyndham Lewis, "The Meaning of the Wild Body," in *The Wild Body: A Soldier of Humour and Other Stories* (New York, NY: Harcourt, Brace, and Company, 1928), 250.

86 Ibid.

87 Lewis, *Paleface*, 237.

88 Wyndham Lewis, *The Apes of God* (Santa Rosa, CA: Black Sparrow Press, 1992 [1930]), 404.

89 Paul Edwards argues that, for Lewis, technology can be a powerful utopian tool for artists – just not for the masses, whom he views through straight-forward "Marxist technological determinism" (*Wyndham Lewis: Painter and Writer* [New Haven, CT: Yale University Press, 2000], 227). Hugh Kenner offers an early version of this claim in attempting to make sense of how Kerr-Orr, the Lewis figure in *The Wild Body*, seems often to be quite similar to the characters he critiques: "the only difference is that they *are* machines, whereas he *operates* one" (*Wyndham Lewis* [Norfolk, CT: New Directions, 1954], 95).

90 Jeffrey Herf, *Reactionary Modernism: Technology, Culture, and Politics in Weimar and the Third Reich* (Cambridge: Cambridge University Press, 1984), 2.

91 Michael E. Zimmerman, *Heidegger's Confrontation with Modernity: Technology, Politics, and Art* (Bloomington, IN: Indiana University Press, 1990), 49–50.

92 Foster, "Prosthetic Gods," 8.

93 There are precedents for this in Lewis's work of this period. For example, he argues that *The Art of Being Ruled* "must of necessity make its own audience; for it aims at no audience already there with which I am acquainted" (*The Art of Being Ruled*, 13). With this emphasis on the need to create a readership, Lewis distances himself from Proudhon and Neitzsche, who, he argues, were happy to write to a "professional critical *corps d'élite*" of a few dozen readers (ibid.).

94 Andrzej Gąsiorek, *Wyndham Lewis and Modernism* (Tavistock: Northcote House, 2004), 78. On the Swiftian interpenetration of utopia and satire in Lewis's work, especially *BLAST*, see Nathan Waddell, *Modernist Nowheres: Politics and Utopia in Early Modernist Writing, 1900–1920* (New York, NY: Palgrave Macmillan, 2012), 140–1 and 146–8.

95 Sherry, for example, sees Lewis's fiction as struggling against the fact that "he cannot halt the temporal momentum of language; cannot carve his pictorial integer onto the page" (*Ezra Pound, Wyndham Lewis, and Radical Modernism*, 127).

96 Jameson, *Fables of Aggression*, 102.

97 Wyndham Lewis, *Tarr* (New York, NY: Penguin, 1982 [1918, rev. 1928]), 332–3.

98 Ibid., 334. Michael Levenson, for example, argues that the novel becomes "a nightmarish literary apparatus that can generate characters without end" ("Form's Body: Wyndham Lewis's Tarr," *MLQ*, vol. 45, no. 3 [September 1984], 261).

99 Jameson, *Fables of Aggression*, 7.

100 Lewis, *Tarr*, 190. Rooms are among Lewis's most characteristic devices of narrative containment. As Jameson puts it: "the incomprehensible requirement for people to come together within walled boxes of various sizes and thicknesses became the occasion for a quasi-existential reflection of the narrative upon its own structural limits" (*Fables of Aggression*, 42). See also Klein, *The Fictions of James Joyce and Wyndham Lewis*, 119–23.

101 Lewis, *Tarr*, 190, 194.

102 Ibid., 190.

103 Ibid., 192.

104 Jameson, *Fables of Aggression*, 31, 32.

105 Lewis, *Tarr*, 190–1.

106 Ann L. Ardis argues that the scene is a sort of test of our willingness to read "as a modernist" – to overlook the sexual violence of the scene's content to appreciate Lewis's formal experimentalism ("Reading 'as a Modernist'/ Denaturalizing Modernist Reading Protocols: Wyndham Lewis's Tarr," in *Rereading Modernism: New Directions in Feminist Criticism*, ed. Lisa Rado [New York, NY: Garland, 1994], 373–90). My reading shifts Ardis's emphasis: the novel itself seems to stage the failure of its own attempts to contain the rape with form.

107 Klein, *The Fictions of James Joyce and Wyndham Lewis*, 144.

108 In Keith Laybourn's widely cited account, he argues that the General Strike crystallized "the problems of declining industries faced with rationalisation" while revealing the tightening limits of trade unionism (*The General Strike of 1926* [Manchester: Manchester University Press, 1993], 120, 6).

109 Rachelle Hope Saltzman, *A Lark for the Sake of Their Country: The 1926 General Strike Volunteers in Folklore and Memory* (Manchester: Manchester University Press, 2012), 6.

110 Christopher Farman details the various elements of the "circus" atmosphere of the strike in cities across the country (*The General Strike: May 1926* [London: Hart-Davis, 1972], 184–5).

111 King George V wrote in his diary, for example, that "[o]ur old country can be well proud of itself, as during the last nine days there has been a strike in which four million people have been affected, not a shot has been fired and no one killed" (quoted in Farman, *The General Strike*, i). See Morag Shiach, *Modernism, Labour, and Selfhood in British Literature and Culture, 1890–1930* (Cambridge: Cambridge University Press, 2004), 200–16 for an analysis of the integral role of violence in syndicalist theories.

112 Virginia Woolf, *The Diary of Virginia Woolf, Volume 3: 1925–1930*, ed. Anne Olivier Bell (New York, NY: Harcourt Brace Jovanovich, 1980), 85.

113 Beatrice Webb, *Beatrice Webb's Diaries, 1924–1932*, ed. Margaret Cole (London: Longmans, Green, and Co, 1956), 95; Lewis, *Men Without Art*, 33.

114 Shiach reads this chapter as an overwhelmingly negative vision: "Decay, corruption, death, and 'dark spasm' are the legacy of the General Strike" in Lewis's novel (*Modernism, Labour, and Selfhood*, 238). At the level of content, such a reading is hard to dispute, but what is particularly interesting about the chapter is how it satirically stages a scene of decay as a redemptive formal moment of containment.

115 Lewis, *The Apes of God*, 619.

116 Ibid.

117 Lewis almost certainly wrote this scene in *Apes* before the taxi-cab driver test, but since he composed the test as a defense against criticism of *Apes*, it seems plausible to read the two passages as responding to each other.

118 Lewis, *The Apes of God*, 621, 624.

119 Ibid., 538.

120 Ibid., 404.

121 Ibid.

122 Ibid., 33.

123 Lewis, *The Apes of God*, 624. Tyrus Miller reads this scene as a parody of the old woman singing wordlessly in Woolf's *Mrs. Dalloway*, and as a site where Lewis mimics the style of Woolf's modernism while polemically rejecting the aesthetic and political positions Woolf stands for (*Late Modernism: Politics, Fiction, and the Arts between the World Wars* [Berkeley, CA: University of California Press, 1999], 71–2, 76). Nathan Waddell, who points out that Lewis criticizes Eliot's use of jazz in *The Waste Land* earlier in *The Apes of God*, argues that the passage's specific reference to Berlin's "What'll I Do?" shows that while Lewis rejected jazz, he had specific, fairly deep knowledge of it ("Wyndham Lewis's 'Very Bad Thing': Jazz, Inter-War Culture, and The Apes of God," *Modernist Cultures*, vol. 8, no. 1 [May 2013], 71–2, 74–5).

124 Lewis, *Apes of God*, 625.

Chapter 4

1 For overviews of West's critical reception, see Bernard Schweizer, Introduction, in *Rebecca West Today: Contemporary Critical Approaches*, ed. Schweizer (Newark, NJ: University of Delaware Press, 2006), 27–30; and Margaret D. Stetz, "Rebecca West's Criticism: Alliance, Tradition, and Modernism," in *Rereading Modernism: New Directions in Feminist Criticism*, ed. Lisa Rado (New York, NY: Garland, 1994), 42–4. Key early feminist recuperations of West included Jane Marcus, "A Wilderness of One's Own: Feminist Fantasy Novels of the 1920s: Rebecca West and Sylvia Townsend Warner," in *Women Writers and the City: Essays in Feminist Literary Criticism*, ed. Susan Merrill Squier (Knoxville, TN: University of Tennessee Press, 1984), 134–60; Bonnie Kime Scott, Introduction, *The Gender of Modernism: A Critical Anthology*, ed. Scott (Bloomington, IN: Indiana University Press, 1990); and Margaret D. Stetz, "Rebecca West and the Visual Arts," *Tulsa Studies in Women's Literature*, vol. 8, no. 1 (Spring 1989), 43–62.

2 See Samuel Beckett, "Dante. . . Bruno. Vico . . Joyce," and William Carlos Williams, "A Point for American Criticism," both in *Our Exagmination Round his Factification for Incamination of* Work in Progress (New York, NY: New Directions, 1972 [1929]). Woolf alludes to "The Strange Necessity" in *A Room of One's Own* (San Diego, CA: Harcourt Brace Jovanovich, 1989 [1929]), 35. In a letter to Harriet Weaver that appears in Ellmann's biography, Joyce reports that he had the first fifty pages of "The Strange Necessity" read to him. Ellman alleges in a note that Joyce "mocked the essay in *Finnegans Wake*" (Richard Ellman, *James Joyce*, rev. ed. [Oxford: Oxford University Press, 1982 (1959)], 605). Bonnie Kime Scott analyzes West's appearance in *Finnegans Wake* – as a version of Anna Livia Plurabelle, often linked to hats, West having recounted going shopping for a hat just after purchasing *Pomes Penyeach* in "The Strange Necessity" – more generously: "I think Joyce took West into the self-mocking spirit" of *Finnegans Wake* (see *Refiguring Modernism Volume I: The Women of 1928* [Bloomington, IN: Indiana University Press, 1995], 55). For an in-depth account of the debate between Joyce and his defenders and West, see Austin Briggs, "Rebecca West vs. James Joyce, Samuel Beckett, and William Carlos Williams," in *Joyce in the Hibernian Metropolis: Essays*, ed. Morris Beja and David Norris (Columbus, OH: Ohio State University Press, 1996), 83–104.

3 Laura Heffernan, "Reading Modernism's Cultural Field: Rebecca West's *The Strange Necessity* and the Aesthetic 'System of Relations,'" *Tulsa Studies in Women's Literature*, vol. 27, no. 2 (Fall 2008), 315.

4 See, for example, Rebecca West, "What Is Mr. T. S. Eliot's Authority as a Critic?" in *The Gender of Modernism*, ed. Bonnie Kime Scott (Bloomington, IN: Indiana University Press, 1990), 587–92. West's opposition to Eliot significantly shaped critics' sense of her aesthetic theory. Stetz, for instance, argues that West posited a theory of art opposed to Eliot's vision of tradition, one that "did not vaunt artistic autonomy over indebtedness to

and connection with past models" ("Rebecca West's Criticism," 60). Carl
Rollyson reads West as a public intellectual who "valued her connection to
her reading audience" more than modernists such as Pound and Eliot did,
and who tried not to be the "bloodless intellectual" she saw in impersonal
Eliot ("Rebecca West as Artist and Intellectual: Roaming Outside the Herd,"
Studies in the Humanities, vol. 35, issue 2 [December 2008], 169, 174).

5 Francesca Frigerio, "Under West(ern) Eyes: Rebecca West Reads Joyce,"
Journal of Modern Literature, vol. 26, no. 1 (Fall 2002), 70.

6 Stetz, "Rebecca West's Criticism," 54. Frigerio similarly outlines West's "organ-
icist aesthetics" ("Under West(ern) Eyes," 69); for Carl Rollyson, "West's
writing never lost its organic quality" (*The Literary Legacy of Rebecca West* [San
Francisco, CA: International Scholars Publication, 1998], 17).

7 Rebecca West, *Harriet Hume: A London Fantasy* (London: Virago, 1983
[1929]), 281. Jane Marcus argues that West's *Harriet Hume* posits a particularly "female version of the pastoral" and exemplifies "[f]emale literary
nostalgia for the lost wilderness" ("A Wilderness of One's Own," 136).
Francesca Frigerio explicitly positions Harriet's naturalized, organic relationship to the piano in opposition to the abstraction promoted by Wyndham
Lewis and T. E. Hulme – "West gives help to this mortified body" that
is excluded from art by modernist classicism ("Music and the Feminine
Art of the Detail in Rebecca West's *Harriet Hume*," in *Rebecca West Today:
Contemporary Critical Approaches*, ed. Bernard Schweizer [Newark, NJ:
University of Delaware Press, 2006], 135).

8 West, *Harriet Hume*, 283.

9 See Nicholas Dames, *The Physiology of the Novel: Reading, Neural Science, and
the Form of Victorian Fiction* (Oxford: Oxford University Press, 2007), 35–6.

10 Ibid., 35.

11 On the complex ways that West's work has been gendered over time, and the
gaps that gendering has produced in critics' accounts of West, see Bonnie
Kime Scott, "The Strange Necessity of Rebecca West," in *Women Reading
Women's Writing*, ed. Sue Roe (New York, NY: Harvester, 1987), 266–9. The
critical literature on the broader gendering of modernist experimentation is,
of course, expansive. Useful overviews can be found in Marianne DeKoven's
"Introduction" to *Rich and Strange: Gender, History, Modernism* (Princeton,
NJ: Princeton University Press, 1991); Rita Felski, *The Gender of Modernity*
(Cambridge, MA: Harvard University Press, 1995), Chapter 1; and Bonnie
Kime Scott's introduction to *The Gender of Modernism*.

12 See Carolyn Burdett, "'The Subjective Inside Us Can Turn into the
Objective Outside': Vernon Lee's Physiological Aesthetics," *Interdisciplinary
Studies in the Long Nineteenth Century*, issue. 12 (2011), n.p.; and Dames,
The Physiology of the Novel, 47–50.

13 Rebecca West, *The Strange Necessity: Essays by Rebecca West* (New York, NY:
Doubleday, 1928), n.p. The note has been omitted from some later editions.

14 Vernon Lee and C. Anstruther-Thomson, "Aesthetic Empathy and Its
Organic Accompaniments," in *Beauty and Ugliness and Other Studies in
Psychological Aesthetics* (London: John Lane, the Bodley Head, 1912), 46.

15 Vernon Lee and C. Anstruther-Thomson, "Anthropomorphic Aesthetics," in *Beauty and Ugliness and Other Studies in Psychological Aesthetics* (London: John Lane, the Bodley Head, 1912), 29.

16 Ibid., 20.

17 Shafquat Towheed, "Determining 'Fluctuating Opinions': Vernon Lee, Popular Fiction, and Theories of Reading," *Nineteenth-Century Literature*, vol. 60, no. 2 (September 2005), 219. Towheed quotes from Vernon Lee's *Belcaro: Being Essays on Sundry Aesthetical Questions* (London: W. Satchell and Co., 1881), 8 (first quotation), 9.

18 Rebecca West, "The Strange Necessity," in *The Strange Necessity: Essays and Reviews* (London: Virago, 1987 [1928]), 89.

19 Ibid., 88.

20 "The so-called psychical phenomena, although observed objectively in animals, are distinguished from the purely physiological, though only in degree of complexity. What can be the importance in how they are designated – 'psychical' or 'complicated nervous' – in distinction from the simple physiological, once it is recognised that the duty of the naturalist is to approach them only from the objective side"? (Ivan Petrovich Pavlov, "Experimental Psychology and Psycho-Pathology in Animals," in *Lectures on Conditioned Reflexes: Twenty-Five Years of Objective Study of the Higher Nervous Activity (Behavior) of Animals*, vol. 1, trans. and ed. W. Horsley Gantt with G. Volborth [New York, NY: International Publishers, 1928], 59–60).

21 Vernon Lee, "On Style," in *The Handling of Words and Other Studies in Literary Psychology* (London: John Lane, the Bodley Head, 1923), 55.

22 See Dames, *The Physiology of the Novel*, 50–3.

23 See Dames, *The Physiology of the Novel*, 247–55; and Joshua Gang, "Behaviorism and the Beginnings of Close Reading," *ELH*, vol. 78, no. 1 (Spring 2011), 1–25. On empathy's role in Richards' behaviorist aesthetics, see Benjamin Morgan, "Critical Empathy: Vernon Lee's Aesthetics and the Origins of Close Reading," *Victorian Studies*, vol. 55, no. 1 (Autumn 2012), 47–50.

24 Pavlov, "Experimental Psychology and Psycho-Pathology in Animals," 50.

25 West, "The Strange Necessity," 84. When Samuel Beckett wishes that West would "assert a more noteworthy control over her salivary glands than is possible for Monsieur Pavlo's [sic] unfortunate dogs," he thus misreads her use of Pavlov ("Dante. . . Bruno. Vico . . Joyce," 13).

26 West, "The Strange Necessity," 181.

27 Carl Rollyson, similarly, argues that for West criticism "is a form of literature and not merely a species of writing about literature" ("Rebecca West as Artist and Intellectual," 170).

28 Rebecca West, "Gide," in *Ending in Earnest: A Literary Log* (Freeport, NY: Books for Libraries Press, 1967 [1931]), 193–4.

29 Rebecca West, "'Journey's End' Again," in *Ending in Earnest: A Literary Log* (Freeport, NY: Books for Libraries Press, 1967 [1931]), 77.

30 West, "The Strange Necessity," 180.

31 Ibid.

32 Ibid., 100. West's phrase alludes to Lee's review of Percy Lubbock's *The Craft of Fiction*, where she brings in Ruskin's "imagination penetrative" to describe the capacity for otherness that, to her, Henry James utterly lacks, causing him to be unable to write three-dimensional characters. See Vernon Lee, "'Imagination Penetrative': Apropos of Mr. Lubbock's *Craft of Fiction*," in *The Handling of Words and Other Studies in Literary Psychology*, (London: John Lane, the Bodley Head, 1923), 279–80.

33 West, "The Strange Necessity," 117–18.

34 On Worringer's influence on Hulme's aesthetics, see Michael H. Levenson, *A Genealogy of Modernism: A Study of English Literary Doctrine, 1908–1922* (Cambridge: Cambridge University Press, 1984), 99–101.

35 West, "The Strange Necessity," 88–9.

36 T. E. Hulme, "Romanticism and Classicism," in *Speculations*, ed. Herbert Read (London: Kegan Paul, Trench, Trubner, & Co., 1936 [1924]), 126.

37 West, "The Strange Necessity," 88.

38 Ibid., 17.

39 Ibid., 22, 17–18.

40 Ibid., 67.

41 Rebecca West, "The Pitoeffs," in *Ending in Earnest: A Literary Log* (Freeport, NY: Books for Libraries Press, 1967 [1931]), 236.

42 West, "The Strange Necessity," 67.

43 Rebecca West, "Concerning the Censorship," in *Ending in Earnest: A Literary Log* (Freeport, NY: Books for Libraries Press, 1967 [1931]), 8.

44 Ibid., 7.

45 See Jenny Hazelgrove, *Spiritualism and British Society Between the Wars* (Manchester: Manchester University Press, 2000), 180–2.

46 West, "Concerning the Censorship," 6.

47 Wilhelm Worringer, *Abstraction and Empathy: A Contribution to the Psychology of Style*, trans. Michael Bullock (New York, NY: International Universities Press, 1953 [1908]), 36.

48 Ibid., 37.

49 Ibid., 44.

50 West, "The Strange Necessity," 178, 188.

51 Worringer, *Abstraction and Empathy*, 3.

52 West, "The Strange Necessity," 84.

53 Ibid., 86.

54 T. S. Eliot, "*Ulysses*, Order, and Myth," *Selected Prose of T. S. Eliot*, ed. Frank Kermode (San Diego, CA: Harcourt, Brace & Co., 1975), 177.

55 West, "The Strange Necessity," 28–9.

56 Ibid., 87.

57 Eliot, "*Ulysses*, Order, and Myth," 177.

58 Ibid.

59 Michael Levenson argues that Eliot attempts to do the opposite in "*Ulysses*, Order, and Myth" – to widen perspectives and create distance from the contemporary (*A Genealogy of Modernism*, 192–207).

60 West, "The Strange Necessity," 194.

61 Rebecca West, letter to Richard Ellman, dated 7 November 1958, in *Selected Letters of Rebecca West*, ed. Bonnie Kime Scott (New Haven, CT: Yale University Press, 2000), 327. Later in this letter, West brings back the term myth, with a dig at Joyce and William Carlos Williams, who, West argued, concocted a "fantastic myth" about West's supposed opposition to Joyce (Ibid., 327). Here, "myth" turns into gossip and fabrication.

62 Clive Bell, *Art* (New York, NY: Frederick A. Stokes, 1913), 17.

63 West, "The Strange Necessity," 131–2.

64 Ibid., 131.

65 Ibid.

66 Ibid., 127.

67 Ibid.

68 Ibid., 127–8.

69 Ibid., 127 (first quotation), 128.

70 Lewis Mumford, *Art and Technics* (New York, NY: Columbia University Press, 2000 [1952]), 15. Sam Weber uses "technics" to translate *Technik* in the title of Heidegger's famous essay. He wants "technics" to include technique and craft but also to reverse the ordinary hierarchy between technologies and science, where we think of science as the site of organization and knowledge that precedes and enables technology. For Heidegger, Weber notes, it is "the other way round" ("Upsetting the Setup: Remarks on Heidegger's 'Questing After Technics,'" in *Mass Mediauras: Form, Technics, Media*, ed. Alan Cholodenko [Stanford, CA: Stanford University Press, 1996], 60).

71 Quoted in West, "The Strange Necessity," 126.

72 Ivan Petrovich Pavlov, "The Cortex as a Mosaic of Functions," in *Conditioned Reflexes: An Investigation of the Physiological Activity of the Cerebral Cortex*, trans. and ed. G. V. Anrep (Oxford: Oxford University Press, 1927), 219.

73 Wells's "World Brain" "would play the role of a cerebral cortex to these essential ganglia" (*The World Brain* [Adelaide: eBooks@University of Adelaide, 2014 (1938)], 50).

74 Wells, *The World Brain*, 11, 14.

75 In one of the more bizarre moments of "The Strange Necessity," West thinks about this group mind almost physically, when she argues that exiles and expatriates suffer mentally when they leave their home countries because they are cut off from the super-cortex. Those who leave, she argues in Chapter 5, wind up relying too much on the individual because they lose access to the collective super-cortex – thus life becomes incoherent, and people become criminals (this is her explanation for Al Capone).

76 Melba Cuddy-Keane, Adam Hammond, and Alexandra Peat define this idea of group thinking as a "keyword" of modernism. They situate West's concept of the super-cortex in the context of other modernist attempts to imagine positive collective thinking – including Jules Romains's *Unanimisme*, Joyce's Here Comes Everybody, and Woolf's mode of mobile, collective narration – and note that like other modernists, West distinguished between super-cortical thinking and a more reductive version she diagnosed in contemporary politics (*Modernism: Keywords* [Malden, MA: Wiley Blackwell, 2014], 40–5).

77 Wells, *The World Brain*, vii.
78 Ibid., viii.
79 Ibid., ix.
80 Ibid., 4, 3.
81 Ibid., 4.
82 Ibid., ix.
83 Ibid., xii.
84 West, *Harriet Hume*, 267.
85 Ibid., 184–5.
86 Ibid., 267.
87 Debra Rae Cohen, "Sheepish Modernism: Rebecca West, the Adam Brothers, and the Taxonomies of Criticism," in *Rebecca West Today: Contemporary Critical Approaches*, ed. Bernard Schweizer (Newark, NJ: University of Delaware Press, 2006), 152. Cohen also reads the novel as a performance of the theory presented in "The Strange Necessity."
88 Charles A. Beard, "Introduction," in *Whither Mankind: A Panorama of Modern Civilization* (New York, NY: Longmans, Green and Co., 1928), 10.
89 Ibid., 14.
90 Ibid.
91 Rebecca West, "Machines and Civilization," *New York Herald Tribune*, 4 November 1928, Books 6.
92 Ibid.
93 Ibid.
94 Bernard Stiegler, *Technics and Time, I: The Fault of Epimetheus*, trans. Richard Beardsworth and George Collins (Stanford, CA: Stanford University Press, 1998), 17.
95 See Gerald Moore, "Adapt and Smile or Die! Stiegler Among the Darwinists," in *Stiegler and Technics*, ed. Christina Howells and Moore (Edinburgh: Edinburgh University Press, 2013), 18.
96 Ibid., 25.
97 Stiegler, *Technics and Time I*, 151.
98 West, "The Strange Necessity," 128.
99 Ibid., 129.
100 See Bernard Stiegler, *Technics and Time I*, 135.
101 Moore, "Adapt and Smile or Die!," 22.
102 Stiegler, *Technics and Time I*, 140.
103 West, "The Strange Necessity," 129.
104 Stiegler, *Technics and Time I*, 141.
105 Ibid., 141, 142.
106 Ibid., 145.
107 West, "The Strange Necessity," 181.
108 Ibid., 137–8.
109 Against Snow's technocratic, managerial optimism, Leavis saw cultural decline, as organic community was replaced by the standardization of a machine-centered mass society. See Guy Ortolano, *The Two Cultures Controversy: Science, Literature and Cultural Politics in Postwar Britain* (Cambridge: Cambridge University Press, 2009), especially 85–6.

110 I. A. Richards, *Science and Poetry* (London: Kegan Paul, Trench, Trubner and Co., 1926), 60.

111 West, "What is Mr. T. S. Eliot's Authority as a Critic?," 591.

112 Ibid., 588–9.

113 Ibid., 591.

114 Rebecca West, "McLuhan and the Future of Literature," *New England Review*, vol. 29, no. 1 (2008 [1969]), 190–1.

115 Ibid., 178.

116 Ibid.

117 Ibid.

118 Ibid.

119 Ibid., 179.

120 As Donald F. Theall notes, McLuhan theorized "communication as participation," a "shared process of human making," in direct opposition to the "transmissional" theories of Claude Shannon, Norbert Wiener, and Warren Weaver (*The Virtual Marshall McLuhan*, [Montreal: McGill-Queen's University Press, 2001], 60, 61, 60).

121 West, "McLuhan and the Future of Literature," 190.

Conclusion

1 Q. D. Leavis, *Fiction and the Reading Public* (London: Chatto and Windus, 1939 [1932]), 231.

2 Ibid., 51.

3 Examples of this commonplace can be found in Chris Hopkins, *English Fiction in the 1930s: Language, Genre, History* (London: Continuum, 2006), 5; and John Mepham, "Varieties of Modernism, Varieties of Incomprehension: Patrick Hamilton and Elizabeth Bowen," in *British Fiction after Modernism: The Novel at Mid-Century*, ed. Marina MacKay and Lyndsey Stonebridge (New York, NY: Palgrave, 2007), 59–61.

4 George Orwell, "Charles Dickens," in *A Collection of Essays* (San Diego, CA: Harcourt, Brace, & Co. 1981 [1946]), 81.

5 Quoted in David Lodge, "The Novelist at the Crossroads," in *The Novelist at the Crossroads and other Essays on Fiction and Criticism* (Ithaca, NY: Cornell University Press, 1971), 18.

6 Ibid., 33.

7 Tyrus Miller, *Late Modernism: Politics, Fiction, and the Arts between the World Wars* (Berkeley, CA: University of California Press, 1999), 20.

8 Jed Esty, *A Shrinking Island: Modernism and National Culture in England* (Princeton, NJ: Princeton University Press, 2004), 2.

9 George Orwell, "Inside the Whale," in *A Collection of Essays*, (San Diego, CA: Harcourt, Brace, & Co. 1981 [1946]), 231. Miller's account of the essay can be found in *Late Modernism*, 7–9.

10 Orwell, "Inside the Whale," 228–9.

11 Ibid., 241.

12 Ibid., 231.

13 F. R. Leavis, "Mass Civilisation and Minority Culture," in *For Continuity* (Freeport, NY: Books for Libraries Press, 1968 [1933]), 16. As Christopher

Hillard notes, Leavis chooses to link these transformations in mass culture to the machine, "even though their emergence might have been more plausibly explained with respect to the logic of capital accumulation or the cash nexus" (*English as a Vocation: The Scrutiny Movement* [Oxford: Oxford University Press, 2012], 62).

14 Leavis, "Mass Civilisation and Minority Culture," 18.

15 Quoted in ibid., 45.

16 Ibid.

17 See, for example, ibid., 32–7; or F. R. Leavis, "What's Wrong with Criticism?" in *For Continuity* (Freeport, NY: Books for Libraries Press, 1968 [1933]), 77–90.

18 See Leavis, "Mass Civilisation and Minority Culture," 22–3, 40–2.

19 Quoted in ibid., 42.

20 F. R. Leavis, "Joyce and 'The Revolution of the Word,'" in *For Continuity* (Freeport, NY: Books for Libraries Press, 1968 [1933]), 217–18.

21 Leavis, "Mass Civilisation and Minority Culture," 31.

22 Ibid., 21.

23 Leavis, "Joyce and 'The Revolution of the Word,'" 214, 210.

24 Ibid., 217.

25 Ibid., 210.

26 Ibid., 215, 211.

27 F. R. Leavis, "John Dos Passos," in *For Continuity* (Freeport, NY: Books for Libraries Press, 1968 [1933]), 109.

28 Ibid., 107.

29 Ibid., 109.

30 Leavis, "Mass Civilisation and Minority Culture," 23.

31 Ibid., 22.

32 Quoted in ibid., 22, 21. Q. D. Leavis also discusses this letter in *Fiction and the Reading Public*, 49–50.

33 F. R. Leavis, "The Literary Mind," in *For Continuity* (Freeport, NY: Books for Libraries Press, 1968 [1933]), 63.

34 F. R. Leavis, "Babbitt Buys the World," in *For Continuity* (Freeport, NY: Books for Libraries Press, 1968 [1933]), 94.

35 Ibid., 92.

36 Leavis, "John Dos Passos," 105.

37 F. R. Leavis, *Two Cultures? The Significance of C. P. Snow, with an Essay on Sir Charles Snow's Rede Lecture* (London: Chatto and Windus, 1962), 21, 23.

38 Snow writes of asking writers "how many of them could describe the Second Law of Thermodynamics. The response was cold: it was also negative. Yet I was asking something which is about the scientific equivalent of: *Have you read a work of Shakespeare's?*" (C. P. Snow, "The Two Cultures," in *The Two Cultures and the Scientific Revolution* [New York, NY: Cambridge University Press, 1961 (1959)], 16).

39 F. R. Leavis, *The Great Tradition* (New York, NY: George W. Stewart, 1950 [1948]), 7.

40 Ibid., 16.

41 Ibid., 26, 16, 24.
42 F. R. Leavis, *D. H. Lawrence: Novelist* (London: Chatto & Windus, 1955), 158.
43 Ibid., 164.
44 Ibid.
45 Quoted in F. R. Leavis, "D. H. Lawrence," in *For Continuity* (Freeport, NY: Books for Libraries Press, 1968 [1933]), 137.
46 Leavis, *D. H. Lawrence: Novelist*, 196.
47 René Wellek, *A History of Modern Criticism: 1750–1950, Volume 5, English Criticism, 1900–1950* (New Haven, CT: Yale University Press, 1986), 251.
48 Ibid., 253.
49 Joseph Frank, "Spatial Form in Modern Literature: An Essay in Two Parts, Part I," *The Sewanee Review*, vol. 53, no. 2 (Spring 1945), 232.
50 Joseph Frank, "Spatial Form in Modern Literature: An Essay in Three Parts, Part II," *The Sewanee Review*, vol. 53, no. 3 (Summer 1945), 437, 438.
51 Frank, "Spatial Form in Modern Literature: An Essay in Two Parts, Part I," 234–5.
52 Ibid., 231.
53 Ibid., 230.
54 Joseph Frank, "Spatial Form: An Answer to Critics," *Critical Inquiry*, vol. 4, no. 2 (Winter 1977), 237.
55 Kermode first posed this issue in *The Sense of an Ending: Studies in the Theory of Fiction* (New York, NY: Oxford University Press, 2000 [1966], 176). Kermode returned to the topic in "A Reply to Joseph Frank," *Critical Inquiry*, vol. 4, no. 3 (Spring 1978), 586.
56 Frank, "Spatial Form: An Answer to Critics," 248.
57 Wellek, *A History of Modern Criticism*, ix.
58 Marshall McLuhan, "Joyce, Mallarmé, and the Press," *The Sewanee Review*, vol. 62, no. 1 (January–March 1954), 55.
59 Ibid., 48.
60 Ibid., 51.
61 Donald Theall and Joan Theall, "Marshall McLuhan and James Joyce: Beyond Media" *Canadian Journal of Communication*, vol. 14, no. 4 (1989), 63n2.
62 Marshall McLuhan, *Letters of Marshall McLuhan*, ed. Matie Molinaro, Corrine McLuhan, and William Toye (New York, NY: Oxford University Press, 1987), 284.
63 Marshall McLuhan, Quentin Fiore, and Jerome Agel, *The Medium is the Massage: An Inventory of Effects* (Corte Madera, CA: Gingko Press, 2001 [1967]), 9.
64 Marshall McLuhan, *Understanding Media: The Extensions of Man*, second ed. (New York, NY: Signet, 1964), 155.
65 Ibid., 136.
66 Ibid., 159.
67 Ibid., 157.
68 Ibid.
69 Ibid., 36.

70 Ibid., 20.
71 Ibid., 27.
72 Ibid., 28.
73 Marshall McLuhan, *The Gutenberg Galaxy: The Making of Typographic Man* (Toronto: University of Toronto Press, 1995 [1962]), 278.
74 McLuhan, *Understanding Media*, 30 (first quotation), 47.
75 Ibid., viii.
76 Ibid., 42.
77 McLuhan, *The Gutenberg Galaxy*, 276.
78 Ibid., 277.
79 Ibid.

Index